THE PSYCHOLOGY OF SUICIDE

87, 88 89

THE PSYCHOLOGY OF SUICIDE

A CLINICIAN'S GUIDE TO

EVALUATION AND TREATMENT

Revised Edition

by
EDWIN S. SHNEIDMAN, Ph.D.,
NORMAN L. FARBEROW, Ph.D.,
AND
ROBERT E. LITMAN, M.D., Ph.D.

JASON ARONSON INC.
Northvale, New Jersey
London

This book was set in 10 pt. Goudy by Lind Graphics of Upper Saddle River, New Jersey, and printed and bound by Haddon Craftsmen of Scranton, Pennsylvania.

Library of Congress Cataloging-in-Publication Data

Shneidman, Edwin S.
   The psychology of suicide : a clinician's guide to evaluation and
treatment / by Edwin S. Shneidman, Norman L. Farberow, and Robert E.
Litman. – Rev. ed.
      p. cm.
   Includes bibliographical references and index.
   ISBN 1-56821-057-4
   1. Suicide – Psychological aspects.   2. Suicide – Prevention.
   3. Suicidal behavior – Treatment.   I. Farberow, Norman L.
   II. Litman, Robert E.   III. Title
   [DNLM: 1. Suicide.   HV 6545 S558p 1994]
   HV6545.S39   1994
   616.85'8445 – dc20
   DNLM/DLC
   for Library of Congress   93-11971

Manufactured in the United States of America. Jason Aronson Inc. offers books and cassettes. For information and catalog write to Jason Aronson Inc., 230 Livingston Street, Northvale, New Jersey 07647.

CONTENTS

III – CONCOMITANTS AND AFTERMATH

PREFACE TO THE

REVISED EDITION

ONE MAIN MERIT that may be especially claimed for this revised edition is its brevity – twelve chapters selected from among the original forty-four, and a comparable reduction in pages. We have tried to retain those chapters that have held up relatively well over the last quarter century and still have something useful – theoretical or clinical – to say to contemporary practitioners.

In the 1950s and '60s there was a great burst of interest in suicide prevention in the United States. The growth in the number of suicide prevention centers from fewer than a half dozen to over two hundred and the emergence of the Center for the Study of Suicide Prevention at the National Institute of Mental Health during the presidencies of Kennedy and Johnson were clear evidences of that surge. Inevitably, as other maladies came to the popular fore, the burning interest in suicide prevention waned somewhat. But a core of focused concern remained, as it ought, considering that the problems of suicide and the challenges of prevention are not likely to disappear in the foreseeable future.

This volume reprints those pieces from our 1967 book that addressed some ubiquitous issues and that continue to reflect today's interests and concerns.

In these days, which see newly minted edited volumes on suicide published each year, we believe that there is a legitimate place for these essays of a generation ago that have survived that temporal span and still speak to us today.

Edwin S. Shneidman
Norman L. Farberow
Robert E. Litman

Los Angeles
November, 1993

EDITORS

EDWIN S. SHNEIDMAN, Ph.D., is Professor of Thanatology Emeritus at the University of California at Los Angeles School of Medicine. In the 1950s he was a co-founder and co-director of the Los Angeles Suicide Prevention Center and then, in the 1960s, first chief of the Center for the Study of Suicide Prevention at the National Institute of Mental Health in Bethesda. He has been visiting professor at Harvard University and at the Ben Gurion University of the Negev in Beersheva; research associate at the Massachusetts General Hospital and the Karolinska Hospital in Stockholm; and a fellow at the Center for Advanced Study in the Behavioral Sciences at Stanford. He was the founder, in 1968, and first president of the American Association of Suicidology. He is the author of *Deaths of Man* (nominated for a National Book Award in science), *Voices of Death, Definition of Suicide*, and *Suicide as Psychache*, and editor or co-editor of a dozen books on death and suicide. He is the recipient of the American Psychological Association Award for Distinguished Professional Contribution to Public Service.

NORMAN L. FARBEROW, Ph.D., is Clinical Professor Emeritus in the University of Southern California School of Medicine. He was co-founder and co-director, with Drs. Shneidman and Litman, of the Los Angeles Suicide Prevention Center, and co-director, with Dr. Shneidman, of the Veterans

Administration Central Research Unit for the Study of Unpredicted Death. He is an honorary member of the Finnish Psychiatric Association, the Finnish Mental Health Association, and the Quebec Association of Suicidology. He is a past president of the International Association for Suicide Prevention and the American Association of Suicidology. He has written (with Glenn Evans) the *Encyclopedia of Suicide*, and has edited, co-edited, and co-authored a number of books, among which are *The Many Faces of Suicide, Suicide in Different Cultures, Suicide Inside and Out*, and *The Crisis of Competence*.

ROBERT E. LITMAN, M.D., M.S., Ph.D., is Clinical Professor of Psychiatry at the University of California at Los Angeles School of Medicine. Dr. Litman's Master of Science degree is in neurology, his Ph.D. is in psychoanalysis, and he has practiced psychiatry and psychoanalysis in Los Angeles since 1950. With Drs. Shneidman and Farberow he helped found the Los Angeles Suicide Prevention Center, and he was the Chief Psychiatrist of the Center for more than thirty years. He was the first director of Psychiatric Inpatient Services at Cedars-Sinai Hospital, Los Angeles. He is a founding member and past president of the American Association of Suicidology. He is the author (or co-author) of *Psychoanalysis in the Americas, Accident or Suicide—Destruction by Automobile, Youth Suicide, Sigmund Freud on Suicide*, and, most recently, *Predicting and Preventing Hospital and Clinic Suicides*.

I
ORIENTATIONS

1

ORIENTATIONS TOWARD

DEATH

Edwin S. Shneidman

IT IS BOTH STIMULATING and depressing to contemplate the fact that at this period in man's history when, at long last, one can find a few genuine indications of straightforward discussions and investigations of death, these pursuits come at the time of man's terrible new-found capacity to destroy his works and to decimate his kind. For these reasons, it may be said that a special kind of intellectual and affective permissiveness, born out of a sense of urgency, now exists for man's greater understanding of his own death and destruction.

The purpose of this chapter is to stimulate a rethinking of conventional notions of death and suicide. A further purpose is to attempt to create a psychologically oriented classification of death phenomena — an ordering based in large part on the role of the individual in his own demise.

Reflections on death, including suicide, are found in some of man's earliest written works. Death and suicide have been depicted and refined in various ways; numerous misconceptions have grown up around these topics. These proliferated intellectual overgrowths are not the specimens that we wish to describe here. Rather, we have to see them as encumbering underbrush that must be cleared away before we can come to the heart of the problem. This is the first task to which we should turn.

3

"IDOLS," OR FALSE NOTIONS ABOUT DEATH AND SUICIDE

Francis Bacon, that great Elizabethan, enumerated four classes of "idols," or fallacies, of inductive thought. Of particular interest to us in the present context are the Idols of the Cave—"the idols of the individual man, for everyone . . . has a cave or den of his own, which refracts and discolors the light of nature." In respect to suicide and death, each person figuratively builds for himself, in relation to the cryptic topics of life and death, his own (mis)conceptual vault of beliefs, understandings, and orientations. I would propose three subcategories of these Idols of the Cave, specifically as they concern: (1) the classification of suicidal phenomena; (2) the classification of death phenomena; and (3) the concept of death itself.

The Idol that the Present Classifications of Suicidal Phenomena Are Meaningful

The use of an illustration may be the best introduction to this topic. A woman of around 30 years of age was seen on the ward of a large general hospital after she had been returned from surgery. She had, a few hours before, shot herself in the head with a .22 caliber revolver, the result being that she had enucleated an eye and torn away part of her frontal lobe. Her chart indicated that she had attempted to kill herself, the diagnosis being "attempted suicide." In the next bed there was another young woman of about the same age. She had come to the hospital that day because she had cut her left wrist with a razor blade. The physical trauma was relatively superficial and required but a few stitches. She had had, she said, absolutely no lethal intention, but had definitely wished to jolt her husband into attending to what she wanted to say to him about his drinking habits. Her words to him had been, "Look at me, I'm bleeding." Her chart, too, indicated a diagnosis of "attempted suicide."

Common sense should tell us that if we obtained scientific data from these two cases—psychiatric anamnestic data, psychological test data, and so forth—and then grouped these materials under the single rubric of "attempted suicide," we would obviously run the risk of masking precisely the differences that we might wish to explore. Common sense might further tell us that the first woman could most appropriately be labeled as a case of "committed suicide" (even though she was alive), and the second woman as "nonsuicidal" (even though she had cut her wrist with a razor blade). But, aside from the issue of what would be the most appropriate diagnosis in each case, it still seems evident that collating these two cases—and hundreds of similar instances—under the common heading of "attempted suicide" might definitely limit rather than extend the range or our potential understanding.

Individuals with clear lethal intention, as well as those with ambivalent or no lethal intention, are currently grouped under the heading of attempted suicide. We know that individuals can attempt to attempt, attempt to commit, attempt to be nonsuicidal. All this comes about largely because of oversimplification as to types of causes and a confusion between mode and purpose. (The law punishes the holdup man with the unloaded or toy gun precisely because the victim must assume that the bandit has, by virtue of his holding a "gun," covered himself with the semantic mantle "gunman.") One who cries "help" while holding a razor blade is deemed by society to be suicidal. Although it is true the act of putting a shotgun in one's mouth and pulling the trigger with one's toe is almost always related to lethal self-intention, this particular relationship between method and intent does not hold for most methods, such as ingesting barbiturates or cutting oneself with a razor. In most cases, the intentions may range all the way from deadly ones through the wide variety of ambivalences, rescue fantasies, cries for help, and psychic indecisions all the way to clearly formulated nonlethal intention in which a semantic usurpation of a "suicidal" mode has been consciously employed. We need to think in terms of a continuum of *lethality*.

The classification of suicide most common in everyday clinical use is a rather homely, supposedly common-sense division, which in its barest form implies that all humanity can be divided into two groupings, suicidal and nonsuicidal, and then divides the suicidal category into committed, attempted, and threatened. That it is neither theoretically nor practically adequate for understanding and treatment of suicide is one of the main tenets of this chapter. It may well be that the word *suicide* currently has too many loose and contradictory meanings to be scientifically or clinically useful.

The Idol that the Traditional Classification of Death Phenomena Is Clear

The International Classification of the Causes of Death lists 137 causes, such as pneumonia, meningitis, malignant neoplasms, myocardial infarctions; but, in contrast, there are only *four* commonly recognized *modes* of death: *natural death, accident, suicide, and homicide*. In some cases, cause of death is used synonymously to indicate the natural cause of death. Thus, the standard U.S. Public Health Service Certificate of Death has a space to enter cause of death (implying the mode as natural) and, in addition, provides opportunity to indicate accident, suicide, or homicide. Apparently, it is implied that these four modes of death constitute the final ordering into which each of us must be classified. The fact that some of us do not fit easily into one of these four crypts is the substance for this section.

The shortcoming of the common classification is that in its over-simplification and failure to take into account certain necessary dimensions it often poses serious problems in classifying deaths meaningfully. The basic ambiguities can be seen most clearly by focusing on the distinctions between natural (intrasomatic) and accidental (extrasomatic) deaths. On the face of it, the argument can be advanced that most deaths, especially in the younger years, are unnatural. Perhaps only in the cases of death of old age might the termination of life legitimately be called natural. Let us examine the substance of some of these confusions. If an individual (who wishes to continue living) has his skull invaded by a lethal object, his death is called accidental; if another individual (who also wishes to continue living) is invaded by a lethal virus, his death is called natural. An individual who torments an animal into killing him is said to have died an accidental death, whereas an individual who torments a drunken companion into killing him is called a homicide victim. An individual who has an artery burst in his brain is said to have died with a cerebral-vascular accident, whereas it might make more sense to call it a cerebral-vascular natural death. What has been confusing in this traditional approach is that the individual has been viewed as a kind of biological *object* rather than as a psychological, social, biological organism and, as a consequence, the role of the individual in his own demise has been neglected.

Dr. Arthur P. Noyes said, "As we grow older, we grow more like ourselves." I believe that this illuminating but somewhat cryptic remark can also be taken to mean that during the dying period, the individual displays behaviors and attitudes that contain great fealty to his lifelong orientations and beliefs. Draper and colleagues assert (1944): "Each man dies in a notably personal way." Suicidal and dying behaviors do not exist *in vacuo*, but are an integral part of the life style of the individual.

The Idol that the Concept *Death* Is Itself Operationally Sound

We come now to what for some may be the most radical and iconoclastic aspect of our presentation so far, specifically the suggestion that a major portion of the concept of *death* is operationally meaningless and ought therefore to be eschewed. Let the reader ask the question of the author: "Do you mean to say that you wish to discuss suicidal phenomena and orientations toward death without the concept of death?" The author's answer is in the affirmative, based, he believes, on compelling reasons. Essentially, these reasons are epistemological; that is, they have to do with the process of knowing and the question of what it is that we can know. Our main source of quotable strength—and we shall have occasion later to refer to him in a very different context—is the physicist Percy W. Bridgman. Essentially, his concept is that death is not experienceable, that if one could experience it, one would not be dead. One can experience another's dying and another's death and his own dying—although he can never be sure—but no person can experience his own death.

In his book *The Intelligent Individual and Society*, Bridgman (1938) states this view as follows:

> There are certain kinks in our thinking which are of such universal occurrence as to constitute essential limitations. Thus the urge to think of my own death as some form of my experience is almost irresistible. However, it requires only to be said for me to admit that my own death cannot be a form of experience, for if I could still experience, then by definition it would not be death. Operationally my own death is a fundamentally different thing from the death of another in the same way that my own feelings mean something fundamentally different from the feelings of another. The death of another I can experience; there are certain methods of recognizing death and certain properties of death that affect my actions in the case of others. Again it need not bother us to discover that the concept of death in another is not sharp, and situations may arise in practice where it is difficult to say whether the organism is dead or not, particularly if one sticks to the demand that "death" must be such a thing that when the organism is once dead it cannot live again. This demand rests on mystical feelings, and there is no reason why the demand should be honored in framing the definition of death. . . . My own death is such a different thing that it might well have a different word, and perhaps eventually will. There is no operation by which I can decide whether I am dead; "I am always alive." [p. 168]

Two further thoughts on death as experience. Not only, as we have seen, is death misconceived as an experience, but (1) it is further misconceived as a bitter or calamitous experience, and (2) it is still further misconceived as an *act*, as though dying were something that one had to do. On the contrary, dying can be a supreme passivity rather than the supreme act or activity. It will be done for you; dying is one thing that no one has to *do*.

In addition to this philosophical aspect of the situation, there is also the reflection that one's own death is really psychologically inconceivable. Possibly the most appropriate quotation in this connection is from Freud. In his paper, "Thoughts for the Times on War and Death," Freud (1915/1925) wrote:

> Our own death is indeed unimaginable, and whenever we make the attempt to imagine it we can conceive that we really survive as

spectators. Hence the psychoanalytic school could venture on the assertion that at bottom no one believes in his own death, or to put the thing in another way, in the unconscious every one of us is convinced of his own immortality. [p. 289]

Indeed, the word *death* has become a repository for pervasive logical and epistemological confusions—"Idols of the Dead." The first order of business might well be to clarify the concepts presently embedded in our current notions of death.

BASIC ORIENTATIONS TOWARD DEATH

The operation which gives meaning to the phrase *basic orientation toward death* has to do with the role of the individual in his own demise. By the *role of the individual* is meant his overt and covert behaviors and nonbehaviors that reflect conscious and unconscious attributes relevant to his cessation. These include at least the following: attitudes and beliefs about death, cessation, hereafter, and rebirth; ways of thinking; need systems, including needs for achievement, affiliation, autonomy, and dominance; dyadic relationships, especially the subtleties of dependencies and hostilities in relation to the significant people in life; the hopefulness and hopelessness in the responses of these people to cries for help; the constellation and the balance of ego activity and ego passivity; orientations toward continuation states. To know these facts about a person would require a comprehensive psychological understanding of that individual's personality.

Three subcategories relating to the role of the individual in his own demise are proposed: (1) intentioned, (2) subintentioned, and (3) unintentioned.

Intentioned Death

By *intentioned*, I refer to those cases in which the individual plays a direct and conscious role in his own demise. These cases do not refer to persons who wish for death or termination, but rather to those who actively precipitate their cessation. (Of course, cessation cannot be avoided by anyone. The entire issue is one of timing and involves postponing and hastening). In terms of the traditional categories of death, no presently labeled accidental or natural deaths would be called intentioned, some homicidal deaths might be called intentioned, and most (but, importantly, not all) suicidal deaths would be called intentioned. In relation to the term *suicide*, intentioned cases may be said to have *committed* suicide. We can list a number of subcategories of intentioned death: (1) death-seekers, (2) death-initiators, and (3) death-ignorers.

1. *Death-seeker*. A death-seeker is one who, during the time that he can be so labeled, has consciously verbalized to himself his wish for an ending to all conscious experience and behaves in order to achieve this end. The operational criteria for a death-seeker lie not primarily in the method he uses—razor, barbiturate, carbon monoxide—but in the fact that the method *in his mind* is calculated to bring him cessation; and, whatever his rescue fantasies or cries for help may be, he does the act in such a manner that rescue (or intervention) is realistically unlikely or impossible. In all, he has a predominantly unambivalent intention or orientation toward cessation during that period. The phrase *during the period* is meant to convey the notion that individuals' orientations toward cessation shift and change over time. A person who was a death-seeker yesterday and made a most serious suicidal act then, could not today be forced to participate in activities that could cost him his life. It is known clinically that many individuals are suicidal for only a relatively brief period of time; so that if they can be given appropriate sanctuary, they will no longer seek death and will wish to continue to live as long as possible.

2. *Death-initiator*. A death-initiator is a death-seeker, but sufficiently different to warrant a separate label. A death-initiator believes that he will suffer cessation in the fairly near future—a matter of days or weeks—or he believes that he is failing and, not wishing to accommodate himself to a new (and less effective and less virile) image of himself, does not wish to let it happen to him. Rather, he wants to play a role in its occurrence. Thus he will do it for himself, at his own time, and on his own terms. We find, on occasion, a case in which an older person, hospitalized in a general medical hospital, in the terminal stages of a fatal disease will, with remarkable and totally unexpected energy and strength, take the tubes and needles out of himself, climb over the bed rails, lift a heavy window, and throw himself to the ground several stories below. What is most typical about such an individual is that when one looks at his previous occupational history one sees that he has never been fired—he has always quit. In either case, the person ends up unemployed, but the role he has played in the process is different.

3. *Death-ignorer*. Consider the following suicide note: "Good-bye, kid. You couldn't help it. Tell that brother of yours, when he gets to where I'm going, I hope I'm foreman down there; I might be able to do something for him." Although it is true that suicide notes that contain any reference to a hereafter, a continued existence, or a reunion with dead loved ones are relatively rare, it is also true that some people who kill themselves believe, as part of their total system of beliefs, that one can effect termination without involving cessation. They seem to ignore the fact that, so far as we know, termination of life always

involves cessation of mind. One can note that even those in our contemporary society who espouse belief in a hereafter as part of their religious tenets still label a person who has shot himself to death as suicidal. This is probably so primarily because, whatever *really* happens after termination, the survivors are still left to live (and usually to mourn) in the undeniable physical absence of the person who killed himself. Thus, this subcategory of death-ignorer, or, perhaps better, death-transcender, contains those persons who, from our point of view, effect their own termination and cessation but who, from their point of view, effect only their physical termination and continue to exist in some manner or another.

This paragraph is not meant necessarily to deny a (logical) possibility of continuation after cessation (life after death), but the concept of death-ignoring (or something similar to it) is a firm necessity in any systematic classification of this type; otherwise we will put ourselves in the untenable position of making exactly comparable a man's shooting his head off in belief and hope that he will soon meet his dead wife in heaven and a man's taking a trip from one city to another with the purpose and expectation of being reunited with his spouse. Obviously, these two acts are so vastly different in their effects (on the person concerned and on others who know him) that they cannot be equated. Therefore, independent of the individual's convictions that killing oneself does not result in cessation but is simply a transition to another life, we must superimpose our belief that cessation is necessarily final as far as the human personality which we can know is concerned.

Subintentioned

Subintentioned death behaviors relate to those instances in which the individual plays an indirect, covert, partial, or unconscious role in hastening his own demise. The fact that individuals may play an unconscious role in their own failures and act inimically to their own best welfare seems to be too well documented from psychoanalytic and general clinical practice to ignore. Often death is hastened by the individual's seeming carelessness, imprudence, foolhardiness, forgetfulness, amnesia, disregard of medical regimen, lack of judgment, or other psychological mechanisms. This concept of subintentioned death is similar, in some ways, to Karl Menninger's concepts of chronic, focal, and organic suicide, except that Menninger's ideas have to do with self-defeating ways of continuing to live, whereas the notion of subintentioned death is a description of a way of stopping the process of living. Included in this subintentioned category would be many patterns of mismanagement and brink-of-death living which result in death. In terms of the traditional classification of modes of death (natural, accident, suicide, and homicide), some instances of all four types can be subsumed under this category, depending on the particular details of each case. In relation to the term *suicide*, subintentioned cases may be said to have *permitted* suicide.

Subintentioned death involves what might be called the psychosomatics of death: that is, cases in which essentially psychological processes (like fear, anxiety, derring-do, hate, and so forth) seem to play some role in exacerbating the catabolic or physiological processes that bring termination (and necessarily cessation), as well as those cases in which the individual seems to play an indirect, largely unconscious role in inviting or hastening cessation itself. The death groups for the subintentioned category are as follows: (1) death-chancer, (2) death-hastener, (3) death-capitulator, and (4) death-experimenter.

1. *Death-chancer.* The death-darer, death-chancer, and death-experimenter are all on a continuum of chance expectation and chance possibility of cessation. The difference lies in the combination of objective and subjective probabilities. If a death-darer has only five chances out of six of continuing, then a death-chancer would have chances significantly greater than that, but still involving a realistic risk of death. It should be pointed out that these categories are largely independent of the method used, in that most methods (like the use of razor blades or barbiturates) can, depending on the exact place of the cut, the depth of the cut, and the realistic and calculated expectations for intervention and rescue by others, legitimately be thought of as intentioned, subintentioned, or unintentioned — depending on these circumstances. Individuals who "leave it up to chance," who "gamble with death," who "half intended to do it" are the subintentioned death-chancers.

2. *Death-hastener.* The basic assumption is that in all cessation activities the critical question (on the assumption that cessation will occur to everyone) is *when*, so that, in a sense, all intentioned and subintentioned activities are hastening. The death-hastener refers to the individual who unconsciously exacerbates a physiological disequilibrium so that his cessation (which would, in ordinary terms, be called a natural death) is expedited. This can be done either in terms of the style in which he lives (the abuse of his body, usually through alcohol, drugs, exposure, or malnutrition) or, in cases where there is a specific physiological imbalance, through the mismanagement of prescribed remedial procedures. Examples of the latter would be the diabetic who mismanages his diet or his insulin, the individual with cirrhosis who mismanages his alcohol intake, the Berger's disease patient who mismanages his nicotine intake. Very closely allied to the death-hastener is the death-facilitator, who, while he is ill and his psychic energies are low, is somehow more than passively unresisting to cessation, and "makes it easy" for death (and accompanying cessation) to occur. Some unexpected deaths in hospitals may be of this nature.

3. *Death-capitulator.* A death-capitulator is a person who, by virtue of some strong emotion, usually his fear of death, plays a psychological role in effecting his termination. In a sense, he gives in to death or he scares himself to

death. This type of death includes voodoo deaths—the type of death reported among Indians and Mexicans from southwestern U.S. railroad hospitals, where the patients thought that people who went to hospitals went there to die, and being hospitalized was thus cause in itself for great alarm—and some of the cases reported from Boston by Weisman and Hackett (1961). All of these individuals play a psychological role in the psychosomatics of their termination and cessation.

4. *Death-experimenter*. A death-experimenter is a person who often lives "on the brink of death," who does not consciously wish either interruption or cessation, but—usually by use of (or addiction to) alcohol and/or barbiturates— seems to wish a chronically altered, usually befogged continuation state of consciousness. Death-experimenters seem to wish to remain conscious but to be benumbed or drugged. They will often experiment with their self-prescribed dosages, always in the direction of increasing the effect of the dosage, taking some chances of extending the benumbed conscious states into interruption (coma) states and even taking some chances, usually without much concern, in a kind of lackadaisical way, of running some minimal but real risk of extending the interruption of consciousness states into cessation. When this type of death occurs, it is traditionally thought of as accidental.

Unintentioned Death

Unintentioned death describes those occurrences in which, for all intents and purposes, the person psychologically plays no significant role in his own demise. He is, at the time of his cessation, going about his business, even though he may be lying in a hospital, with no conscious intention of effecting or hastening cessation and no strong conscious drive in this direction. What happens is that something from the outside—the outside of his mind—occurs. This something might be a cerebral-vascular accident, a myocardial infarction, a neoplastic growth, some malfunction, some catabolism, some invasion—whether by bullet or by virus—which, for him, has lethal consequences. It happens to him. Inasmuch as all that anyone can do in regard to cessation is to attempt some manipulation along a temporal dimension (that is, to hasten or to postpone it), one might suppose that unintentioned death is synonymous only with post-poner, but it appears that there are other possible attitudes.

In terms of the traditional categories of death, most natural, accidental, and homicidal deaths would be called unintentioned, and no presently labeled suicidal deaths would be so called. In relation to the term *suicidal*, unintentioned cases may be said to have *omitted* suicide.

The death categories for unintentioned cessation are: (1) death-welcomer, (2) death-acceptor, (3) death-postponer, (4) death-disdainer, and (5) death-fearer.

1. *Death-welcomer.* A death-welcomer is one who, although playing no discernible (conscious or unconscious) role in either hastening or facilitating his own cessation, could honestly report an introspective position of welcoming the end of his life. Very old people, especially after long, painful, debilitating illness, report that they welcome the end.

2. *Death-acceptor.* The slight difference between a death-welcomer and a death-acceptor lies in the nuance of activity and passivity that distinguishes them. The death-acceptor is one who has accepted the imminence of his cessation and is resigned to his own fate. In this, he may be relatively passive, philosophical, resigned, heroic, realistic, or mature, depending on the spirit in which this enormous acceptance is made.

3. *Death-postponer.* Most of the time most of us are acute death-postponers. Death-postponing is the habitual, indeed the unthinking, orientation of most humans toward cessation. The death-postponer is one who, to the extent that he is oriented toward or concerned with cessation at all, wishes that it would not occur in anything like the foreseeable future and further wishes that it would not occur for as long as possible. (This death-postponing orientation should not be confused with the ubiquitous human fantasies of immortality.)

4. *Death-disdainer.* Some individuals, during those moments when they consciously contemplate cessation, are disdainful of the concept and feel that they are above being involved in the cessation of the vital processes that it implies. They are, in a sense, supercilious toward death. It may well be that most young people in our culture, independent of their fears about death, are habitually death-disdainers, as well they might be—for a while.

5. *Death-fearer.* A death-fearer is one who is fearful of death and of the topics relating to death. He may literally be phobic about this topic. He fights the notion of cessation, seeing reified death as a feared and hated enemy. This position may be related to conscious wishes for omnipotence and to great cathexis to one's social and physical potency. Hypochondriacs, fearing illnesses and assault, are perhaps also death-fearers. (A person who, when physically well, is a death-fearer might, when physically ill, become a death-facilitator.)

Imagine five people, all older men on the same ward of a hospital, all dying of cancer, none playing an active or unconscious role in his own cessation. Yet it is still possible to distinguish among them different orientations toward cessation. One wishes not to die and is exerting his "will to live" (death-postponer); another is resigned to his cessation (death-acceptor); the third is disdainful of what is occurring to him and will not believe that death can "take him" (death-disdainer); still another, although not taking any steps in the direction of hastening his end, does at this point in his illness welcome it (death-welcomer); and the fifth is most fearful about the topic of death and the implication of cessation and forbids anyone to speak of it in his presence (death-fearer).

It might be protested, inasmuch as the assessments of these intentioned states and death categories involve the appraisal of unconscious factors, that some workers (especially lay coroners) cannot legitimately be expected to make the psychological judgments required for this type of classification. To this, one answer would be that coroners throughout the country are making judgments of precisely this nature every day of the week. In the situation of evaluating a possible suicide, the coroner often acts (sometimes without realizing it) as psychiatrist and psychologist and as both judge and jury in a quasijudicial way. This is because the certification of a death as suicide does, willy-nilly, imply some judgments or reconstruction of the victim's motivation or intention. Making these judgments—perhaps more coroners ought to use the category of "undetermined"—is an inexorable part of a coroner's function. My position is that it is much better to make these psychological dimensions explicit and to attempt, howsoever crudely, to use them, than to employ these psychological dimensions on an implicit and unverbalized level. The dilemma is between the polarities of a usable, oversimplified classification, on the one hand, and a complex, but more meaningful classification, on the other. The goal would be to try to combine greatest usefulness with maximum meaningfulness.

DISCUSSION*

Avery D. Weisman, M.D., Department of Neurology and Psychiatry, Harvard Medical School

Dr. Shneidman is understandably impatient with the prevalence of false notions about death and suicide. In fact, he thinks that the word *suicide* is too ambiguous to be either scientifically or clinically significant. He also wants to avoid the term *death* and to replace it with operational terms. Like other investigators of suicide and death, he is deeply aware that the line that divides living from dying is often difficult to determine. Semantic confusion, oversimplification, prejudice, and unexamined assumptions impose still further obstacles to understanding.

Dr. Shneidman's central concept is that of *cessation*. It refers to conscious experience. An analogous concept, *termination*, applies to physiological functions. The relation of cessation to termination is approximately that between psychic death and physical death. While termination presumably puts an end to conscious experience, it is possible for cessation to occur without concomitant termination. This distinction underscores the contrast between extinction of individual consciousness and objective death as an inescapable fact of nature.

---

*This section is reproduced from *The International Journal of Psychiatry* 2, no. 2 (March 1966): 190–200 by permission of the publisher.

Dr. Shneidman focuses on the concept of cessation, and shows how people may, knowingly or not, bring about or delay their own cessation. Thus, there are cessation-fearers, cessation-ignorers, cessation-postponers, and so forth. According to the degree in which a person's conscious motivation participates in his own cessation, Dr. Shneidman distinguishes between intentioned, subintentioned, and unintentioned deaths.

Concepts of Death

It is extremely difficult to learn what people think about death and dying. Not only are most people burdened by assumptions and prejudices that have been uncritically absorbed in the course of life, but their personal attitudes toward death are likely to change as they grow older, fall sick, and are themselves threatened with death.

The concept of cessation allows us to recognize how people affirm the reality of death at various stages of life and under different circumstances. Patients are not expected to say *what* death means to them, or *how* they expect to die. Although Dr. Shneidman's classification of cessation behavior is largely contingent upon reports and observations made by sophisticated, observant investigators, the choice of category is broad enough to reduce unwarranted inferences. He demonstrates that *cessation attitudes are not necessarily suicidal, nor is there a specific cessation attitude for suicide.* With equal relevance, cessation attitudes are both vital and lethal, covering a wide range of comprehensive versions of life as well as death.

Perhaps the most prevalent concept of death is that it is an unmitigated evil, never to be sought, always to be avoided as long as possible. Although cessation and termination cannot be postponed indefinitely, most people also believe that suicide is wrong—far more than those who believe that suicide is a sickness. Even sophisticated thinkers find that death is deplorable, and that hastening the inevitable is a sign of disability or defeat, not merely of disease. In Dr. Shneidman's sense, most of us are *doomed* to be cessation-postponers and cessation-fearers. Mankind concedes the universality of objective death, but still regards personal extinction either as an illusion or a tragic fault. Because Dr. Shneidman shows that the inner attitude of suicidal patients cannot be reduced to a single formula, he urges us to think again about our conventional notions of life and death.

Appropriate Death

Dr. Thomas Hackett and I (1961) reported a group of patients who approached death with a minimum of anxiety and conflict. Several of our patients anticipated death as a fitting solution to their problems. It was apparent that for some people death is not deplorable, but desirable as a means of attaining resolution of conflict, fulfillment of desire, and rewarding quiescence. We termed this concept *appropriate death.*

Although we were quite explicit about our meaning, so strong are the forces of habit and prejudice that the concept of appropriate death has been misunderstood in different ways. First, it is not intended to be merely a poetic metaphor, or a sentimental afterthought when someone has died. Second, appropriate death has no etiological significance. It is not a conspiracy of emotional, social, and biological forces that come together and dispose patients to an unwelcome death. Third, we understand that because the world is filled with so many needless and meaningless deaths it is difficult to imagine that death can ever be either acceptable or appropriate. The judgment about whether or not death was appropriate could not be made with finality, nor could we dogmatically declare that death was wholly acceptable to our patients. We defined an appropriate death as one in which there is reduction of conflict, compatibility with the ego ideal, continuity of significant relationships, and consummation of prevailing wishes. In short, an appropriate death is one which a person might choose for himself, had he an option. Death is therefore a harmonious end point of motivated acts within the context of the ego ideal. It is not merely conclusive; it is consummatory.

It is quite simple to define appropriate death in whatever way we choose. It is another matter when we try to discover if there are appropriate and acceptable deaths among patients who are not predilected to death and who manage to survive.

We can ask a hypothetical question: If no one died until he chose to, who would ever be ready for death? For the vigorous, healthy adult, the question is clearly unthinkable, because his affiliation with life is strong. However there are other people, for example, the chronically ill and extremely aged, in whom the margin between life and death is obscure. They may be quite willing to slip into oblivion, without being either depressed or suicidal. But to be willing to die is not equivalent to being able to die. Death may be acceptable and not appropriate, or it may be appropriate and not acceptable. We have known a patient who survived a series of hazardous operations for brain abscess. Despite numerous postoperative complications, he recovered. Three weeks after hospital discharge, he committed suicide. Evidently, his drive to survive persisted during his hospital weeks, but collapsed shortly after discharge! What kind of cessation was this? Had he died in the hospital, his death would have been subintentioned or unintentioned. He was a death-acceptor at this time. After discharge, he became a successful death-seeker. We may speculate that he was not suicidal in the hospital because he was cared for with unusual dedication and was not expected to fulfill social obligations. After discharge, however, he was once again a homeless drifter, living on the margins of life. No one can tell if this patient, deep in his mind, expected to destroy himself, nor can we be sure whether he was a death-welcomer or a death-fearer. In other words, although Dr. Shneidman has provided us with a valuable system of taxonomy, it is still not quite completely operational. We require quite a bit of understanding of a patient's attitude toward survival before we can appraise his attitude toward extinction.

Any concept of death is a version of life. The range of possible deaths is a catalogue that depicts many kinds of acceptability and appropriateness. Because there is a difference between cessation and termination, some kinds of death may be highly appropriate in the interpersonal and intrapersonal dimension, without involving a suitable impersonal or biological termination. We have studied several patients in whom social and emotional factors were consistent with both an acceptable and appropriate death, and yet they did not die. Naturally, we do not understand the specific biological, social, and emotional conjunction that eventuates in death. The concept of appropriate death does not require this kind of information. It does require that cessation and termination have a meaning in the life-style of a patient, that a patient does not die merely as a passive victim of a disease, and that dying is a positive act that protects his responsibility.

Suicide and Appropriate Death

What is the relation of suicide to appropriate death? Is it not an appropriate death that a suicidal patient wants to bring about? Does each variety of cessation correspond to a different context in which death is appropriate? Suicidal patients seek harmony, relief, and resolution of conflict. They apparently choose to extinguish themselves in order to find an idealized version of life.

Despite their similarities, suicide and appropriate death differ. There are, to be sure, many illustrious men who have chosen to terminate their lives rather than to survive with diminished creative powers. There are many other instances in which murder may be defensible. Whether a man's life is always his to dispense with is a moral question, and cannot be decided by psychiatrists or psychologists. Knowledge of the psychopathology of suicide is still rudimentary, but we have reason to believe, with Dr. Shneidman, that self-destruction may be "murder in the 180th degree." In other words, a suicidal act may replace and relieve a homicidal fantasy. Moreover, suicidal impulses are inconstant. A man who is suicidal today may find the idea unthinkable tomorrow. In suicide there are critical phases; one part of a person takes over the autonomy of the rest, and decrees its extinction—usually in opposition to his life-style, his ego-ideal, and the longitudinal meaning of his life.

A suicidal patient has *appropriated* death, without achieving an appropriate death. The availability of suicide carries many people through sleepless nights, but I doubt if many people choose suicide, quietly and dispassionately, as the culmination of a life plan. Any of us may choose suicide rather than suffer the tyranny of disease or despotic forces, but those people who do destroy themselves are usually suffering from an inner agony, not an external crisis.

The statement "I have nothing more to live for" may be a sentiment expressed by someone whose feasible work is done, or, in contrast, an utterance wrung out in a moment of despair. Despite verbal similarity, one statement is an expression of quiescence, the other, of pain. This is the interface where Dr. Shneidman's work and our own will meet. We are deeply appreciative of the contributions that he and his colleagues have made to these basic problems.

Karl Menninger, M.D., The Menninger Foundation, Topeka, Kansas

There is much in the lives of individuals and communities that is puzzling: bickerings, hatreds, and fightings over trivia, useless waste and self-destructiveness. People extend themselves to injure others, and expend time, trouble, and energy in shortening that pitifully small recess from oblivion which we call life. As if lacking aught else to destroy or failing to accomplish it, many turn their weapons directly upon themselves.

Death Instinct

It was such observations as this that led Sigmund Freud to the formulation of the theory of a drive toward self-destruction which he called the death instinct. There exist from the beginning in all of us strong propensities toward self-destruction and these come to fruition as actual suicide only in exceptional cases where many circumstances and factors combine to make it possible.

Freud makes the further assumption that the life and death instincts—let us call them the constructive and destructive tendencies of the personality—are in constant conflict and interaction just as are similar opposing forces in the concepts of physics, chemistry, and biology. To create and to destroy, to build up and to tear down, these are the anabolism and the catabolism of the personality, no less than of the cells and the corpuscles—the two directions in which the same energies exert themselves.

These forces, originally directed inward and related to the intimate problems of the self, continuously tend to be directed outward, focused on other environmental objects. Managed with sufficient skill and with the maintenance of a certain balance and control, this may resolve in growth, development, social integration. An incomplete turning outward of the self-directed destructiveness *and* also of the constructiveness with which we are—by hypothesis—born, results, of course, in permanent lack of development. Instead of dealing with people such individuals avoid them. Instead of fighting their enemies, such individuals fight themselves; instead of loving friends or music or the building of a house, such persons love only themselves. Hate and love are the emotional representatives of the destructive and constructive tendencies.

But no one evolves so completely as to be entirely free from the upsurge of the self-destructive tendencies; indeed, the phenomena of life, the behavior peculiar to different individuals, may be said to express the result of the measures taken to control these conflicting factors. An equilibrium of sorts, oftentimes very unstable, is achieved, maintained until disturbed by new developments in the environment which cause a rearrangement with perhaps quite different outcome.

Freud repeatedly emphasized that the manifestations of the self-destructive instinct were never nakedly visible. In the first place, the self-destructive instincts get turned in an outward direction by the very process of life, and in the second place, they get neutralized in the very process of living. Self-destruction in the operational sense is a result of a return, as it were, of the self-destructive tendencies to the original object. It is not *quite* the original object as a rule, because the object of redirected aggression, aggression reflected back upon the self, is usually the body. And since a part of the body may be offered up as a substitute for the whole, this partial suicide, as we have called it, is a way of averting total suicide. But if that part of the body is a vital part, the partial suicide becomes actual suicide.

On this basis we can understand how it can be that some people kill themselves quickly and some slowly and some not at all, why some contribute to their own deaths and others withstand valiantly and brilliantly external assaults upon their lives to which their fellows would have quickly succumbed. So much of this, however, takes place automatically and unconsciously that it will seem at first blush like an impossible task to dissect the details of a particular bargain or compromise between the life and death instincts.

Early in my professional career I was impressed with the central position in all psychiatry held by the phenomenon of suicide. It is considered irrational in most cultures; in some societies it is unknown; it is strangely overprevalent in certain very civilized countries. It increases with prosperity. Rationalized as it may be by intellectuals, its occurrence is always somewhat uncanny, incredible, inexplicable. It is a little difficult for survivors to conceive of anyone having been *quite* so hopeless, *quite* so heartless, *quite* so unrealistic. It is, indeed, a last act, an irreparable, irreversible, final blow. Its dreadfulness, its aggressive impact, is felt by relatives and friends and physicians, which, of course, was part of its victim's intent.

Three Components in the Suicidal Act

First of all suicide is obviously a *murder*. In the German language it is, literally, a murder of the self (*Selbstmord*), and in all the earlier philological equivalents the idea of murder is implicit.

But suicide is also a murder committed *by* the self as murderer. It is a death in which are combined in one person the murderer and the murdered. We know that the motives for murder vary enormously; so do the motives for wishing to be murdered, which is quite another matter and not nearly as absurd as it may sound. For since in suicide there is a self that submits to the murder and would appear to be desirous of doing so, we must seek the motives of this strange submission.

If the reader will picture to himself a battlefield scene in which a wounded man is suffering greatly and begs someone to kill him, he will readily appreciate that the feelings of the *murderer* would be very different, depending upon whether he were a friend or a foe of the wounded man; those of the man who desires to be murdered, that is, to be put out of agony, however, would be the same in either case.

In many suicides it is quite apparent that one of these contributing factors is stronger that the other. One sees people who want to die but cannot take the step against themselves; they fling themselves in front of trains or, like King Saul and Brutus, they beseech their armor bearers to slay them.

Probably no suicide is consummated unless—in addition to these wishes to kill and be killed—the suicidal person also wishes to die, if we understand the word *wish* here to relate to the resultant of motivational factors, conscious and unconscious wishes. Many suicides, in spite of the violence of the attack upon themselves and in spite of the corresponding surrender, paradoxically seem to be unwilling to die. Every hospital intern has labored in the emergency ward with would-be suicides who beg him to save their lives. The fact that dying and being murdered achieve the same end so far as personal extinction is concerned leads the practical-minded individual to think, "If a person wants to murder himself, or if he feels so bad about something that he is willing to be murdered, then he surely must want to die." But the illustration just given is only one of many indications that this is not so. Murdering or being murdered entails factors of violence, while dying relates to a surrender of one's life and happiness. In attempted suicide the wish to die may or may not be present, or may be to quite a variable degree, as Shneidman has described in his concepts of cessation, termination, interruption, and continuation. Freud emphasized the fact that instincts were never conscious and that we should not equate the death instinct with the wish to die or the life instinct with the wish to live. What I am proposing is that many other factors enter the formula. Stengel and others have pointed out how a certain amount of playacting is always involved whereby the drama of suicide is played with a childish and unrealistic King's X cross: "It really isn't going to happen even though I am doing it." "I am doing it not to end all but to portray all." "I am showing what I have suffered." "I am dramatizing the need I have for help." Such feelings as this represent a wish to live, despite the actions which seem to indicate a wish to die.

Suicide must thus be regarded as a peculiar kind of death, which entails three basic internal elements and many modifying ones. There is the element of dying, the element of killing, and the element of being killed. Each is a condensation for which there exist complexes of motive, unconscious and conscious. What we call a suicide is for the individual himself an attempt to burst into life or to save his life. It may be to avoid something far more dreadful, to avoid committing murder or going mad. After all, the reasoning processes of the suicidally impelled person cannot be expected to be logical or rational or even consistent. From my own point of view the suicidal determination—determination, I say, in fantasy, not enactment, not motivation—the suicidal determination as such, the surrender of all hope, is a final catastrophe of dissolution, which the organism so greatly dreads. In a sense suicide is a flight from death, using death in a very broad sense.

Some Additional Comments on Methods and Prevention

In the end each man kills himself in his own selected way, fast or slow, soon or late. We all feel this, vaguely; there are so many occasions to witness it before our eyes. The methods are legion and it is these which attract our attention. Some of them interest surgeons, some of them interest lawyers and priests, some of them interest heart specialists, some of them interest sociologists. All of them must interest the individual who sees the personality as a totality and medicine as the healing of the nations.

I believe that our best defense against self-destructiveness lies in the courageous application of intelligence to human phenomenology. If such is our nature, it were better that we knew it and knew it in all its protean manifestations. To see all forms of self-destruction from the standpoint of their dominant principles would seem to be logical progress toward self-preservation and toward a unified view of medical science.

Robert E. Litman M.D., Chief Psychiatrist, Suicide Prevention Center, Los Angeles, California; Clinical Professor of Psychiatry, School of Medicine, University of Southern California, Los Angeles

Dr. Shneidman applies psychodynamic concepts to the classification of deaths. The result is a new scientific view of self-destruction, avoiding the sociolegal connotations of suicide.

The academic reader will enjoy this essay for its literary style and marks of philosophic erudition. But style should not obscure the essential content, which is a bold proposal that the prevailing classification of death, honored by centuries of use, should be discarded as unclear in favor of a new classification that assigns the deceased into categories according to his orientation toward death.

The traditional classification of death has served the sociolegal need to assign blame for every death, either to God (natural, accident) or man (homicide, suicide). By analogy with homicide, suicide might be "justifiable" (as in heroic self-sacrifice), "excusable" (as in simple carelessness), or "culpable" (a deliberate social wrong). The concept of the role of the individual in his own demise cuts across these categories and serves a different need, that of furthering the scientific understanding of self-destruction.

Is Suicide a Useful Term?

Dr. Shneidman suggests, "It may well be that the word *suicide* currently has too many loose and contradictory meanings to be scientifically or clinically useful." This is a statement with which I must agree. As a term, *suicide* leads more to scientific confusion than to clarity. In clinical practice the word suicide has an affectual shock value which is useful in a few limited communication situations but often leads to ambiguous discourse and misunderstanding between practitioners. In talking about suicidal behavior, it promotes clarity if the clinician specifies whether the given act, thought, impulse, or affect was mildly suicidal, moderately suicidal, or seriously suicidal. Suicide is not a unitary syndrome, but rather a collection of different acts by dissimilar people for various motives.

However, I do not feel that the community is ready for a new taxonomy of death. Rather we should encourage the legal profession, coroners, and police officials to use the customary and accepted classifications more consistently and conscientiously. By contrast, behavioral scientists working in the vanguard of research on self-destruction do need new designs for ordering their observations. To classify certain people as "death-seekers," "death-darers," "death-experimenters," and so forth, is dramatically descriptive and stimulates new views of human lives and deaths.

Is It Dynamic?

"The operation which gives meaning to the phrase *basic orientation toward death* has to do with the role of the individual in his own demise. By *role of the individual* is meant his overt and covert behaviors and nonbehaviors that reflect conscious and unconscious attributes relevant to his cessation."

By his concept *role of the individual*, Shneidman ties orientation to behavior (and nonbehavior). These behaviors are understood to reflect all the multidetermined complexity of shifting drives and defenses ambivalently balanced against each other. Obviously the whole purpose of this classification is to introduce psychodynamic concepts into the descriptive terminology of death. For this effort the essay deserves general recognition and evaluation.

Probably the greatest difficulty from the standpoint of personality dynamics involves Shneidman's snapshot focus on a limited unit of time. By tying orientation to action behavior, the concept freezes psychodynamics at one particular moment of time, that moment appropriate to the behavior "relevant to his cessation." Although this focus on a segment of time and a segment of behavior-action is in some respects artificial and does not do justice to the complexity of total personality, it provides a tremendous gain in clarity and, we hope, in useful diagnostic divisions. A difficulty in the path of clinical application is that over periods of time patients tend to change, sometimes rapidly, in their orientations and behaviors.

REFERENCES

Bridgman, P. W. (1938). *The Intelligent Individual and Society*. New York: Macmillan.
Draper, G., Dupertuis, C. W., and Caughley, J. L. (1944). *Human Constitution in Clinical Medicine*. New York: Hoeber.
Durkheim, E. (1897/1951). *Suicide*. Glencoe, IL: Free Press.
Freud, S. (1915/1925). Thoughts for the times on war and death. In *Collected Papers, vol. 14*. London: Hogarth.
Weisman, A. D., and Hackett, T. (1961). Predilection to death: death and dying as a psychiatric problem. *Psychosomatic Medicine* 23: 232–256.

2

THE SUICIDE PREVENTION CENTER: CONCEPTS AND CLINICAL FUNCTIONS

Norman L. Farberow, Samuel M. Heilig, and Howard J. Parad

T HE MODERN ERA of suicide prevention began in the United States in 1958 with the establishment of the Los Angeles Suicide Prevention Center (LASPC). In the succeeding three decades, the LASPC has changed considerably, although its basic principles remain the same. The first part of this chapter briefly reviews these changes and describes current practices; the second part focuses on the clinical functioning of a suicide prevention center (SPC) telephone crisis service, presenting examples of the people who use its services and the kinds of demands that are made upon the center and staff. The final section illustrates "in-person" crisis therapy with a suicidal client and summarizes guidelines for suicide prevention.

The LASPC was established as a result of comprehensive research on the status of suicide in Los Angeles County from 1954 to 1957 (Farberow and Shneidman 1961). Information was obtained about suicides, suicide attempts, and other self-destructive behaviors from mental hospitals, psychiatric clinics, emergency rooms, and mental health professionals and general practitioners throughout Los Angeles County. As the data were collected, it became evident that no agency in the county provided immediate response to suicidal crisis.

THE FIRST DECADE

The first conceptualization of a suicide prevention center (proposed to the National Institute of Mental Health) was an evaluation unit within the Los Angeles County Hospital through which all hospitalized persons who had attempted suicide would be processed before discharge. The principal aim was to evaluate the suicide potential of the individual upon discharge and to provide the person with an appropriate resource in the community from which continuing treatment could be obtained. While functioning in this way during its first 5 years, the LASPC gathered information and experience about suicidal persons and their treatment.

In an overview of the field of suicide prevention, Farberow (1968) described the changes that occurred in the first decade. The initial concept of evaluation and referral before hospital discharge changed radically as the community became aware of the agency and its services. The first major change was due to burgeoning telephone calls by persons calling for help before attempting suicide. What had been a 9:00 A.M. to 5:00 P.M., five-day-a-week operation became a crisis or emergency service that operated 24 hours a day, 7 days a week, every day of the year. Professional resistance to the use of the telephone in working with highly disturbed persons was overcome by the growing recognition that the telephone provided an early and readily available means of contact for desperate people seeking immediate help. Thus the service was reconceptualized as a crisis-oriented response center, part of a network of helping resources. The focus was on resolution of the emergency followed by help in finding the resources in the community most suitable for the person's specific needs.

A second major change occurred in 1966 with the introduction of nonprofessional volunteers to respond to telephone callers (Heilig, et al. 1968), the only way the center could function on a full-time 24-hour basis within budget constraints. Although this change was initiated reluctantly, the selection, training, and supervision of volunteers and their performance in providing the services of the LASPC proved to be highly successful. By 1968 a number of SPCs had been established throughout the country, and a range of models with considerable variation in staffing, forms of support, places of operation, and types of service were developed according to the needs of the individual communities.

At that time, the major clinical problems for suicide prevention were identified as the development of effective evaluation criteria, responding to the needs of the chronic borderline suicidal person who required continually available but not constant care, reaching the persons at highest risk (for example, the elderly, white, sick male) who were not making use of the services, and dispelling the taboo against discussion of suicide that prevented people from asking for help as well as their significant others from responding to a cry for help. Ideas for prevention of suicide, such as teaching suicide prevention in schools, were just beginning to appear; possibilities for primary prevention were being explored; and interventive activities prior to a suicidal crisis were being developed.

THE SECOND DECADE

The second decade witnessed continued expansion of clinical and research activities as well as a growing sense of professional identity in the field of suicide and suicide prevention. Motto (1979) summarized specific changes that occurred using a survey of seventy suicide prevention and crisis intervention centers — forty-seven in the United States and twenty-three abroad. Questionnaires asked each of the centers to describe services or activities that had been added to or that had modified the traditional model of 24-hour crisis service offering telephone counseling and referral. Additional services for a variety of crisis situations were reported, including programs for treatment of disturbed adolescents, drug and alcohol abusers, victims of rape and crime, sexual abuse, and wife battering. Respondents reported that ancillary programs were developed for parents concerned with child abuse, for single-parent families, and for the special needs of the deaf and mentally retarded. Some centers had formed clubs and social groups for repeat callers and were offering the use of a meeting place within the center.

Many of the agencies had extended their services with family counseling for suicide problems, sex counseling, marital counseling, and face-to-face as well as telephone hotline counseling offered in their own agencies. Group therapy used traditional insight and supportive methods, but also developed nontraditional methods such as open-end, drop-in, socialization, and art therapy groups (Farberow 1976). An innovative center in Australia reported an arrangement to provide group interaction by telephone.

Some outreach programs included special groups that visited hospitals to provide emotional support for rape victims undergoing the required medical procedures; crisis counseling for inmates on referral from the jail chaplain; and crisis counseling for hospitalized patients who had attempted suicide. In Asia special efforts were made to meet with at-risk students who failed their studies or encountered difficulty in school and were afraid to tell their parents.

Emphasis on the emergency aspect of suicide prevention was reported in many SPCs. In some places the evaluation and disposition of evening and weekend emergency psychiatric requests to the county emergency medical services were handled by the emergency telephone lines of the local SPC. These centers were empowered to dispatch an ambulance to an emergency anywhere in the county. In one center, crisis intervention staff covered the hospital psychiatric emergency service during nights and weekends. They also made home visits to patients who declined alternative resources. Conspicuously absent were programs for special populations (such as the elderly or survivors of a significant other who committed suicide) and bereavement counseling following deaths due to accidental and natural causes as well as suicidal deaths.

Motto (1979) summarized the trends over the decade by noting that the services of the SPC were now broader in scope, had increased in depth, and were less dependent on referral sources. Services were less passive in that staff took a more active case-finding approach toward suicide prevention; programs had greater visibility and were more available. In addition, centers became a more integral part of the community care system by collaborating closely with key elements of the community's crisis-response network. At the same time they continued to conform to the important original characteristics of the SPC, that is, accessibility, availability, and unquestioning acceptance of the caller's need.

THE 1980s

The third decade has seen the emergence of focused concern for specific groups in the field of suicide prevention: youth, AIDS victims, and family survivors.

Youth

The suicide rate among the young in the United States, especially among the 15-to-24-year-old age group, increased from 4.5 per 100,000 in 1950 to a peak of 13.3 per 100,000 in 1977, an increase of 196 percent, nearly triple the 1950 rate (Farberow et al. 1987). Although the rate declined slightly to about 12.8 in 1988, it continues to be distressingly high. Suicide is the second-leading cause of death among 15-to-24-year-olds (accidents are first). It is the eighth-leading cause of death among persons of all ages in the United States (Lamb 1988).

To meet the challenge of the precipitous rise in suicide rates among the young, programs have been developed to teach suicide prevention in schools (California State Department of Education 1987). The most common signs of suicidal feelings are taught along with simple recommendations of what to do, such as listening with understanding, not being judgmental, and encouraging the individual to talk to parents and/or a responsible adult in the school. Information is provided about possible resources in the community. Suicide prevention centers, available for consultation, service, and training, are identified as a primary resource for the schools. In most programs a major aim has been to enlist the aid of students in the identification of at-risk students. A primary source of resistance is the reluctance to reveal the "secret" of a friend, especially if sworn to secrecy. The students soon see, however, that it is better to get help and to keep their friend alive than to keep the secret and lose the friend.

AIDS

Another population increasingly at risk for suicide consists of persons with AIDS and their families (Frierson and Lippman 1988). Although the extent of the problem of suicide among AIDS patients is unknown, it is anticipated that the rate will be high due to the guilt and shame, the loss of social status and supportive networks, the extensive medical and physical debilitation, and the accompanying financial pressures that stress the patient. Although systematic data are not yet available, the risk of suicide is probably also greater among persons with AIDS-related complex (ARC) and the "waiting well," that is, those individuals in groups at high risk for the disease because of their prior sexual activities, who are apprehensively waiting to see if symptoms will appear. Calls to SPCs from persons affected by AIDS are rising.

Survivors after Suicide

Increasing attention has been focused on survivors—family members who experience a crisis of bereavement after the suicide of a loved one (Dunne et al. 1987). Family members have been found to be more vulnerable to stress reactions, including prolonged unresolved grief and ongoing depressive disorders, and at higher risk for suicide themselves.

Survivor groups, a specialized type of bereavement group, now number approximately eighty across the country. Most groups have been started by survivors who felt a need for help not available through traditional facilities. Groups usually meet monthly for indefinite periods.

At the LASPC, a "Survivors after Suicide" program was developed according to a crisis intervention model. Groups of six to ten members meet for eight weekly sessions to deal with the following problems: reactions to the loss of a loved one, shame due to attitudes about suicide, guilt about not having done something to prevent the suicide, and anger that the deceased chose to die this way. Family and social relationships change because many family members, friends, and colleagues are too embarrassed to talk about a suicide, thus weakening the usual sources of support. A special problem experienced by survivors is that of disbelief or puzzlement: Why did he or she do this?

It is helpful for survivors to meet in a group with others who share the same trauma. Group members always report that they feel less alone, less shame, and more understood after attending. The group is co-led by a professional and a survivor, the latter having gone through the group experience and received training in group process. The survivor-facilitator serves as a positive role model, exemplifying the success of the program and the fact that it is possible to live through and overcome the grief despite the intensity of the current pain.

When the 8-week program is concluded, members are invited to participate in monthly meetings. Some feel they need additional time and help. Grief is often aroused around anniversaries and holidays, or members may simply need the ongoing support offered by the group.

STANDARD SETTING

The American Association of Suicidology (AAS) had assumed as one of its primary responsibilities the development of standards for the certification of its member agencies and individual members (AAS 1984). The criteria for certification do not attempt to assess outcome of intervention but rather focus on "adequate functioning" of an SPC, defined in terms such as organization, operation, and role in the community. The criteria establish levels of functioning (unacceptable, minimal, and optimal) that may exist in the various operations of the SPC. Two components of the SPC—the general service delivery system and service in life-threatening crisis—are summarized below.

General Service Delivery

The general service delivery category is evaluated in terms of the response the crisis program provides to its clients. It determines the availability of the five components of the service delivery system as well as the levels at which they operate: telephone service, walk-in crisis service, outreach crisis service, the degree to which crisis cases can be followed up, and client record keeping. The last component evaluates the completeness of the record-keeping system, the availability of the records, and the confidentiality with which they are maintained.

Services in a Life-Threatening Crisis

The components that are evaluated in the area of services in a life-threatening crisis include whether an assessment of lethality is routinely made, the capability of rescue, the degree to which follow-up occurs of persons attempting or threatening suicide or violence, provision of services to survivors of suicide, follow-up for victims of violence, and involvement in community education. Rescue capability is not necessarily required of the agency itself but liaison with other community resources such as telephone company tracing services, police and ambulance services, and other types of rescue services should be evident. The follow-up for victims of violence includes victims of assault, such as rape, child abuse, or battering, and the survivors of victims of traumatic death.

CLINICAL PRINCIPLES AND PROCEDURES

The basic principles and clinical procedures in suicide prevention have broadened as the field has expanded over the past three decades. First developed with the aim of crisis intervention and resolution, the early procedures were emergency-oriented and directed toward resolution of problems. Their objective was to provide immediate relief from tension by evaluating the lethality of the situation through structured interviewing and focused fact gathering, identifying and rallying resources, developing an action plan, and authoritative management. The broadened concept now includes the acceptance of an ongoing relationship (especially with persons who make repeat attempts) and the use of modified long-term techniques to accommodate the large group of borderline, poorly adjusted, relatively fragile, chronically suicide-prone persons who become the responsibility of the SPC after having exhausted virtually all the other treatment resources in the community. Additional treatment procedures, such as controlled and limited use of the telephone for regular contacts, maintenance of the relationship by telephone outreach, and varied forms of brief and long-term group therapy have been developed to address the special needs of this latter group.

Despite the involvement of many other kinds of medical and community helpers, mental health personnel still have the primary responsibility of providing care to suicidal people. The additional helpers, often termed "gatekeepers" because they are among the first to come in contact with persons whose suicidal impulses are surfacing, include probation officers, school counselors, clergy, physicians, and others involved in ongoing care in the human services sector. Psychological autopsy studies have indicated that many persons who committed suicide had received some type of treatment or counseling just before their death. These cases indicate missed opportunities for early recognition and treatment that might have prevented a suicide.

There are three core elements in suicide prevention: (1) recognition, (2) evaluation of risk, and (3) treatment. Suicidal thinking and behavior is so prevalent that it is useful to ask all clients who are interviewed for counseling or therapy whether they have thought about suicide or have ever felt suicidal. The ubiquity of such thoughts was demonstrated in a study in which youngsters were asked whether they had ever made a suicide attempt or thought about suicide (Farberow et al. 1987). The results indicated that 3 percent to 5 percent of high school students ages 16 to 19 years had made a suicide attempt, whereas approximately 10 percent had thought about it in the previous week. Also striking was the finding that 40 percent to 60 percent were aware of suicidal activity among their peers. These findings are even more disturbing when one realizes that they relate to young people who had not previously been identified as troubled.

Persons with certain kinds of problems are at higher risk for suicide. These problems include one or more of the following: borderline personality disorders, alcohol and drug addiction, chronic life-threatening illness, and severe emotional and mental disturbance. People who are deeply depressed and feeling helpless and/or hopeless; who are psychotic, isolated, withdrawn, and detached; or who are chemically dependent and acutely agitated are at greater risk for succumbing to suicidal impulses than are persons who are more capable of responding to and accepting offers of help.

It is important to listen carefully to what people say when they come for help. Verbal statements range from remarks that can be understood as indirect suicidal comments to overt suicide threats: "I can't stand this pain," "I can't go on like this," "I can't live without him," "I'd be better off dead," "I wish I were dead," "I'm going to kill myself." Suicidal comments need to be explored. However, such comments are often resisted by therapists and counselors because they fear taking responsibility for a case in which death is a real possibility. Such cases can provoke a lot of anxiety as well as demand extra time, energy, and work from the therapist.

After a suicidal problem is identified, it is important to talk openly and directly about it. Most people who think or behave in a suicidal fashion are not at immediate high risk; most people who think about suicide will not try to kill themselves. Moreover, most people who make suicide attempts will not die. Suicidal feelings can best be understood as an indication of the depth of a person's feelings about his or her problems. The important question is how to evaluate the more serious risks within a population already identified as suicidal (Farberow et al. 1968). Over the past 25 years many experts in the field of suicidology have developed various suicide lethality scales that are helpful to clinicians. However, the best use of these scales is in conjunction with clinical judgment. Although various criteria are useful in evaluating the seriousness of risk for suicide, the following three criteria are most important:

1. *Prior suicidal behaviors.* A history of prior suicide attempts greatly heightens a person's risk for suicide. Moreover, if past attempts have been of high lethality as reflected by the method (gunshot or jumping from high places)

or circumstances (cases in which the person survived a suicide attempt due to fortunate and unforeseeable circumstances), the risk is even further heightened. In general, people who have continuing, chronic struggles with suicidal impulses make increasingly serious suicide attempts. Frequently, a suicide attempt is used as a means to put the crisis behind the person; that is, it serves as an ordeal or test to determine whether to live or die. When clients have a history of suicidal behavior, it is useful to learn what brought them to the point of overt suicidal behavior. If the aim was to die or to manipulate responsive behavior from significant others, this information will be important in planning current treatment.

2. *Suicide plan.* People who have arranged a plan to kill themselves, for example, by buying pills or a gun and ammunition, selecting a place and time when they will kill themselves, writing farewell notes or preparing a will, and taking care of last-minute affairs, are obviously at higher risk than are those who have no specific plan. When a person reports that he or she has acquired the means to kill him- or herself, such as a loaded gun, it is extremely important to offer to take the gun for safekeeping or to urge that it be given to someone else so that the person can be protected from his or her own lethal impulse. Surprisingly, many suicidal persons respond favorably to such requests. Most suicidal people are ambivalent and would rather find a solution other than suicide. The opportunity to be protected from their own impulses as well as the offer of help in solving problems can be a life-saving combination.

People who exhibit psychotic symptoms and who act impulsively or unpredictably need external controls and should be evaluated for hospitalization or appropriate medication. A significant clue is the client's responsiveness to an offer of help. Being able to accept help is a positive sign that militates against the hopelessness that frequently characterizes the suicidal person. It is also important to observe the progress of the symptoms. If symptoms remain or get worse, one must be concerned about the possible occurrence of a suicide attempt, and the treatment program should be modified or strengthened.

3. *Resources.* The resources of the suicidal person represent the third most significant factor in evaluating lethality. If the person indicates that he or she has money, a therapist, a close and caring family, and good friends, the risk of suicide lessens considerably. When people are isolated and have no helpful network, the risk increases. Available resources should be enlisted as quickly as possible, especially when risk is high. Suicidal people feel lonely, isolated, and rejected. When feasible, the involvement of friends and family is preferred, but even incorporating community and social services helps to break through the client's feelings that he or she is unworthy and no one cares.

The criteria outlined above should be considered interrelated rather than independent factors. In treatment, the practitioner should remember that although the problems are serious, most suicide cases are not life-threatening emergencies. Rather, they often represent an expression of desperation about the person's inability to cope with life events or perceived existential meaninglessness. The person's feelings progress through stages of depression, anxiety, guilt, and anger to the end stages of feeling worthless, helpless, and hopeless. Most cases are identified and in some kind of care long before the final stages are reached. The greatest risk is associated with feelings of helplessness and hopelessness. Regardless of stage or degree of risk, it is important for the therapist to convey a sense of hope to counteract the client's feelings of hopelessness.

The suicidal person must feel that his or her communication about suicide has been heard and that his or her feelings and predicament are understood, recognized, and taken seriously. The problems precipitating the suicidal reaction may then be explored, for example, losses through separation or divorce, the death of a spouse, a life-threatening or painful physical illness, a serious personal humiliation. Such problems occur within the context of the patient's personality and possible psychiatric conditions, such as depression, borderline personality disorder, alcoholism, manic-depressive disorder, and schizophrenia. Often these conditions are preceded by a lack of success in jobs and personal relationships, and a diminished sense of well-being. Approximately 75 percent of the people who call an SPC come from diagnostic groups characterized by failures in living and disordered relationships. The remaining 25 percent who call an SPC are reacting to an unusual life crisis, for example, the death of a loved one. In general, persons who have had a successful life course but are reacting to an extreme, sudden life stress with depression and a suicidal response are good candidates for therapy. With some relief from the stress, they can usually return to a well-functioning life-style.

With chronic suicidal persons who have a history of failure in prior treatment, the therapist should take a long-term, maintenance/supportive approach, with minimal expectations for improvement. These clients need ongoing contact with a therapeutic agent rather than actual therapy. Such clients make repeat suicide attempts and call the SPC when they become disturbed and suicidal. Simply knowing that someone is available to talk with them when they become confused, depressed, or are struggling with a problem helps them get through these episodes. These people are often involved with a number of different helping agencies. Knowing this relieves the full burden from the therapist who is treating these difficult clients. Coordination among the various helping agencies, however, is vital.

It is important to remember that the potential for suicide continues to be present even though the context of the call to the SPC may have shifted to other matters. Clients should be asked if they still have suicidal thoughts. When a chronically suicidal person drops out of long-term counseling, the therapist should question whether the patient is depressed or discouraged about the therapy and/or has been feeling hopeless and suicidal. Effort should be made to locate the person, possibly through one of the other agencies with which the person has contact, to make certain that the person at least stays in contact with a helping professional.

CASE EXAMPLES

The following examples of suicide calls present brief diagnostic information on each caller and the evaluation and treatment plan for various cases. Although each caller is unique, some callers fall into categories that may be readily recognized and that most mental health professionals can identify in terms of diagnosis and difficulty. The first category, chronic repeat callers, presents the most difficulties for telephone counselors.

The Chronic Repeat Caller

Brenda. A repeat caller for a number of years, Brenda lost her supervisory job 3 years ago when she falsely accused her own supervisor of sexual harassment. On discovery that the charge was false, she was told that she could be reinstated if she made a formal apology to her colleague. She refused and was subsequently discharged. In discussing this incident she vacillated between blaming the other supervisor and blaming herself. Most of the time her calls focused on regrets over her actions, her wish to undo her "mistakes," and her ruined career. Currently, she works in another business setting but shows much anxiety over her performance.

Because Brenda has high expectations of herself as an achiever, any failure is a source of much anxiety. Diagnosed as manic-depressive, she has been hospitalized seven times since the first incident 3 years ago. She takes lithium regularly, has a therapist, and indicates that she calls many other crisis lines. Her father is deceased, but her mother continues to be supportive. She has a boyfriend who lives nearby, and she frequently spends the night with him.

Brenda was viewed as an obsessive, highly anxious person with an alternative manic-depressive diagnosis. Her suicide risk has continued to be high, especially in light of a recent serious suicide attempt when she took more than fifty sleeping pills. However, Brenda has received adequate support from a longtime therapist and a supportive mother and boyfriend. Her use of the suicide prevention telephone service is attributed to her need to have a service available at any hour of the day or night and her fear that she will be without such support. Counselors were instructed to encourage Brenda to call her therapist when she is in crisis and to persuade her to use her outside resources as well as her own inner capabilities. They were told to remind her gently that the SPC's purpose is not to do ongoing therapy over the telephone but to help people in crisis find and work with their own resources. Her calls were to be limited to no longer than 5 minutes unless there was a high suicide risk, in which case the therapist was to be informed and rescue procedures were to be initiated.

Marvin. A 45-year-old white male who had been a truck driver, Marvin had brain damage and seizures as a result of being mugged 8 years before. Following the mugging, his wife divorced him and he lost his home and child. Currently, he lives with his parents and several pets.

For many years Marvin was permitted to call the SPC for support because he was so lonely. However, in recent years he has learned to make other contacts and now has a much wider social network. Classes at a nearby adult school have provided additional social stimulation. He takes care of his own needs, including grocery shopping and family errands. Even though his abilities and resources have expanded, he continues to call the SPC for social contact.

Marvin's calls have generally been social as opposed to crisis oriented. He talks about his activities, his classes, his walking the dog, and his conversations with others. He has never reported being suicidal. Although he often sounded as if he had been drinking, he always denied it and stated that it was caused by his medication. He has been easy to talk to except that he becomes belligerent when drinking.

During a case conference, SPC counselors decided that their objective with Marvin should be changed from providing a social outlet to weaning him gradually from the service, because he was not suicidal. He had widened his social activities, which needed to be reinforced and encouraged. Workers would also provide him with referrals to new resources such as church, adult day-care, and other organizations. It was decided that an important new resource might be Alcoholics Anonymous, where he could meet many new people and learn to control his drinking. He did not have to be alcoholic to attend the meetings. If it was determined that he was drinking when he called, he was to be told that counselors would not talk with him while he was drinking. No calls were to go beyond 5 minutes; if he called on a busy shift, he was to be told firmly that the lines had to be kept open for crisis calls.

Loss

Among the most common problems presented to a suicide prevention counselor is that of loss of a significant other, most often through separation or divorce, sometimes by death. The following two cases illustrate the loss of a best friend and a lover.

Bill. Bill indicated that he was a suicide survivor; his best friend, Mary, had killed herself 2 days prior to his call. Mary's funeral was scheduled for the next day, and he was anxious about the funeral and unsure how he would behave. He did not want to attend the funeral but felt that it was necessary for him to do so. Most of the discussion revolved around Mary's suicide and the pain he felt at her action, along with his feeling of anger, resentment, and love. It was difficult for him to talk about his feelings of resentment, and he needed reassurance that such feelings were not unusual.

Bill had not anticipated that Mary would commit suicide and was angry, particularly that she had succeeded in killing herself, whereas he had failed in his six previous attempts. He reported strong feelings of guilt because when she called him the night before she had killed herself, he told her that he was very busy and cut their conversation short. She had not told him about her suicidal intentions. He felt he could have helped if he had only known, although they had not been as close as they once had been.

Mary was a victim of incest, both by her father and brother. This experience served as a close bond between them because Bill also had been incestuously maltreated by his father when he was young. His anger at Mary centered partly on her inability to deal with the problem, which made him feel that he was unable to overcome his own. He assumed that the incest was the reason for Mary's suicide.

Bill was not currently in therapy or on any medication. He was urged to attend the funeral and told that he would feel worse if he did not attend. He was advised to seek outpatient counseling and was asked to call back after the funeral to tell counselors how things had gone. He called back within 5 days to report that he continued to feel very suicidal and that the only thing that kept him from killing himself was the possibility of hurting his friends. He revealed for the first time that he was bisexual and that he accepted his orientation. He did have a close friend with whom he was able to talk and other friends who were quite supportive. He continued to feel guilt about not having talked with Mary when she called.

Bill initially failed to follow through on the advice to seek outpatient counseling and was again urged to do so. He was given a specific referral to an agency in his area and invited to apply to the Survivors After Suicide program conducted by the center. Bill applied to the agency for continuing outpatient therapy but did not take advantage of the suicide survivor program. He stated that he would not commit suicide because a friend had threatened to kill himself if Bill committed suicide, and he did not want to feel responsible for another person's death.

Bill was considered a moderate risk for suicide. Although he continued to feel some guilt over Mary's suicide, he had an excellent network of supportive friends. Moreover, he finally entered therapy.

Tom. Tom, who was gay, said that his lover, an AIDS victim, had died 2 months previously. Tom said that they had a good relationship for over 2 years. Although Tom expressed thoughts of suicide, he had no plans to kill himself; the first lethality rating was moderate to low. Tom showed no indication of substance abuse and stated that he had good family support, although his family was not close geographically. He talked about the possibility of visiting his lover's sister and family in another city.

On a second call 4 days later, Tom indicated he still had suicidal thoughts, but careful inquiry indicated that he had not formulated a specific plan. However, his ambivalence about his homosexuality had increased, apparently as a result of contact with his family, who rejected his life-style and told him that it was just as well that his lover had died because it indicated the error of Tom's ways. Tom continued to talk about his plans to visit his lover's family, who accepted his gay life-style.

Two weeks later Tom called to say that he was leaving the city and he wanted to thank the counselors for their help. He did not wish to talk any further and terminated the call quickly. On a second call 2 days later, Tom's pain from his loss seemed to be deepening. He was now talking about dying and admitted that he possessed an unloaded gun that he kept in the trunk of his car. He was still in contact with his lover's family, who were urging him to visit. Tom's suicidal risk was considered much higher after this call; he was urged to accept a referral to a therapist in Los Angeles or to find one after he had visited his lover's family. Later that day a counselor from another SPC telephone service in the city called and reported that Tom was threatening to kill himself by drowning; the counselor was trying to get him to come to the office for help. He refused. The counselor was told to remind Tom that he had promised his lover, who had died slowly of AIDS, that he would take care of himself. Tom continued to feel extremely depressed and to refuse all offers of help. He had never provided any telephone number or address and thus could not be traced.

Two weeks later Tom's family called to report that Tom had killed himself the night before. The family felt guilty and angry. Tom had called the family from Canada but had hung up on them. He refused to accept their suggestions for seeking help. There was no information on how Tom had killed himself.

The staff discussed at length how this case might have been handled differently or how Tom might have been persuaded to seek help. Because he had never given identifying information that would allow staff to contact him, any outreach or rescue activity was impossible. His deepening depression and increasing determination to kill himself, which became evident over the succession of calls, was especially frustrating to counselors in that he did not allow any intervention. He was only 23; his death was sad and needless—and especially difficult for a suicide prevention staff to bear because a series of contacts had occurred. In the staff meetings that followed, it was emphasized repeatedly that Tom had refused all help and that the center had exhausted every avenue in its efforts to help.

Borderline Personality Disorder

Dan. A 43-year-old Vietnam veteran, Dan worked as a salesperson after the war but had deteriorated over the past 3 or 4 years. He lost his job and fiancée, and attempts to find work had been disastrous. He lived with a disturbed father and was supported financially by public assistance.

According to the Veteran's Administration (VA), Dan's diagnosis was borderline personality disorder. The VA claimed that his problems started before Vietnam and therefore limited its services to him. Dan felt that he had been treated badly and became very angry when talking about his experience with the VA.

Dan had been prescribed antipsychotic and antidepressant medication but took his pills irregularly. When he was depressed, he preferred to diet and exercise. He often turned to nontraditional treatments such as yoga, dianetics, and fasting.

Dan had attempted suicide several times. Although some of these attempts were relatively serious, he claimed that he had intended to injure rather than to kill himself. He had a history of alcohol use but tended to deny it was a problem. He had been hospitalized several times over the past half-dozen years.

Dan was depressed and exhibited moderate psychomotor retardation. He felt hopeless and lacked energy. He felt that he no longer fit in or belonged to society. He described Vietnam flashbacks and felt guilty because he was the only man in his squad to survive a fire fight. Lacking finances, he could not afford to move out of his father's house. His suicidal status varied from moderate to high. His history of suicide attempts and his rejection of help from resources that were available to him indicated a higher risk for suicide. However, he did not seem to have any suicidal plan worked out, and his suicidal behavior in the past was more or less impulsive.

Dan continued to use the VA, although he resented the VA's efforts to limit its responsibility to help him. He continued to seek help from the SPC as well as other agencies but was not able to feel comfortable with any single source of help. Currently, he continues to rely primarily on his inner resources, a philosophical and somewhat spiritual approach to life; he is involved in reading, meditating, exercising, and yoga.

The SPC counselors were urged to validate Dan for the growth and progress that he had made and to reassure him that he was not a failure. He was encouraged to use the VA as an always available, no-cost resource, especially when he felt depressed and had impulses to injure or kill himself.

The Abusive Violent Caller

Jim. A 44-year-old white male, Jim had called the SPC for several years, usually to complain about the women he met in Los Angeles, how terrible Los Angeles was, and how difficult it was to meet nice women. Frequently, his calls would start out controlled; however, as they progressed he would become more abusive and enraged.

Information was difficult to obtain, because Jim was a nonstop talker and did not answer many questions. Both his father and mother were deceased; he had siblings in other cities. Jim seemed to be active in the community and to participate in several community clubs. He stated that he paid for his sex and did not have any steady female companion. He had one male friend with whom he spent time.

Jim, a clerical worker who had been unemployed for the past 5 to 6 years, lived on Social Security disability benefits. He had been fired from his last job after an altercation with a female employee who pressed charges against him. He did not go to prison, but he continued to complain bitterly about the woman and to express angry, violent feelings toward her. He stated that he had harassed her on the telephone for a long time after he was discharged.

Jim first called the SPC 6 years ago, after which there was a 4-year gap about which he would provide no information other than to hint that he had been in a mental hospital for a while. He indicated that he has been in counseling for more than 15 years and was currently attending a group at a local mental health center. Diagnosed as manic-depressive, he was taking both antipsychotic and antidepressant medication.

Jim had a history of several prior suicide attempts but provided no detailed information about them. When he called, he either threatened to kill himself or someone else. His anger toward women was general and nonspecific, and his threats against women were either to kill or rape them because that was what they deserved.

A case conference about Jim clarified the appropriate responses to make with him. Because of his abusiveness, especially toward women counselors, he was to be told that he could call only during certain shifts and that there would be a particular counselor (male) who would be available to talk to him. If he called at any other time, he was to be told that it was impossible to speak with him now but that someone would be willing to talk with him at the specified times. Confrontations were to be avoided, and statements to him were to be impersonalized; that is, the SPC, as opposed to an individual, would make decisions and establish the procedures for him to follow. In addition, he was to be referred back to his therapist with the reminder that the center could not conduct therapy with him and that he should take advantage of his therapeutic relationship to work through his feelings about women. This plan was approved by Jim's therapist, who stated that Jim's continuous venting of his feelings to the SPC had seemed to impede his progress in therapy.

The objective was to wean Jim away from using SPC services because its counselors, rather than helping him, were providing an outlet for him to be hyperabusive.

The Psychotic Caller

Nan. A 30-year-old black female, Nan had been diagnosed schizophrenic and was taking medication irregularly. Her alcoholic mother had been unable to take care of her, so Nan had been placed in foster care at an early age. She stated that she had been disabled since childhood. Her history of hospitalization was confusing. At one time she stated that she was first hospitalized at age 10; another report said age 16.

She lived in board and care homes and on the streets, although recently she had been living with a boyfriend in a halfway house operated by the state. She reported that she would have to leave the halfway house at the end of the week and was not sure where she would live—either on the street or in her boyfriend's car. Nan depended on her boyfriend to provide for her. He paid for her stay in the home and for her medication.

Unable to read or write, she stated that she received no help from community agencies because she could not fill out the necessary forms. She could not get to the agency offices because she would not take the bus and was unable to drive. Nan called the SPC to complain about her boyfriend's abuse of her. He beat her because she could not work and he had to support her.

Nan frustrated the counselor because she rejected offers of help or referrals. She always terminated her calls very abruptly, possibly because someone came into the room and made her hang up. At other times, it seems she just tired of the conversation and chose to hang up on her own.

Nan was viewed as a high-risk caller, based partly on her statement that she had made more than fourteen suicide attempts using methods such as overdoses and cutting her wrists. Her mental illness, lack of support system, chronic suicide history, and generally chaotic life-style made her a high risk for suicide under any kind of stress.

The Elderly Caller

Rose. Rose, a 61-year-old woman living with her husband and stepdaughter, called several times within a period of 2 weeks. She had been married to her second husband for 10 years; he was an alcoholic and was physically and psychologically abusive. Rose's children by her first marriage were grown and lived elsewhere. They offered no support in her present situation; Rose expressed much bitterness about their lack of support.

She said that she had no friends because she and her husband moved so often that it was difficult to form lasting relationships. She was unable to work; they lived primarily on her husband's Social Security and occasional odd jobs. Her husband retained tight control over finances and did not give her any money for the house or to spend on herself. She had a continuing medical problem of herpes.

At first, Rose refused to identify herself when she called. Eventually, she provided her first name and the area in which she lived. Her calls generally focused on her feelings of loneliness and helplessness. Her husband frequently spent his evenings with friends and often did not return home until morning. Often she called while he was out. Although she was willing to talk about various options for helping herself, she usually ended up rejecting them. She left her husband a number of times but always went back to him. She felt incapable of supporting herself and living alone.

Rose never attempted suicide and never described a suicide plan. However, she stated that she thought of suicide often and felt very depressed. She had nowhere to go, no one to help her, and no way to help herself.

Rose was evaluated as having moderate to low suicide potential in light of her lack of prior suicidal behavior and any suicide plan. She had relatively few resources and stayed in the relationship with her abusive husband for support. Although referred to various community resources, such as Al-Anon, Women Helping Women, and a psychiatric clinic in her neighborhood, she did not follow through on any of these recommendations. Even though it was unlikely that she would do so, the counselors were instructed to continue to urge her to take advantage of the community resources in her area and to point out her opportunities for increasing her social supports through them.

Sharon. A 72-year-old white woman, Sharon was semiretired, working part time as a substitute bookkeeper. She is representative of a group of elderly, lonely, angry callers who are not so much suicidal as depressed, unhappy, and feeling rejected.

Although Sharon claimed she was active and in good health, she also stated that she had no friends and could not seem to get help from the numerous physicians whom she consulted. When the therapist to whom she was referred prescribed medications, Sharon stopped seeing him. She also refused medications prescribed by her physician, claiming bitterly that they could only offer pills but not any evidence that they cared.

Sharon reported suicidal thoughts but never any attempts. She stated that she would either use a gun or overdose on drugs; however, she did not own a gun and had refused all prescriptions offered by her physician.

Sharon was angry and hostile; she rebuffed the counselor's efforts to help the first time she called, which was early in the morning. When she called again later in the day, she complained about the counselor she had spoken with earlier, stating that she did not like all the questions. She said that she wanted to let the center know that if she killed herself it would be the center's fault because the counselors did not help her. However, she promised to call back later that day.

Sharon's suicidal risk was rated low because she had no prior suicidal behavior and her suicidal thoughts were vague and unformed. However, her anger, bitterness, and depression put her at some risk. She had no friends and challenged anyone who might care about her. Because she had a therapist, it was recommended that counselors listen to Sharon for a short period, then urge her to continue with her therapist.

Youthful Callers

Cecily. Fifteen-year-old Cecily called twice. Her presenting problems revolved around the recent loss of her boyfriend and some delinquent acting out. She felt that she received little support from her family because her brother, who was in poor health, required constant attention. She had few friends. She attended high school and worked part time as a clerk in a clothing store.

She had been cutting school for the past several months as well as drinking and smoking marijuana. Recently, she had been dating men in their late twenties. Once she had stayed out all night on one of her dates.

Cecily complained of depression and described feeling lonely and being unable to communicate with her parents. She claimed that her mother blamed her for the breakup of her first marriage because her natural father left when her mother became pregnant with Cecily. Information about prior suicidal behavior was conflicting. At one point she stated that she had made no suicide attempts, but on another call she indicated that she had made one attempt. She reported frequent suicidal thoughts and indicated that she would use drugs to kill herself, although she had none on hand. She had no counseling and rejected all efforts to get her to talk to her school counselor, her teacher, or her physician. She "knew" that her mother would not go with her to counseling.

It was apparent that Cecily was living a confused and disorganized life that could possibly lead to delinquency and suicidal behavior. The staff considered her to be at moderate risk at this time but at high risk for eventual suicide. Her friends seemed to contribute to her self-destructive behavior and she felt alienated from her family. Reconnecting Cecily with her family was the counselors' highest priority, but she would not provide a telephone number or any information that would let the counselors establish contact with her family. She was urged to call Teen Lines, whose teen workers might be able to establish a more direct relationship with her. Meanwhile, she was urged to call the SPC, where someone would always be available to talk to her. Counselors told her that they considered her situation serious and that they would be there to help her.

Stewart. A single, 24-year-old-man, Stewart lived with a roommate and was recently unemployed. His parents were separated; his only brother lived in another city. Stewart called the SPC because he felt completely overwhelmed by all the bad things that were happening in his life. His girl friend of 6 months had just broken up with him because she felt too young to commit herself to a permanent relationship. In addition, Stewart lost his job, and another job that he had anticipated had not come through. He felt that it never would.

During the call, Stewart reported that he had had no prior suicidal behavior but that he now wished that he had a gun. He talked about jumping off an overpass into the freeway traffic below. However, he was hesitant about doing this because he was afraid that he might hurt someone and might cause an accident on the freeway.

Stewart's parents were only recently separated. He was angry at both of them because he felt that they used him to get back at each other. He resented this but was afraid to say anything to his parents for fear he might alienate them. Stewart's mother was alcoholic and could not be counted on for support.

Stewart was rated relatively low in suicide risk because he had no prior suicidal behavior. The counselor felt that his jumping off a bridge was more a fantasy than a possibility. Despite feeling overwhelmed, he had resources; his father was still available to him and his roommate could also be counted on to assist him. Stewart was urged to apply at one of the several psychiatric clinics in the area where he lived and was assured that although he felt very unhappy and depressed at this point, depressions were usually of brief duration and that he could help himself considerably by talking with a therapist.

Barbara. Barbara, a 28-year-old white woman who lived with her father and her 4-year-old son, worked full time as an executive secretary. Her husband had died within the previous month after a serious industrial accident. She was extremely angry and bitter at his physicians because they did not prepare her for his death. She felt alone, empty, and panic-stricken by the immensity of her loss.

Barbara called because she had begun to experience frightening suicidal thoughts within the past week. When questioned closely, however, she had no history of suicide attempts, nor did she have a suicide plan. She appeared to need support, which she felt that she could not get from her family at that point.

Barbara was reassured that her thoughts were normal, considering the immensity of her loss and the suddenness with which it had occurred. She was assured that help was available for her grief and that her bereavement could be made more easy to bear with counseling. She was referred to counseling at the psychiatric clinics in her area and to the Widow-to-Widow hotline.

Evaluation and Treatment in a Clinical Setting

Most of the above case examples illustrate problems of assessment and management by a telephone crisis service of suicidal risk in chronically disordered crisis-prone persons. The following case example by H. Parad illustrates the evaluation and treatment of suicidal risk presented by a relatively high-functioning client experiencing an acute crisis state of loss following betrayal by her boyfriend.

Ann. Ann, a divorced 33-year-old fashion designer, had apparently coped well in her everyday work and social life, despite considerable childhood deprivation and trauma at the hands of her abusive alcoholic father. A few days previously she had learned that Jim, her 51-year-old lover, had deceived her by having an affair with another woman. Discovering her lover's duplicity suddenly activated old and painful memories of her former husband's infidelity as well as her father's womanizing (which led to her mother's nervous breakdown). Jim had falsely assured Ann of his intent to marry her and his desire for children, but now her dreams were shattered. She was having trouble sleeping, had little or no appetite, was avoiding her friends, and was barely able to concentrate on her job. Ann described feeling worthless, unlovable, and suicidal. She had a loaded pistol at home and said she had been about to blow her brains out the previous night but had called a friend instead. The friend calmed her and referred her for immediate crisis therapy.

In the first session, Ann refused to (1) bring in the pistol, (2) give the bullets for safekeeping to her girl friend (who had referred her to the crisis clinic), (3) consider hospitalization, (4) permit the therapist to communicate either with her girl friend who lived in the apartment next door or her mother who lived nearby. Mindful of Ann's extremely high risk for suicide, the therapist offered to see her in frequent therapy sessions to help her cope with her despair and agitation. The therapist said decisively, "Ann, you are in a severe and overwhelming crisis. I don't think you really want to die—what you want is to stop hurting inside. I'm here to help you."

Sobbing, Ann gradually responded to the therapist's overtures and reluctantly agreed to call the SPC round-the-clock hotline if she felt like using the pistol. But she would not surrender the pistol until she had time to sort out her thoughts. She felt miserable and unlovable. She was having flashbacks to her adolescence, when her father, after being especially abusive toward her and her mother, suddenly abandoned the family to live with another woman. Ann also flashed back to the nanny who had raised her and who often slapped her face cruelly. "When I was 8, Nanny burned me by putting my hand on an electric stove." Ann then confided she had taken an overdose of pills when she was 15 after her father had called her a bitch because she had behaved assertively toward him. Medical help had been called and her stomach pumped out, but apparently she had not been hospitalized.

Ann cried as she talked about her father's death last year from cirrhosis of the liver. She said she was through with Jim, all that she had now were her two dogs ("my babies"), a few friends, and a job she could barely perform.

An unusually thoughtful and self-observing client, despite the intensity of her pain, Ann requested that we tape record the sessions so that she could review (between sessions) what she and the therapist had said. The following verbatim vignettes convey the intense interplay between Ann (A) and the therapist (T):

A (crying): I asked Jim outright, "Were you with another woman when you went out of town?" and he finally said, "Yes."

T: Your feelings were badly hurt. Any woman would be hurt by that. You were lied to. You're entitled to feel hurt and angry.

A: And betrayed.

T: How do you make the leap from what happened with Jim to thinking of killing yourself?

A: Oh, it's not just that. That's just one more thing. That would be overreacting if that were the only thing. This is just the stone gathering up the moss.

T: This is the way life is? Every time you meet a man and are disappointed?

A: This is what continues to happen to me. This is the pain. This is just . . . this is the end of another thing that I put my hopes into, to have something nice in my life. This is another painful thing in my life. I just looked around, no more, I cannot do it, I can't do it anymore. . . . I'm not talking about just this one thing. . . . The problem is I have nothing good in my life. . . . There is nothing! All I see is more pain coming down, all failure, more problems. True, there have been some nice things that have happened in my life, but I've always been in pain and, as you've said, there are no buffers between me and the pain. . . . I'm beginning to believe that this is my destiny. . . . I'm beginning to believe the way it was yesterday is not what a human being can do. I can't . . . I can't do it. I can't continue. . . . I need a sign. I need a little something, some hope. I need a little something nice, not a lot, just a little something and I don't think that's greedy (sobbing).

T: Of course not.

A: Yesterday the pain didn't stop. It went on and on. So many hours. I took a tranquilizer but that didn't stop it. It went on all night. There is an enormity to it that frightens me.

T: Enormity?

A: It's unbearable. It doesn't stop. The enormity of the hope-lessness.

T: Could it be that the pain you're experiencing is the little girl in you that feels rejected?

A: It's all the pain of everything.

T: You have success in your life. You've been a really first-class fashion designer.

A: Yes, that's true.

T: You have lots of friends.

A: Yes, that's right too.

T: Right now you don't have a relationship with a man.

A: No. I have men friends but not on a sexual basis.

T: You've done a lot of things in your life, so how come a man is given so much power—in his greed and betrayal—that he has the power of life and death over you?

A (firmly): He doesn't have that power over me. It's just proof positive. It's not these things. It's that there is nothing in my life. . . . But I'm all right today. I'm alive today. I'm coping today. I'm trying to get positive again. What I'm trying to say to you is I'm trying to push myself in that mode. There's a part of me that yearns to be healthy, yearns to be O.K. And I'm here and I'm listening to you.

T: And you called me yesterday twice.

A (proudly): That's right. And better than that, I got through the day without seeing you in the office. I got through it without anyone.

T: So there really is a thrust toward life and healing in you.

A: There is! There is a thrust, every bit as strong as the other thrust [death]. I wouldn't give one more power than the other. They are both very strong in me and very equal and at different times. And one of them is going to win—and one of them is going to win really big—because when I get very healthy, if that's what happens, I won't feel this way anymore. . . . And if I do away with my life I won't have the other [the thrust toward life]. Maybe they are the same thing, that is, different ways of getting healthy.

T: I want to ask you some important questions.

A (interrupts): Yesterday, as the pain increased, I liked it. I knew where I'd be. I was going to take care of my dogs. I was going to give them to two neighbors.

T: You were going to blow your brains out?

A nods

T: How many bullets do you have?

A (defiantly): Enough.

T: Do you know how to use the pistol?

A: Yes. I took lessons.

T: So you're very much at risk.

A (quietly): But I didn't use it [the pistol].

T: That's right! And I'm glad you didn't! It's not good for you to be alone. It's good for you to be with people.

A: I called some people I thought could help me by giving me some advice. A girl friend wanted to come over. I didn't want to talk with her.

T: Did you tell her you were thinking of killing yourself?

A: No, but I told her today that I was frightened. I insinuated that there was a danger, a dangerous situation.

T: That's right. It is dangerous.

A: I don't want to be this way.

T: You have a dangerous weapon. Can you give it to me? I want you to bring me the pistol today after our session. I don't want you to kill yourself. I can only try to imagine the depth of what you're feeling. No matter how much it hurts, and only you know how painful it really is, I don't want you to kill yourself.

A maintains eye contact.

T: You believe you have a spirit [previously discussed by A] that will live on in your next life and that your next life will be better, which neither of us can prove or disprove. That's why I try to stay with what we know in this life. You have friends and a career. You have very high intelligence. You have many, many talents and, in my opinion, much to live for. [Therapist waits for Ann's comments. She nods and tells therapist to go on.]

T: And the thing that seems to have stirred up your pain is Jim's affair, which reminds you of the little girl in you that felt abandoned, rejected, and unloved years ago. That's what I think your pain is about to a very significant degree.

A: I haven't dissociated all this from my father.

T: Yes, you say your father left your mother for another woman. Did she try to harm herself after that?

A: She had a nervous breakdown, but I don't think she tried to kill herself.

Toward the end of her next session, Ann gave the therapist the pistol and the bullets; the therapist agreed to provide "safekeeping" for the weapon until further notice. Ann carries a card with the SPC hotline number; although she hasn't called the hotline, she is reassured by the knowledge that someone will always be there to listen to her. Although she declined psychiatric evaluation for antidepressant medication, Ann did agree that she would now consider hospitalization if her suicidal thoughts made her feel out of control again. Like the hotline, the availability of the protective milieu of the hospital was a source of comfort to her. She did not use either resource.

Working closely with the therapist, Ann undertook the following actions, which were discussed over the next four sessions: (1) She confronted Jim about his affair, expressed her outrage at him, and angrily terminated the relationship. (2) She phoned and later visited her mother, with whom she shared her recollections of her father's abusive and tyrannical behavior. The mother and daughter cried and hugged each other. Ann's stepfather, Frank, was unusually supportive toward her, which meant a lot to Ann. (3) She resumed her relationship with three of her closest friends, started swimming lessons, and briefly discussed with her supervisor at work the fact that she had been under a lot of stress due to the breakup of her relationship with Jim. (4) Through frequent role plays, she ventilated her rage against Jim and her father.

Ann gradually began to understand that her depression was triggered by (1) feelings of loss and abandonment and (2) turning her rage against herself instead of expressing it in an appropriate way to the targets of her anger. A prolific dreamer, she kept a dream book; in discussing her dreams, she was able to see that her attraction to older men (Jim, among others) was, in her words, "a wish and a longing for a father." Similarly, she thought of the therapist as "a good dad."

In subsequent sessions, Ann shared the following notes, which she wrote after listening to the tape recordings of the sessions under the heading: "Things that helped me in my sessions":

1. Experiencing my natural state as one of vitality and happiness.
2. Unexpressed rage (which is against others), which I turned against myself and would finally destroy me. Target the rage outward.
3. Expressing yourself empowers yourself.
4. Curse from my father: "I don't have a right to be." "As long as you feel you don't have a right to be, you'll hold on to the depression" (said by therapist).
5. Wallowing. Turning away from inside pain to the world outside would help.
6. Reidentifying myself as myself. Not identifying with my father, who killed himself through alcoholism.

These interrelated notes were reviewed in a therapy session. Ann submitted another account of her observations of the therapy sessions 2 weeks later:

1. Confrontation. Proving to myself that I can confront and *have the power to no longer be a victim!*
2. Your [therapist's] concern for me! (That helps.)
3. When the therapist said, "You don't want to be dead, you just don't want to hurt so much," that helped a lot too. Then I found out there was a way to avoid pain.
4. I felt you [therapist] understand my pain as much as another person could. Your sympathy meant a lot.
5. Understanding that I am not really a victim and that I don't have to spend my life in victimization.

Within 3 months Ann resumed dating. In her words, the themes in therapy were "mourning, men, and mother." She regained her enthusiasm about work, resumed an active social life, and, at the time of termination, was involved in a positive relationship with a recently divorced man who was interested in having a family with her.

Last Christmas, Ann sent the following note to the therapist:

May this Christmas and the coming year be joyous and fruitful for you and your family. My boyfriend and his children by his former marriage and I are doing very well. We never get to see enough of each other and I'm occasionally intimidated by his small son but for the most part I'm thrilled with him. His daughter and I have developed a wonderful relationship, and I'm extremely fond of her and I think I've taken an important place in her life too. She, my boyfriend, and I had a family confrontation one day, instigated and led by me, and in my best therapy-like tradition (learned in our sessions), I got all of us to air our feelings; and as a result we are communicating beautifully. Some things happened between my boyfriend and his daughter that I think represent a turning point for them and maybe for me too. She's a changed girl, definitely less moody and much happier. Bravo, your influence stretches even farther than you imagine! Again, I wish you the best and send you all my thanks again for our work together. Its success shows in the loving and communicative relationship I now enjoy with my boyfriend. Best, Ann.

In a recent follow-up interview, Ann indicated that she would probably remarry soon, looked forward to having a family, was doing well in her work, and had not had any preoccupation with suicide for the past 2 years.

At Ann's request, her pistol and bullets (she had a license to use the pistol for self-defense) were returned. Both therapist and client felt comfortable with this arrangement.

GUIDELINES: A SUMMARY

The following guidelines are generally helpful to the mental health professional doing crisis intervention work with suicide-prone clients.

1. Directly explore the possibility of suicidal thoughts with all depressed and distressed clients. Do not be afraid to ask the client if he or she has had self-destructive thoughts or has ever tried to harm him- or herself. Consider suicidal thoughts and behavior as a cry for help.

2. If the client has suicidal thoughts or plans, evaluate the degree of suicidal risk by checking the client's health, history of psychiatric disorder, marital and employment status, attachments to significant others, chemical dependency, previous suicide attempts, suicidal thoughts or suicidal behavior, and, most important, whether the client has a specific suicide plan, the lethal means (pills, weapons, automobile) and the intention to carry out the plan.

3. If the suicidal plan includes potentially lethal medication, knives, or guns, try to persuade the client to surrender them to you or other reliable person(s).

4. If the client is isolated and if hospitalization is not desirable or feasible, actively reach out to his or her significant others; alert them to the danger of the client being alone; encourage the client to communicate his or her suicidal thoughts and plans. Remember, talking about suicide is healthier than doing it!

5. Contract with the client to call you (or a hotline) if he or she feels like carrying out a suicidal intent. Be sure to have back-up help. Do not be overly heroic. Make sure you give your at-risk client the number of a reliable 24-hour hotline; instruct the client to call the hotline at any time of the night or day if you are not available at a time of need.

6. Seek consultation from colleagues who are knowledgeable about lethality assessment and suicide prevention. Remember, those who give support must also receive support to avoid burnout.

7. When it is possible to do so, refer suicidal clients to self-help support groups (for example, Alcoholics Anonymous) while continuing your therapeutic contact with them. If you are not able to offer the client short-term therapy beyond your initial emergency assessment and intervention, refer the client to an appropriate crisis clinic or other mental health service for short-term or ongoing individual and/or group therapy.

8. Although most suicide-prone persons do not kill themselves, always take suicidal gestures seriously, even if the client seems to act manipulatively.

9. Finally, and perhaps most important, remember that the healing power of the volunteer's and mental health professional's caring, concerned availability, and reaching out is crucial to the suicidal client's struggle for and affirmation of life.

CONCLUSION

The LASPC program and clinical approach described here are to some degree representative of SPC programs throughout the United States and in other countries. Suicide prevention centers serve all ages, from the adolescent to the elderly. Volunteers who staff the telephone lines experience many frustrations, especially when they deal with young, high-risk callers who will not provide identifying information to enable contact with their family or other possible sources of support. Loss of loved ones, health, jobs, and self-esteem are pervasive themes that run through all of the clinical examples. Despite the fact that many callers refuse help, the knowledge that the center may make the difference between life and death sustains staff and volunteers in their efforts.

REFERENCES

American Association of Suicidology. (1984). *Certification Standards Manual*, 3rd ed. Denver: American Association of Suicidology.

Dunne, E. J., McIntosh, J. L., and Dunne-Maxim, K., eds. (1987). *Suicide and Its Aftermath: Understanding and Counseling the Survivors*. New York: W. W. Norton.

Farberow, N. L. (1968). Suicide prevention: a view from the bridge. *Community Mental Health Journal* 4:469–474.

———— (1976). Group psychotherapy for self-destructive persons. In *Emergency Mental Health and Disaster Management: a Mental Health Source Book*, ed. H. Parad, H.L.P. Resnik, and L. Parad. Bowie, MD: Charles.

Farberow, N. L., Heilig, S. M., and Litman, R. E. (1968). *Techniques in Crisis Management: a Training Manual*. Los Angeles: Suicide Prevention Center.

Farberow, N. L., Litman, R. E., and Nelson, F. L. (1987). Youth suicide in California. Paper presented at American Association of Suicidology/International Association for Suicide Prevention Meeting, San Francisco, September.

Farberow, N. L., and Shneidman, E. S., eds. (1961). *The Cry for Help*. New York: McGraw Hill.

Frierson, R. L., and Lippman, S. B. (1988). Suicide and AIDS. *Psychosomatics* 29:226–231.

Heilig, S. M., Farberow, N. L., Litman, R. E., and Shneidman, E. S. (1968). Role of nonprofessionals in the suicide prevention center. *Community Mental Health Journal* 4:287–295.

Lamb, D. (1988). Support groups help: Rugged West—A climate for suicide. *Los Angeles Times*, December 6.

Motto, J. A. (1979). New approaches to crisis intervention. *Suicide and Life-Threatening Behavior* 9:173–184.

Suicide Prevention Programs for California Public Schools. (1987). California State Department of Education, P.O. Box 271, Sacramento, CA 95802.

3

PREPARATORY AND PRIOR SUICIDAL BEHAVIOR FACTORS

Norman L. Farberow

INTRODUCTION

Suicide does not just occur. Experience has shown that it is more often the end result of a process that has developed over a period of time and within which have been many fluctuations in the course of reaching the decision to act against oneself. Fortunately, experience has also shown that during that period, the individual engages in a number of behaviors that have become available as signs and portents. There are, of course, many kinds of signs such as epidemiological, demographic, family characteristics, personality disorders, cultural factors, and others. Although inevitably there will be some overlap with other areas, this chapter will focus on behavioral factors only; that is, acts and actions engaged in by the person that indicate the potential for a self-destructive act to occur in the future.

Because of the large amount of pertinent research in the area of behavioral factors, this review, necessarily, is arbitrary and selective. For example, no effort has been made to examine all the so-called suicide potential scales containing predictive items. First, there are no scales specifically constructed to evaluate suicide potential in adolescents; second, the behavioral items on the scales are almost all considered individually in this chapter anyhow; and third, many of the scales depend on clinically reported items rather than on research-substantiated factors. Finally, it must be remembered that, while considering each factor separately, the factors almost always will appear in a context that will contain other clues, some of which may affect considerably the significance of the factor discussed.

PRIOR SELF-DESTRUCTIVE BEHAVIOR

Prior self-destructive behavior, whether in the form of suicide attempts, threats, ideation, or gestures, has been identified by many investigators as a powerful indicator of completed suicide risk (Farberow and Shneidman 1955; Farberow et al. 1966; Shneidman and Farberow 1957, 1961; Dorpat and Ripley 1967). However, the research was conducted primarily on adults in psychiatric settings, general hospitals, and in the community. This chapter will focus on children, adolescents, and youth. For the most part, studies reviewed are limited to those whose subjects are aged 20 or below, but occasional research that includes older ages is included. The format will look at studies of completed suicides, then attempted suicides within each risk variable. The research on children or young adolescents is presented first. In addition, the studies are further divided on the basis of the presence or absence of control or comparison groups.

PRIOR SUICIDAL BEHAVIOR

Completed Suicides – Control Groups

The risk factors of previous self-injuries, suicide attempts, threats, ideation, and gestures have been grouped under the general heading of prior suicidal behavior. Most of the time, the prior suicidal behavior refers to suicide attempts. However, many researchers have not differentiated between suicide attempts and gestures, or between suicidal ideation and threats, and often, not between suicide attempts and threats. When such distinctions appear it is uncertain how much overlap has occurred, for suicide attempts are almost always preceded by threats and ideation. The best approach was deemed the conservative one of assuming that all the forms of suicidal activity, verbal and behavioral, are equivalent for the purposes of risk evaluation and prediction. As seen later in this chapter, this view is substantiated by other investigators. Dorpat and Ripley's (1967) review of studies of committed suicides from the United States and England led them to the conclusion that between 20 percent and 65 percent of individuals who commit suicide have made prior suicide attempts. In an additional fifteen studies that determined the incidence of completed suicides in groups of attempted suicides by follow-up, the authors found that the percentages ranged from 0.03 percent in one short follow-up study to 22.05 percent in the longest follow-up study. The researchers estimate the incidence of committed suicide among the suicide attempts to be between 10 percent and 20 percent, but add their belief that the actual number of attempted suicides who go on to commit suicide is greater than the percentage given.

Relatively few investigators over the past 10 to 15 years have used control groups in their studies of completed adolescent suicides, a fact that does not surprise too much in terms of the problems involved in obtaining appropriate groups for comparison. One approach has been through the use of matched peers. Shafii and colleagues (1985) at the University of Louisville conducted psychological autopsies on twenty adolescents, ages 12–19, who committed suicide in Jefferson County, Kentucky. Their highly relevant control group was made up of seventeen matched-pair living peer friends, the same age and sex as the adolescent suicide, from whom the same extensive set of data were gathered. The researchers found that the suicides were significantly more often likely to have a history of suicide threats (p < .02) and suicidal ideation with expressions of the wish to die (p < .02) than did the controls.

Rich and colleagues (1984) also conducted psychological autopsies. The subjects were all 283 completed suicides in San Diego County over a period of 20 months. The investigators compared the 133 suicides under age 30 with the 150 suicides age 30 and over and found that prior suicide threats and attempts were high in all ages of completed suicides. Prior "suicide talk," 71 percent, and suicide attempts, 42 percent, were noted in the under 30 age group, but were not significantly different from the frequencies of 63 percent suicide talk and 35 percent attempts found in the over 30 age group. The comprehensive psychological autopsy study of Maris (1981a) compared completed suicides (from Cook County, Illinois) with attempted suicides and natural deaths (from Baltimore, Maryland). The study covered all ages, including thirty-six young adults, adolescents, and children ages 10 to 29, among his study population of 414 subjects. In analyzing his data on all subjects with highly sophisticated statistical methods, Maris found that the single factor with the greatest discriminatory power (beta .64) was the number of prior suicide attempts; however, that factor separated the two suicidal groups from the natural deaths, but not from each other. The interesting factor that distinguished the completed suicides was that they had one relatively serious prior attempt, while the attempters had several low-lethality prior suicide attempts. When Maris (1981b) later compared his group of thirty-six young completed suicides with the remainder of his completed suicide group, using the same statistical procedures, he found that the factor most significant in differentiating the young suicides from the older suicides continued to be the greater number of prior suicide attempts in their histories.

Seiden's (1966) study compared a group of twenty-five students at the University of California at Berkeley who committed suicide over a 10-year period, with the entire UCB student body population during the same period. Information from newspaper clippings, police files, university records, and reports of friends and acquaintances indicated there were "numerous warnings" in almost every case of suicide, and 22 percent had made prior suicide attempts. They had also given subtle warnings, such as making wry jokes about killing themselves, or crossing out the word "emergency" in the question "Whom shall we notify in case of emergency?" on the medical history form, and substituting the word, "death."

PRIOR SUICIDAL BEHAVIOR

Completed Suicide – No Control Group

Control groups for completed suicide are often neither available nor feasible. Noncontrolled studies are nevertheless valuable in providing information and generating direction and hypotheses for further study. Some of the following suicide studies of children and adolescents are marked by extensive exploration into background, personality, behavioral, physical, and communication factors. As in the case of controlled studies, prior suicidal behavior is referred to often as a significant risk-indicator in the histories of the completed suicides the investigators studied.

Shaffer's (1974) study is well known and often referred to because of its study population completeness – all the children and younger adolescent suicides under age 14 occurring in England and Wales over a 7-year period, 1962 to 1968 – and its exhaustive search for information from a wide variety of sources – government, school, medical, social service, and family. The histories of his thirty cases disclosed that 46 percent, almost half, had previously attempted or threatened suicide, or revealed their suicidal thoughts before their death, with 27 percent having done so in the 24-hour period before their death.

Three studies, in widely separated parts of the world, using coroner's office reports and hospital records, where available, of completed suicides, found that prior suicide attempts were significant. Cosand and colleagues (1982) gathered data on 315 suicides between ages 10 and 24 that occurred in Sacramento County, California, between the years 1925 and 1979. They compared the older youth with the adolescents aged 15 to 19 and found that the older age group had made significantly more suicide attempts than the younger age suicides and that the females in both age groups had significantly more prior suicide attempts than the males. In another long term study, Marek and colleagues (1976) compared seventy-six cases of committed suicides among "juveniles" occurring between the years 1881 and 1960, with seventy-six similar cases occurring over 15 years, 1960 to 1974, in Cracow, Poland. Data were obtained from hospital records and coroners' offices. In the more recent seventy-six cases, they found prior suicidal attempts in 17 percent of the cases and suicide threats and ideation in an additional 13 percent. In a large-scale study of Ontario, Canada, Garfinkel and colleagues (1979) examined all the data available in the coroner's office records for the 1,554 suicides aged 10 to 24 that occurred between January 1971 and August 1978. They found that a history of threats, note-leaving, general manifestations of depression, and other suicidal behavior "accounted for the majority of prior symptoms" in the cases for which information on prior conditions was available.

In summary, studies of the histories of completed suicides, whether control or comparison groups are used or not, indicate that prior suicidal behavior in the form of attempts, threats, or ideation, or combinations of these, is one of the strongest indicators of high risk in adolescents as well as in adults. Percentages of frequency of this factor, supported by good methodology and statistical evaluation, vary from 22 percent to 71 percent in study populations from university, government, and city hospital settings; in psychiatric and general populations; and from coroner's office records.

PRIOR SUICIDAL BEHAVIOR

Suicide Attempts, Threats, Ideation – Control Groups

The presence or absence of prior suicidal behavior has been explored in controlled studies even more frequently among suicide attempters than among completed suicides. Some studies have been retrospective, others prospective.

Two studies serve as landmarks in this area. Jacobs' (1971) and Teicher's (1970) carefully designed research compared fifty adolescent suicide attempters treated at Los Angeles County General Hospital with a matched control group of thirty-one adolescents at a suburban high school. They reported 44 percent of the attempters had one or more previous suicide attempts, while there were no attempts among the controls. The other landmark early study was a total population study in Sweden carried out by Otto (1972) on all the children and adolescents under age 21 who made a suicide attempt and came to the attention of health authorities. A control group consisted of adolescents from the general population matched for age, sex, and geographical region. Otto found that 16 percent of his study population of the 1,727 young suicide attempters had made previous suicide attempts. Prior attempts were more common among boys (21 percent) than girls (14 percent).

In three studies of overdosers, prior suicide attempts were frequent in the experimental groups and absent in the controls. McIntire and Angle (1973) found that 26 percent of fifty poison center patients, ages 6 to 18, had made similar suicide gestures in the past, whereas no such gesture was reported by any of the controls. McKenry and colleagues (1983) noted that prior suicide attempts were marked in their study population of forty-six adolescent attempters admitted to a university hospital primarily for overdoses. The nonsuicidal comparison group from the same hospital had no prior suicide attempts in their history. In a study from England, Hawton and colleagues (1982) followed up fifty adolescents who were treated for suicide overdoses at the Oxford General Hospital Psychiatric Service in England. The investigators found that 40 percent of the attempters — versus none of the controls from a sample of the general population — had either taken an overdose or injured themselves prior to the attempt that brought them into the study.

Clarkin and colleagues (1984) studied two different age groups of adolescents with suicidal behavior in a New York hospital; the first group had a mean age of 16 and the second a mean age of 25.5. The researchers noted that 58 percent of the adolescents and 75 percent of the young adults had made at least one prior attempt. Apparently, prior suicide attempts appear in significant numbers in the younger, as well as the older, adolescents and youth.

PRIOR SUICIDAL BEHAVIOR

Attempts, Threats, Ideation — No Control Groups

Selected studies of young suicide attempters seen in psychiatric hospitals and in private practice note the presence of prior suicide attempts in the history. Shafii and Shafii (1982) reviewed 340 cases of children and younger adolescents mostly aged 13 to 15, for suicidal or severe self-destructive behaviors seen on an emergency basis at the Child Psychiatric Services at the University of Louisville Hospital; Diekstra (1982) reviewed 158 admissions of adolescent suicide attempters to a hospital in Holland. Both studies noted that the risk of suicide is significantly increased when a previous suicide attempt has been made. Diekstra found that previous suicide attempts and suicide threats or ideation ranked first and second in significance among the indicators.

Schneer and colleagues' (1975) interesting study reported that the admissions during one year for a hospital in Brooklyn at two different times, 11 years apart, indicated that the number of suicidal adolescents had almost doubled, from 13.6 percent to 26.7 percent, although the census of admissions had remained practically the same. Concomitantly, the percentage of admissions with repeated episodes of suicidal behavior had increased five-fold, from 4 percent to 20 percent. Gabrielson and colleagues (1970) studied a special risk group, fourteen pregnant females, aged 13 to 17, who had made suicide attempts and were admitted to the Yale-New Haven Hospital, and found that 21 percent had histories of prior suicide attempts. Crumley (1979) reviewed the histories from his own private practice of forty adolescents, aged 12 to 19, in treatment following a suicide attempt. He found a history of numerous prior attempts was common in seventeen, or 40 percent.

In summary, retrospective studies of histories of adolescent suicide attempters, all except one from hospital populations where they were treated, indicated substantial levels of prior suicidal behavior, ranging from 16 percent to 38 percent. At least half the studies were controlled.

SUBSEQUENT SUICIDAL BEHAVIOR

Follow-up Studies — Control Groups

The preceding studies were retrospective; they started with groups of completed suicides or attempted suicide and then sought information in the young people's histories that indicated identifying or predictive behavior, especially prior suicidal behavior. The following group of studies use a prospective approach, taking groups from their index suicidal behavior and following them for various periods of time, noting the kinds and frequencies of suicidal behaviors that subsequently appeared.

As in the previous studies of attempted suicides, the presence of a prior suicidal behavior is a good predictor of the index suicidal behavior, which in turn becomes a valuable clue to predict suicidal behavior in the follow-up period. Barter and colleagues (1968) and Stanley and Barter (1970) provide two reports on a follow-up study of a group of adolescents, under the age of 21, hospitalized for suicide attempts in the Colorado Psychiatric Hospital over a 3-year period. A follow-up interview on forty-five patients indicated continued suicidal behavior by 42 percent of the youngsters. Stanley and Barter (1970) extended the study to include psychiatrically ill adolescents hospitalized at the same time but with with no history of suicidal behavior. The follow-up data indicated that suicide attempts occurred in 50 percent of the experimental subjects and in only 16 percent of the controls, a highly significant difference.

Otto's (1972) study, referred to earlier, was actually a 10-year follow-up of 1,727 child and adolescent suicide attempters in Sweden. They were compared with nonsuicidal children equivalent demographically. A huge undertaking, it was possible only in a country where data are routinely kept on its citizens from the time they are born until they die. Otto found that mortality was significantly higher in the suicidal group than in the controls, with 5.4 percent deceased in the experimental group and 1.8 percent deceased among the controls. Of the attempters who died, 80 percent committed suicide. Repeated attempts were more common among boys than girls, 21 percent versus 14 percent.

Four additional controlled studies reported on the occurrence of suicidal events following treatment for suicide attempts. Cohen-Sandler and Berman's (1981) well-designed investigation conducted with young suicidal children, ages 6 to 16, followed for 3 years twenty suicidal children, twenty-one depressed but not suicidal children, and thirty-five psychiatric controls, nonsuicidal and nondepressed. Five percent of the children had engaged in multiple suicide attempts before the index hospitalization. Twenty percent of the suicidal children were suicidal again after discharge. No further suicidal behavior was reported in the other two groups.

Rauenhorst (1972) followed a group of fifty Caucasian female attempters, ages 16 to 30, and compared them with matched controls, who had been treated for minor or accidental trauma. Follow-up continued for 14 to 21 months after discharge. Among the thirty-eight experimentals and forty-four controls located and interviewed, five of the experimentals, 38 percent, and none of the controls had made a subsequent suicide attempt. One person made several subsequent attempts.

As part of his larger study, Motto (1984) followed for 10 years male adolescents who had been admitted and treated in psychiatric inpatient hospitals in San Francisco because of a suicidal state or depressive mood. He focused on the 122 boys in this population who were ages 10 to 19 and found that eleven suicides, 9 percent, occurred within a mean of 38 months after discharge. Motto further reports that 43 percent of the 119 subjects had a history of one or more attempts before the index hospitalization, and that 9 percent of those who reported no prior suicide attempts went on to commit suicide, whereas 10 percent of those with a history of prior attempts did so.

In a study in Oxford, England, Hawton and colleagues (1982) did two follow-ups of fifty adolescent overdosers aged 18 and under, at 1 month and 12 months after discharge. He compared his group, divided into two subgroups, one 15 and below and the second 16 to 18, with a general population sample previously collected. In the year following the overdose, 14 percent of the patients made further suicide attempts, all but one of them in the 16 to 18 year age group.

SUBSEQUENT SUICIDAL BEHAVIOR

Follow-up Studies – Not Control Groups

Two researchers report follow-up studies but do not use control groups. White (1974) surveyed fifty consecutive patients aged 14 to 19 admitted to a general hospital in Birmingham, England, following suicidal overdoses. Information on forty of the cases in 1 year of follow-up indicated that 10 percent of the patients had further self-poisoning episodes. Crumley's (1979) group of forty adolescents in his private practice who had entered treatment following a suicide attempt yielded one patient, 3 percent, who committed suicide within 2 years following his treatment.

In summary, the follow-up studies of suicidal behavior support further the usefulness of prior suicidal behavior as an indicator of suicide risk. Further suicide attempts ranged from 10 percent to 50 percent, and completed suicides occurred in from 3 percent to 10 percent subsequently. As one would expect, most of the study populations were hospital patients. The follow-up times varied considerably, ranging from several months to 10 years.

In general, from the studies of completed suicides, attempts, threats, and ideation suicidal behavior – with and without control groups and retrospectively in case histories or prospectively through follow-ups – prior suicidal behavior is a significant and valuable clue for further self-destructive behavior. The risk factor seems valid both for children and adolescents and for boys and girls and also seems to increase in significance with increasing age among adolescents.

RELATIONSHIP BETWEEN COMPLETED SUICIDE, SUICIDE ATTEMPTS, AND SUICIDE THREATS

Most efforts to explore the relationship between the various kinds of suicide have approached the problem from two directions – similarities and differences between demographic characteristics, suicide methods and motivations, and/or the extent to which all the suicide behaviors occur in the same persons. Stengel and Cook (1958) were the first to demonstrate the demographic and personality differences between completed and attempted suicides in their London study. Those differences, that is, that attempters are younger, use less lethal methods, have more women than men, more often occur where others can rescue, have been substantiated regularly. The role of intention to die has been found to be critical, with the attempters more often motivated to influence others than to die. The concept of attempted suicide has been incorporated in Kreitman's term, parasuicide, in which he emphasized the nonfatal aspect of the act when an "individual deliberately causes self-injury or ingests a substance in excess of any prescribed or generally recognized therapeutic dosage" (1977, p. 3). Kreitman and his colleagues find their studies have confirmed the traditional view that parasuicides and suicides are epidemiologically distinct. Sex and age patterns are different, rates are very different, and motivations may be different. At the same time they note the close relationship between the two, with 1 percent of parasuicides going on to commit suicide within 1 year and 41 percent of the completed suicides having a history of parasuicide. Although Kreitman's populations refer to the general population, their studies included ages down through 15.

Marks and Haller's (1977) large scale study on the relationship between attempts and threats compared adolescents who had made suicide attempts with adolescents referred for both suicide attempts and for suicidal thoughts and threats, and with adolescents referred for suicidal thoughts and/or threats but with no suicide attempts. The comparison group was the rest of their large sample of disturbed adolescents not referred for suicidal behavior. The groups were compared on family, school, friends, leisure time interests, emotions, and so forth, using psychological tests, interviews, and therapists' ratings. Marks and Haller concluded that there was little evidence to support the assertion that those teenagers who threatened suicide were markedly different from those who attempted it. The results also indicated the same distinctions in personality and demographic characteristics between commits and threats as had been found between commits and attempts. For suicide attempts, the 3:1 ratio of females to males was confirmed; for suicidal thoughts, the ratio was more 2:1 female to male. There were apparently enough sex differences to emphasize the need to study the sexes separately.

Goldberg's (1981) study aimed at identifying characteristics that may be the same for people with suicide ideation, those who attempted suicide, and those who completed suicide. A variety of schedules were administered to 489 persons and the presence or absence of thoughts of suicide during the previous month were related to the various factors as the outcome variables. Goldberg concluded from the similarities reported by the subjects that suicide ideation, attempts, and completions, if not on a continuum, are at least overlapping phenomena. Persons with these different kinds of suicidal manifestations, she felt, might be essentially equivalent.

In summary, the overlap to which all the suicide behaviors, commits, attempts, threats, and education occur in the same population has been noted at length in the studies surveyed in the preceding sections of this chapter. While it is possible, as Kreitman (1977) has done, to focus on the differences between the populations, it is the similarities and overlap that seem more impressive. It is also unlikely that an overlap group exists as a separate group, as has been suggested.

In general, it seems justifiable to conclude that the presence of any of the overt forms of suicidal behavior, such as attempts, threats, and/or ideation in the prior history of any individual can be considered valuable indicators of high risk for further self-destructive acts. The usefulness of the presence of high levels of indirect self-destructive behaviors as predictive clues is much more uncertain.

PREPARATORY BEHAVIORS

While the risk factors reviewed above, prior and subsequent attempts, threats, and ideation, rate as excellent indicators of suicide risk, they have the disadvantage of occurring late in the process of identification, and mark the fact that a suicidal state has already existed. The obvious aim is to identify factors that occur earlier, before any overt suicidal behavior has appeared, so that intervention to prevent possible injury or death can take place. The following section reviews studies that note activities aptly termed *preparatory behaviors* that may be considered as risk factors for potential suicide.

INDIRECT SELF-DESTRUCTIVE BEHAVIOR

Indirect self-destructive behavior (ISDB) has long been recognized as an important aspect of self-destructive behavior (Durkheim 1897/1951), but it has not been systematically investigated until relatively recently. Menninger (1938) developed the concept psychodynamically as *focal or partial suicide* while Farberow (1980) has conducted research on a number of the behaviors felt to be indirectly self-destructive, or suicidal equivalents. Whereas a number of behaviors have been identified as indirect self-destructive behavior, only the research by Farberow will be discussed in this chapter.

   No studies, except those of Farberow and his colleagues, have specifically explored the parameters of these behaviors from the point of view of determining the personality characteristics, attitudes, prevalence, and demographic features of persons who consistently engage in this kind of behavior. Farberow (1980) selected various groups of persons engaging in ISDB and conducted controlled studies of their characteristics. One specifically involved young people, juvenile delinquents. Studies were conducted of groups of patients who were diabetic, had thromboangiitis obliterans or Buerger's Disease, were elderly and chronically ill, hyperobese, or on renal hemodialysis. Control groups were made up of cooperative patients in each disease group. In addition, a file survey determined the presence and kind of ISDB in five treatment groups: two drug rehabilitation programs, a youth delinquency program, and two hospital populations, one of completed and one of attempted suicide. Briefly summarized, the major results obtained from these studies characterized the patients with levels of ISDB as: high impulsivity, low frustration tolerance, present orientation, minimal tolerance for frustration or delay, and little future orientation or concern. These characteristics were frequently accompanied by strong drives toward risk taking, pleasure seeking, and a need for excitement. In the case file study, the methadone maintenance group had the highest ISDB scores, especially on noncompliance with medical regimen, not making recommended changes in life activities, and disregarding treatment requirements. Alcohol abuse was one of the most frequent forms of ISDB, appearing in from one-half to one-third of the drug abusers. In the youth diversion group, where the ages were 18 and under, 5 percent were noted to be problem drinkers and 20 percent to be drug abusers. Overt suicidal behavior in any of the groups was absent or minimal, except among the elderly chronically ill. There was a high inverse correlation between suicide potential and life satisfaction, leading to the conclusion that ISDB among the elderly, chronically ill was generated by feelings of isolation and loss, variables also known to arouse direct suicidal behavior. It may be that the elderly, chronically ill person uses ISDB as a way of avoiding the stigma and taboos characterizing overt suicide. The extent to which the ISDB frustrates the hospital staff may also bring some feeling of power into an environment in which the patients have, for the most part, lost control of their lives.

In general, indirect self-destructive behavior as an indicator of suicide risk is behavior about which there is still far too little understood to function as a reliable clue. The difficulty seems to lie in its complexity in that different degrees of certain kinds of ISDB may serve different purposes in the same individual, protecting the individual in some instances (as substitute behavior) or putting him at greater risk (by becoming part of the problem and making it even larger). Substance abuse seems to be at least a low level indicator of risk but will be useful only if accompanied by other, more reliable indicators.

SCHOOL PROBLEMS

School plays an important role in the life of the young person, eventually occupying at least a third of the individual's day. As the second major social system in which children and adolescents are involved, it adds its own pressures and stresses to the traditional ones of family and home. A number of investigators of suicide have found school behaviors such as failures, discipline, and truancy significant as risk factors for potential suicidal behavior.

Academic Performance

A number of investigators noted school failures and falling behind the appropriate grade among both completed and attempted adolescent suicides. Seiden (1966) found that although undergraduate suicides did much better than their fellow classmates in terms of grade point average, 3.18 versus 2.50, there was a continuous deterioration of their performance as they progressed through school. The students were filled with doubts of adequacy and were despondent over their general academic aptitude. Iga (1981) describes the pervasive concern about gaining entrance into school and performing in school well enough to stay in it as a primary contributing factor in suicides of Japanese youth. Education is virtually the only means for achieving security in a society that is highly status conscious. Preparation for the examination begins in early childhood for many Japanese. At least 80 percent of the children attend a neighborhood cram school for further preparation after school hours.

Shafii and colleagues (1985) report conflicting data about school performance from their studies of committed suicides versus attempted suicides. They found that poor academic performance or being a school drop-out did not differentiate their suicide subjects. However, acting-out behavior resulting in disciplinary problems and suspension from school did significantly differentiate the suicides from the controls. In contrast, Shafii and Shafii (1982) found that failure in academic performance was a marked characteristic of young suicide attempters, 15 and younger, when compared with nonsuicidal psychiatric patients.

Pfeffer and colleagues (1979, 1980) found differences in suicidal behavior between inpatients and outpatients of latency age. As a result of a higher incidence of multiple deficits in ego functioning in both the suicidal and nonsuicidal inpatient groups, at least three-fourths of each group tested below grade level. However, the suicidal children were much more worried about doing poorly in school than the nonsuicidal controls, 48 percent versus 19 percent. In contrast, among the outpatients, both suicidals and controls worried about doing poorly in school, but showed no significant difference in the percentage functioning at the appropriate school grade level.

The percentage performing poorly in school was noted as high (78 percent) in the study by Barter and colleagues (1968); 58 percent by Hawton and colleagues (1982); and 35 to 38 percent by Garfinkel and Golombek (1983). Garfinkel and Golombek found that more than half were experiencing failure in school or were drop-outs, but closer inspection indicated that the severity of the attempt made a difference. Those attempts rated most severe were correlated most highly with success at school while minor or moderate ratings of severity of suicide attempts were more significantly associated with failure at school. They felt this corroborated results in a previous study of completed suicides in which the suicides had been associated with industrious and productive performances.

Stanley and Barter (1970) found that disturbance in school adjustment was an early and frequent indicator of emotional disturbance in adolescence. However, they were not able to demonstrate a significant difference in adequate school adjustment between their experimental and control groups. In their follow-up, they did find a difference, with patients who repeated suicide attempts after discharge having significantly poorer school records than the control groups.

Otto (1972) noted school problems also in his extensive follow-up of suicide attempters. However, the levels of school problems he found for his experimental group, 7 percent, was considerably lower than those reported in the preceding studies. The nature of the school problems were primarily unsatisfactory school results, desire to quit school, problems relating to teachers and school friends, and severe fear of examinations. Otto said that it is unusual for the school to be the direct cause of a suicide attempt. When an attempt does occur it is more likely to be in the higher grades where the demands may be too much for some children. Marek and colleagues (1976) found school failures to be the primary motive for suicide deaths in their study of juvenile suicides in Poland.

Among uncontrolled studies, Rohn and colleagues (1977) found that 75 percent of the teenagers hospitalized for a suicide attempt at the University of Maryland Hospital had exceptionally poor school records. Tishler and colleagues (1981) felt that deteriorating school marks and worry about failing school were typical of their adolescent suicide attempters seen at a children's hospital in Columbus, Ohio.

Strong contradictory evidence is reported by Cohen-Sandler and colleagues (1982) in their well-controlled study that divided subjects into four developmental stages from birth to 15 years. Their control groups were depressed and nonsuicidal psychiatric children. They found, in contrast to the high frequency of school adjustment problems reported by other investigators, that school refusal, poor concentration, and poor school work failed to discriminate among the children. Indeed, school problems were reported generally for only 20 percent or fewer children in the entire sample.

Disciplinary Problems

Shaffer (1974) found that it was primarily in this school behavioral area that children and adolescents who committed suicide were expressing their emotional problems. The most frequent precipitant was a disciplinary crisis, occurring in 31 percent of his cases. Five of his subjects had learned that a letter describing their anti-social behavior in school and their truancy was about to be sent to their parents. Four had been in a fight with another child and two had been dropped from a school sporting team. Three had presented school problems because of a dispute with one or the other parent.

Rohn and colleagues (1977) found 35 percent of their suicide attempters were having behavior or discipline problems. White (1974) found adverse school reports more likely to occur in the younger adolescents than in the older. He reported 67 percent were labeled as idle trouble-makers or a bad influence. When the subjects were in secondary schools there were only 14 percent with similar adverse reports. Barter and colleagues (1968) noted disciplinary actions in 78 percent of their suicide attempters.

Truancy or Drop-outs

Shaffer (1974) noted truancy in seven boys and two girls, and that twelve of the twenty-one boys had not been in school the day before their death. Three of these had been chronic school refusers while five had been absent for less than a week. Two had been away from home and school during the 24 hours preceding their deaths. Truancy was also noted as a problem by Barter and colleagues (1968), Otto (1972), and Garfinkel and Golombek (1983).

Isolation and Withdrawal

Otto (1972) noted a desire to quit school in 12 percent of his subjects. Nilson (1981) found a number of school problems in her study of runaways. However, she felt that school problems and the process of running away are interactive so it was useless to decide which was primary or to determine the relationship of school problems to suicidal behavior in her runaway group.

Wenz (1979) conducted an interesting sociological study related to this problem by looking for sociological correlates of alienation among two hundred adolescents, aged 12 through 18, who were telephone callers to a crisis intervention center or suicide attempters treated in emergency medical facilities. He found significant negative correlations of school performance with alienation in 20 percent of the above-average students, 25 percent of the average students, and 56 percent of the below-average students. Like Nilson, he assumes that school difficulties themselves are not a primary factor in the suicide attempt but rather problems that have been present for a long time and are the result of alienation.

In summary, almost all the researchers confirm the use of school problems and poor school performance as significant risk factors. However, the evidence produced in the well-controlled studies of Pfeffer and colleagues (1979, 1980) and

Cohen-Sandler and colleagues (1982) indicate that caution needs to be used in evaluating the presence or absence of this factor, for school problems may be more generally predictive of emotional disturbance (which would include suicide) than primarily of suicide alone. However, school problems may be highly age-related, and so less differentiating in the younger ages than in the older ages. While still an important clue, school problems rank more as moderately predictive, but clues that provide considerable additional supporting weight when other factors are present.

ANTI-SOCIAL BEHAVIOR

Anti-social behaviors appear in many forms. We have included in this category such behaviors as aggression, rage, hostility, violence, delinquency, homicidal impulses, fire-setting, stealing, and disobedience. References are primarily to behavior indices although at least one investigator, McAnarney (1979) relates the tendency to national attitudes. She sees Denmark, Sweden, and Japan as suppressing aggression and notes the higher rates of suicides occurring in their countries, and contrasts them with the Norwegians who enjoy more freedom in expressing anger and have a markedly lower rate of suicide.

Some of the most intensive work in evaluating the role of aggression in suicidal behavior has come from two sources, Pfeffer and her colleagues (1979, 1980, 1982, 1983) in New York, and Cohen-Sandler and colleagues (1982) in Washington, D.C. Earlier studies from Pfeffer and colleagues (1979, 1980) on inpatient and outpatient children of latency age compared four groups: children who were suicidal recently, suicidal in the past, nonsuicidal recently, and nonsuicidal in the past. They found aggression high in all groups, 90 percent for the suicidal groups and 80 percent for the nonsuicidal groups, a nonsignificant difference. All the children displayed severe aggression that included fights, temper tantrums, a tendency to hurt and tease others, a destructiveness toward objects, defiance, and restlessness. Fire-setting and stealing were prevalent among both suicidal and nonsuicidal children. When their desires were not fulfilled, they displayed intense rage.

Often both suicidal and homicidal impulses were present, and to defend against the rage, the children denied, projected, and displaced hostile feelings onto others. A similar research design applied to a group of outpatient children who were latency-aged yielded exactly the same results (1980). The sole specific indicator of potential suicidal behavior was an increase in hypermotor behavior both within the inpatients and the outpatients.

Pfeffer and her colleagues (1982, 1983) then conducted two studies of children aged 6 to 12, with one group predominantly from a low social status and the second from a middle social status. The subjects were divided into four groups: those with suicidal tendencies alone, those who showed assaultive tendencies alone, those with both suicidal and assaultive tendencies, and those with neither suicidal nor assaultive tendencies. The results showed that the degree of expression of aggressive tendencies was a significant predictor of group membership for each of the four groups of children. Aggression was greatest in the group classified as both assaultive and suicidal; lying, stealing, and truancy were present among both children who were suicidal only and assaultive only. One important contribution of this study was the delineation of two types of children: the first, an assaultive and suicidal group who had distinct ego deficits and exhibited rage episodes and serious assaultive tendencies; the second, a group with relatively stable ego functioning who decompensated and were more likely to become overtly depressed under extreme environmental stress. The authors pointed out that from a theoretical point of view, the results did not deal directly with the question whether suicidal behavior is an expression of inhibited aggression or aggression turned inward. Rather, different groups of variables were producing different patterns of behavior expressed as assaultiveness and suicidal behavior. These different sets can occur in isolation, producing groups of children who are assaultive alone or suicidal alone. However, they can also occur together, in which case they produce highly intense aggression.

In Washington, Cohen-Sandler and colleagues (1982) noted especially the appearance of aggression in their four progressive developmental life-stages from infancy to 15 years of age. They concluded that, as a result of experiencing a disproportionate number of losses of all kinds, suicidal children, in contrast to the experiences of depressed and psychiatric controls, developed a greater loss of self-esteem and an increase in aggrieved rage. A review of their life events showed that suicidal children remained more intensely involved with family members and peers during childhood than the children in the control groups who were more often separated from their families. The frustrated investment of the suicidal children in these relationships was expressed as rage. Nearly two-thirds of the suicidal children made homicidal threats, gestures, and even attempts.

The presence of aggressive, violent feelings in the young suicidal child was reported by Paulson and colleagues (1978) who found violence, internalized hate and anger, marked preoccupation with fire-setting, and homicidal behavior toward family members and peers in 20 percent of suicidal children hospitalized for suicidal behavior.

Aggressive, violent, and anti-social behaviors have been noted in varying proportions by a number of investigators of older adolescents. Among those with control subjects, Jacobs (1971) and Teicher (1970) hypothesized that rebelliousness of suicidal adolescents is one phase they go through until they reach the final suicidal stage. McIntire and Angle (1973) found a mean score for hostility significantly higher for their experimental group of self-poisoners than for control subjects. Tishler and colleagues (1981) found that suicide attempters between ages 12 and 18 had a significantly higher score on the hostility scale of the Brief Symptom Index when compared with a group of nonattempters, and Otto (1972) reported that one group of youngsters in his extensive follow-up of suicide attempters in Sweden could be characterized as showing increased irritability, aggressiveness, instability, and peevishness. Otto hypothesized that it was depression that was hidden behind the antisocial activities such as vagrancy, theft, and truancy. Smith (1983), comparing highly suicidal teens with highly suicidal adults, found that the high-risk teens were much more overtly angry, explosive, and less well-behaved than the adults.

Two of the three psychological autopsy studies using controls, Shafii and colleagues (1985) and Rich and colleagues (1984) found that anger, irritability, and outbursts characterized the younger subjects who suicided. Rich and colleagues classified 9 percent of their under-30 cases as antisocial personality compared with only 1 percent of the group aged 30 and over. The under-30 aged group also experienced legal trouble more significantly, p < .001. Shafii and colleagues reported antisocial behavior including involvement with legal authorities, shoplifting, fire-setting, fighting, school disciplinary problems, drug selling, and prostitution significantly more often in the suicidal group than in the control group, p < .003. Maris (1981) reported that younger subjects who completed suicide were significantly more often motivated by revenge and likely to commit suicide based in anger and irritability than were older suicides.

In studies of committed suicide with no control groups, Shaffer (1974) reported antisocial symptoms in 73 percent of thirty children he studied. Crumley (1979) found antisocial and violent behavior a prominent feature in two studies of suicide attempters from his private practice, with intense rage appearing when the teenager was disappointed when the person on whom he was leaning was unavailable. Hendin (nd) related the increase in the suicide rate of young blacks in the United States to their struggle to deal with conscious rage and murderous impulses.

Among studies of attempted suicides with no controls, Goldberg's (1981) extensive epidemiological investigation of suicidal ideation found that persons who denied overt aggression had the highest percentage of suicidal thoughts, 16.5 percent. Rosenberg and Latimer (1966) found evidence, in the records of seventy-seven suicidal adolescents at a state hospital, of patterns of sexual delinquency, running away, truancy, and destructive behaviors for the girls, and considerable acting-out, running away, destructiveness, stealing, and defying authority for the boys. Alessi and colleagues (1984) found that 63 percent of juvenile delinquents considered seriously suicidal were committed for one or more violent felonies and 31 percent had a history of assaultive in-program behavior.

Summarizing, antisocial behavior, especially assaultiveness, when expressed along with suicidal behavior, seems to be an excellent risk factor for suicidal potential. All of the researchers quoted noted its significance in contrast to control groups. It seems likely that antisocial behavior is more important as a clue in the younger ages, so long as it is accompanied by suicidal expressions. It does not appear to be as significant in adult suicides, as indicated by Rich and colleagues (1984) and Maris (1981b).

POOR IMPULSE CONTROL AND ACTING-OUT

Impulsive and acting-out behavior are closely related to the antisocial behaviors just discussed and are frequently included among the list of various behaviors when antisocial behaviors are identified by researchers. For example, Maris (1981b) found that younger children who completed suicide had more intense deep feelings, more aggressive feelings, and higher levels of impulsivity and dissatisfaction with their life accomplishments than older completed suicides. Shafii and Shafii (1982) found the risk of suicide was significantly increased when there was impulsivity and lack of regard for danger in the histories of suicidal children and adolescents.

Impulse and acting-out behavior were both noted by Crumley (1979) in his review of his private practice patients and by McIntire and Angle (1973) in their study of self-poisoners in children and adolescents. The researchers in both studies considered the impulsivity and the activity as part of the antisocial, hostile, and aggressive behavior that characterized their populations.

Among suicidal children of latency age, Pfeffer and colleagues (1979, 1980) found an inability to tolerate frustration, delay actions, tolerate deprivation, or plan for the future. However, this poor impulse control was present for both suicidal and nonsuicidal children. The researchers found an increase in hypermotor behavior, possibly providing an increased potential for dangerous acting-out behaviors. Finally, Pfeffer (1979) noted in an earlier study that an unrealistic, repetitive acting-out of life-endangering and omnipotent fantasies, such as being a superhero, was another important clue of high risk. The confusion and loss of reality from acting out such fantasies were thought to arise from feelings of intense vulnerability and helplessness.

In summary, poor impulse control and acting-out behavior are often seen as part of the pattern of behaviors included as antisocial. Impulsivity appears to characterize suicidal persons in the studies reviewed, although Pfeffer and colleagues found it did not differentiate suicidal children from the nonsuicidal children. In general, impulsivity and acting-out serve as good clues especially when found in the context of antisocial behavior. It may be that, because of the lack of preparation and planning, impulsivity will produce more suicidal events, but that they are less likely to be lethal.

SUGGESTIBILITY

Involvement in Fantasy Games and Imitation

In recent years increasing attention has been focused on the growing degree of violence appearing in television programs, many of them screening at times when they can be watched by adolescents and children. Sometimes the violence has involved suicidal behavior, as in the Russian roulette scene of the Academy Award-winning film, *The Deer Hunter*. Concomitantly, there has been widespread popularity of various fantasy games involving an array of violent activities, including instructions to the youngsters that they should try to become in real life the characters that they are fulfilling in the game. Now in its seventh year, the National Coalition on Television Violence (NCTV) has been conducting lobbying and educational campaigns among both the public and the government in an effort to control the violence shown on television and the continuing development of violent fantasy games. They point out that prime time violence has increased over recent years. For the fall-winter season shows on the major television networks, ABC, NBC, and CBS in 1980 to 1981, the average number of acts of violence per hour was 5.6. By the winter of 1985, the average had increased to 13.9 acts of violence per viewing hour.

To illustrate the process of imitation and the way in which violence on TV can stimulate similar acts of violence in young viewers, NCTV gathered information on verified imitations of the Russian roulette suicide that was featured in *The Deer Hunter*. The Coalition was able to find forty-one shootings with thirty-seven deaths. Most of the time the information about the event was attributed to newspaper reports; in other instances it was attributed to notification by a friend or the family. In each instance, the act was reported to have occurred within a short time of having seen the movie, or with specific identification of the action as an imitation of the movie scene by friends or family. Of the forty-one shootings, approximately half, or twenty, of the victims were below the age of 19.

NCTV has also been concerned with toys requiring violence in fantasy, such as war games and fantasy games. A survey of fifty different fantasy role-playing games found that all had a basic violent theme, such as medieval sorcery and combat, wild west battles, outer space combat, postnuclear holocaust violence, urban thievery, espionage, assassinations, samurai brutality, war violence, and others. Frequently the violence is intense and gruesome.

One of the most popular and widely played games is the adolescent fantasy role-playing game Dungeons and Dragons (D&D). The game has been claimed to be a major factor in causing at least fifty suicides and murders, according to the evidence accumulated by the NCTV and by a group calling itself Bothered About D&D (BADD), founded by the mother of one of its victims. The game requires attacks, assassinations, spying, theft, and poisonings. The players arm their characters with any of sixty-two different types of weapons. An extreme number of monsters from horror and demonology are involved, including twenty-two types of satanic demons and devils. Players can be cursed with twenty different types of insanity. D&D is played in groups under the direction of a Dungeon Master, primarily by males, age 12 to 20, and there are an estimated three to four million players in the United States. The game can last for months and even years with the goal being not to get killed and to accumulate as much power as possible. Power is earned by the murder of opponents. Players can be good or evil and are encouraged to identify with their own character in the game. In the group of related deaths, twenty-two, or 44 percent, of the suicides or murders involved youngsters aged 19 and under.

All the evidence about the game is primarily anecdotal. The publishers of NCTV quote, without sources, various authorities on whose work they rely for their evidence of the harm from violent, fantasy role-playing games, violent toys and play, and the desensitization effect of continued exposure to role-playing violence.

Although specific research is lacking on the relationship between magical thinking/fantasy and suicide, a hypothesis might be drawn from the results of the study by Gould (1965). Magical thinking implies a loss of ability to recognize the boundary between fantasy and reality. Thus, for young people or children who have either lost or not developed the ability to maintain the boundary, fantasy games, such as war games and Dungeons and Dragons, become more and more engrossing and all-encompassing.

The games themselves become the reality. Pfeffer (1986) calls attention to this in her comments on ego functioning often seen in suicidal children: "As the pace, pitch, and content of the child's play intensify, suicidal children may lose the ability to discriminate between themselves and play objects. . . . Another aspect of ego boundary diffusion of suicidal children is manifest when play ceases and becomes a form of personal acting out" (p. 201).

SOCIAL ISOLATION

Social isolation appears in many forms including withdrawal, alienation, asocial behavior, poor or inadequate peer relationships, and similar behaviors. It is usually considered fairly often to be the hallmark of a depressive syndrome. However, social isolation may appear in suicidal persons even when depression is not evident.

In their comprehensive description of the development of the suicidal state, Jacobs (1971) and Teicher (1970) identify one stage as a process of progressive social isolation from meaningful social relationships. The first stage of exacerbated problems is followed by a period of dissolution and disappearance of meaningful social relationships. The feelings of isolation that follow then become both the problem and the barrier that prevents resolution of it. Withdrawal into self appears as gloominess, silence, and social alienation and the physical withdrawal frequently takes the form of running away from home. Sometimes the adolescent will try to reestablish a relationship with a significant other in a romance. About 36 percent of the suicide attempters were found to be engaged in a serious romance that was failing or terminating.

Both Seiden (1966) and Hendin (1975) found in their studies of suicidal college students that they were often asocial, withdrawn, shy, friendless, and alienated from all but the most minimal social interactions. Often, they almost totally absorbed themselves in their school work, which may then have served as a protective device. Hendin hypothesized the psychodynamics as one in which the students saw their relationship with their parents as dependent on their emotional, if not physical, death. The depression and isolation that developed was actually a form of protection that sometimes shielded the individual and even made suicide unnecessary.

The adolescent suicide attempters treated by Shafii and Shafii (1982) and Rohn and colleagues (1977) at their university hospitals and the self-poisoners seen by McIntire and Angle (1973) at their poison control center were characterized as loners, preoccupied with self, involved in failed romantic relationships, withdrawn, and isolated. Rohn and colleagues found the social aspects characteristic of the boys in his study. However, Marks and Haller (1977) found that their suicidal girls were more likely to have few or no friends during their childhood, to be socially isolated, and to be unable to talk about their personal problems with anyone.

In two follow-up controlled studies, Stanley and Barter (1970) in Colorado found that young people who went on to make further attempts after their hospital discharge were much less likely to have adequate peer relationships, less likely to be living with their parents, and to have more social agency contact than those who did not make further suicide attempts. Otto (1972) found social isolation much more prominent in his suicide attempters than in his nonsuicidal controls. He hypothesized that behind much of the antisocial behavior may be found loneliness and isolation, listlessness, contact difficulties, feelings of guilt, emptiness, and apathy.

Wenz's (1979) interesting sociological approach hypothesized alienation as a highly significant factor among adolescent suicide attempters. Applying Dean's Measure of Alienation to adolescents who called a suicide prevention center and adolescent attempters treated at emergency rooms, he found the variable with the strongest negative association was social contact with peers, indicating the less the relational involvement with peers, the greater the feelings of social isolation. Wenz concludes that alienation sets in motion a train of events that leads to attempted suicide. As a result of alienation there is an atrophy of interpersonal relations. The greater the communication blockage, the greater the adolescent's sense of isolation and the more the person withdraws from further contact with others. The process is circular and leads to ever-greater degrees of isolation and withdrawal. His reasoning is strikingly similar to that of Jacobs (1971).

Summarizing, controlled studies indicate that social isolation consistently identifies the suicidal person when comparisons with nonsuicidal persons are available. It thus appears to be a good clue, but not in and of itself; social isolation appears in depressed persons who are not suicidal and in nondepressed nonsuicidal persons. However, when social isolation appears with suicidal expression, it emerges as a significant high risk predictor.

RUNNING AWAY

Runaways are inherently a suicide risk group inasmuch as the behavior is associated with emotional disturbance, family conflicts and strife, school and learning problems, social alienation, and other negative conditions, all of which are associated with suicidal risk. Nilson's (1981) study of twenty-eight runaways compared them with other court referrals who were not runaways. Half the runaway group, fourteen, made suicide attempts or gestures and twelve showed suicidal ideation only. In the nonrunaway control group, only two of the eighteen made an attempt or gesture, while eleven showed signs or ideations. The difference between the two groups is significant, $p < .02$.

The presence of a history of having been a runaway is noted by Rosenberg and Latimer (1966) and White (1974) in their research on attempted suicides among adolescents, and Shaffer (1974) also notes the presence of runaways in the histories of younger adolescents who completed suicides.

Four well-controlled studies sharply diverged on the usefulness of a history of running away. Jacobs (1971) considers it the third stage in his theory of the development of the suicidal state, following the second stage of withdrawal. Marks and Haller (1977) find the presence of running away a significant differentiator between suicidal boys and emotionally disturbed nonsuicidal boys, but not a differentiating factor between the girls. The strongest evidence against running away as a distinguishing feature comes from the studies by Pfeffer and colleagues (1979, 1980) and Cohen-Sandler and colleagues (1982). Their carefully designed studies find that running away is more a symptom of emotional disturbance than necessarily of suicidal risk.

In summary, the usefulness of running away as a significant risk factor, while seemingly positive, has been thrown into doubt by the results of Pfeffer's and Cohen-Sandler and colleagues' studies. It is true, however, that the population of their studies are young, ranging in age from 5 to 14 at the most. It may be that the usefulness of this factor changes with older adolescents. At this point, the value of a history of running away as a suicide risk indicator is useful but not necessarily predictive unless accompanied by other self-destructive clues.

THINKING PATTERNS AND STYLES

Shneidman (1961) has pioneered in the study of suicidal thinking. His approach has been an analysis of the logical substructures of syntax in the writings of suicidal people, primarily through the comparison of genuine suicide notes with simulated suicide notes. Shneidman stimulated a number of other researchers. Using the matched pairs of real and simulated suicide notes, Tripodes (1976) applied twenty-four aspects of reasoning patterns, including the cognitive maneuvers, and the idio-, contra-, and psycho-logic categories of analysis to the thinking of suicidal people. The picture of the suicide note-writer obtained was impressively similar to that described in clinical face-to-face contact, but with the added special features of the suicide logic and style of thinking.

Tripodes used a comprehensive approach, covering all aspects of style of thinking. Neuringer (1976) focused on dichotomous thinking or the tendency to polarize thought in an extreme manner. Using the semantic differential with groups of suicide attempters, psychosomatic patients and normal patients, Neuringer (1961) found in two separate studies that suicide attempters were overwhelmingly more dichotomous in their thinking on the activity and potency factor scales than were the other two groups of subjects. While polarization of values was apparently a common characteristic of individuals in psychological stress, the dichotomization of the activity and potency factors seemed to be an exclusive hallmark of suicidal thinking. The results were even more extreme when only highly serious suicide attempters were compared with the psychosomatic and normal patients. Neuringer and Lettieri (1971) extended the earlier studies by taking daily measures of dichotomous thinking from high-risk, medium-risk, and zero-risk individuals over a 3-week period following a suicidal crisis. The results were the same, but the investigators were even more alarmed that the extreme dichotomous thinking did not seem to diminish over time. They raised the concern that the process of dichotomous thinking associated with suicidal action might always be present, ready continuously to distort the world in such a way that suicide is an ever-present possibility.

Levenson and Neuringer (1971, 1974) conducted a number of studies on rigidity and constriction of thinking in the suicidal individual and found that person to be more socially rigid and inflexible, to show an inability to shift in problem-solving strategies, as did Linehan and colleagues (1981), to be consistently high in field dependency, and to have difficulty solving arithmetic problems.

To summarize, Neuringer (1976) stated that suicidal individuals seemed to have difficulty in utilizing and relying on internal, imaginative resources; to polarize their value systems; and to tend to be rigid and constricted in their thinking. The process was the result of emotional stress affecting the cognitive structures, and decreasing cognitive capacity.

Kaplan and Pokorny (1976) tested the hypothesis that the level of self-derogation in the thinking of individuals might predict subsequent suicidal behavior. In a longitudinal study of junior high school students in Houston, they administered a questionnaire three times at annual intervals, and obtained measures of self-derogation over periods of time. By correlating them with the number of self-destructive behaviors appearing between the measures, the investigators confirmed their hypothesis that high levels of self-derogation were positively associated with suicidal thoughts, threats, and suicide attempts.

In summary, style of thinking, while apparently useful and intriguing, is limited in its predictive value for suicide because few professionals have the specialized knowledge of logic and language to apply the suggested analysis. Dichotomous and self-derogatory thinking seem like positive risk factors, especially after suicidal behavior appears. Such modes of thinking serve as evidence of increasing constriction and rigidity, boding ill for an individual's ability to see alternative possible courses of action.

SUICIDE NOTES

Shneidman (1980) is also the person who discovered and initiated the use of suicide notes and personal documents as a source of valuable insights, not only into the thinking and reasoning styles of suicidal persons, but also as a means of determining personality and emotional state immediately preceding the suicide.

Researchers in this area have indicated that suicide notes do not appear until about age 15. Shneidman and Farberow (1960) collected notes in Los

Angeles County from people ranging in age from 13 through 90, with the median age in the fifties. Suicide notes come primarily from completed suicides; they are rarely obtained from attempted suicides. In a statistical comparison of attempted and committed suicides, Shneidman and Farberow (1961) found suicides notes in 36 percent of the committed suicides and only 1 percent of the attempted suicides.

Shneidman (1980) has held three different positions on the relationship of suicide notes to suicidal phenomena since he began their study. At first, the notes would offer special opportunities for observing the thinking and feeling that went into the act; second, that it is understandable that the views into the thinking and feeling were so limited considering the stress under which the notes were written; and third, that the notes' value was increased measurably when seen in the context of the history of the suicidal person. In such instances the note then "illuminates many aspects of the life history."

Shneidman (1976) reviewed all the studies that had been conducted on suicide notes up to 1976 and reported that research had been carried out on the logic of suicide, changes in suicidal dynamics over age, the socioeconomic and psychological variables of suicide, suicidal life-space, the emotional content, the effects of motivational level on language, comparisons with ordinary letters to friends and relatives, language characteristics, relations to persons, and computer count of key tag words.

Shneidman summarized by saying that, as a whole, the studies indicated that it was possible to distinguish between genuine and simulated suicide notes, and that the genuine suicide notes were primarily characterized by dichotomous logic, greater degree of hostility and self-blame, more use of specific instructions to the survivors, less evidence of thinking about how one is thinking, and much evidence of the variety of meanings attributed to the word *love*. The content of the notes frequently reflects unrequited love, intellectual self-assertion, shame and guilt related to disgrace, the wish to escape from the pain of insanity, the wish to spare loved ones from further anguish, and a sense of inner pride and autonomy connected to one's own fate in the manner of one's own death. Often the writing is directed to his survivors-to-be as though he were going to be alive to supervise his wishes.

Peck (1980) conducted a content analysis of suicide notes of suicide victims below the age of 35 (15.3 percent below age 25) in a large Midwest city. He found that elements of fatalism were most prevalent in victims under the age of 20, that they decreased for each of the subsequent older age groups, and that they were more frequent among single persons. The author concludes that the young fit a fatalistic model of suicide, which is described as a condition of excessive constraint or regulation that may trigger a reaction when the individual moves from excessive regulation to a state of alienation and a break in social ties. This almost seems a definition of adolescence.

Edland and Duncan (1973) categorized the notes written by about 23 percent of the committed suicides in Monroe County, New York, into a system that focused on the psychodynamics and attitudes toward death. The authors felt that indications of such thoughts and concerns in individuals, while they were alive, should serve as significant predictive clues for high-risk potential suicide.

In summary, suicide notes have yielded much information about suicidal persons, information that has been useful in identifying risk factors, such as dichotomous thinking, constriction, ambivalence, and age-related dynamics. Further exploration will undoubtedly yield more. As predictive clues, however, the usefulness of suicide notes seems limited, for they are rarely discovered until after the fact of a suicide and so serve more to indicate what did happen rather than what might.

CONCLUSIONS AND SUMMARY

A number of summary conclusions can be made about behavioral clues as risk factors.

1. Prior suicidal behavior of any kind is unquestionably as strong a risk factor indicator for adolescents as it is for adults. It is consistently substantiated in both retrospective and prospective studies, in both well-controlled and no-control studies, and identifies from 22 percent to 71 percent of completed suicides and from 16 percent to 38 percent of attempted suicides retrospectively, and from 3 percent to 10 percent of completed suicides and 10 percent to 50 percent of attempted suicides prospectively.

2. Indirect self-destructive behaviors seem to play too complex a role in the personality of the individual to serve as reliable risk indicators. For some individuals, such behavior may play a protective role against suicidal behavior, whereas for other persons, the same behavior can become a significant self-destructive behavior on its own. Much more needs to be learned of the role of indirect self-destructive behaviors in the personality of the individual before they can achieve a consistent value as a risk factor.

3. Suicide attempters and committers among adolescents still seem most appropriately viewed as separate but overlapping populations.

4. While prior suicide attempts, threats, and ideations may be excellent clues for further suicidal behavior, it is also true that they are late clues in the progression toward suicide, indicating that a suicidal state has

already occurred. Primary prevention objectives encourage the identification of preparatory suicidal risk behaviors at earlier states that
may prevent the development of an overt suicidal state.

5. School problems have been identified consistently in histories of
   children and adolescents who have either committed or attempted
   suicide. These problems include deteriorating academic accomplishments, disciplinary problems, and truancy. However, they also identify general emotional disturbance and need other suicidal clues to be
   most useful as risk factors.

6. Antisocial behavior, especially assaultiveness and threatening people,
   and including rage and hostility, are highly useful clues of suicide
   potential, especially among children and younger adolescents.

7. Social isolation and impulsivity are also often noted. However, these
   behaviors are found to characterize the general psychiatric population
   just as frequently as they do the suicidal group. These factors appear
   to be of greater value when they occur with other evidence of suicide
   potential and help to substantiate the evaluation.

8. Suggestibility and imitation probably play a role in suicide. However,
   this has been shown primarily in large-scale group and social reactions. The role suggestibility and imitation play, especially in violent
   role-fantasy games and television violence, in stimulating suicidal
   behavior in the individual is unclear.

9. Suicide notes can be highly useful in delineating the suicidal person's
   style and pattern of thinking. Dichotomous thinking, especially, may
   serve as a useful clue in reflecting increasing rigidity and loss of ability
   to seek alternatives as the person becomes more and more suicidal.

10. Running away may also be considered another kind of indirect
    self-destructive behavior, possibly substitutive or protective, possibly
    overtly self-harmful, probably both. Because running away and suicidal behavior are both highly associated with family conflict, it is
    highly likely they will be found together.

REFERENCES

Alessi, N., McManus, M., Brickman, A., and Grapentine, A. (1984). Suicidal behavior
    among serious juvenile offenders. *American Journal of Psychiatry* 141:286–287.
Barter, J. T., Swaback, D. W., and Todd, D. (1968). Adolescent suicide attempts: a
    follow-up study of hospitalized patients. *Archives of General Psychiatry* 19:523–527.
Clarkin, J. F., Friedman, R. C., Hurt, S. W., et al. (1984). Affective and character
    pathology of suicidal adolescent and young adult inpatients. *Journal of Clinical
    Psychiatry* 45:19–22.
Cohen-Sandler, R., and Berman, A. L. (1981). A follow-up study of hospitalized suicidal

children. *Proceedings of the 14th annual meeting of the American Association of Suicidology*, 42–44.

Cohen-Sandler, R., Berman, A. L., and King, R. A. (1982). Life stress and symptomatology: determinants of suicidal behavior in children. *Journal of the American Academy of Child Psychiatry* 21:178–186.

Cosand, B. J., Bourque, L. B., and Kraus, J. F. (1982). Suicides among adolescents in Sacramento County, 1950–1979. *Adolescence* 17:917–930.

Crumley, F. E. (1979). Adolescent suicide attempt. *Journal of the American Medical Association* 214:2404–2407.

Diekstra, R. F. W. (1982). Adolescent suicidal behavior: building blocks for a social learning theory. *Proceedings of the 15th annual meeting of the American Association of Suicidology*, ed. C. Pfeffer and J. Rickman, pp. 30–31.

Dorpat, T. L., and Ripley, H. S. (1967). The relationship between attempted suicide and committed suicide. *Comparative Psychiatry* 8:74–79.

Durkheim, E. (1897/1951). *Suicide*. Glencoe, IL: Free Press.

Edland, J. F., and Duncan, C. E. (1973). Suicide notes in Monroe County: a twenty-three year look (1950–1972). *Journal of Forensic Sciences* 18:364–369.

Farberow, N. L., ed. (1980). *The Many Faces of Suicide*. New York: McGraw-Hill.

Farberow, N. L., and Shneidman, E. S. (1955). Attempted, threatened and completed suicide. *Journal of Abnormal and Social Psychology* 50:230.

Farberow, N. L., Shneidman, E. S., and Neuringer, C. (1966). Case history and hospitalization factors in suicide of neuropsychiatric hospital patients. *Journal of Nervous and Mental Disease* 142:32 49.

Gabrielson, I. W. et al. (1970). Suicide attempts in a population pregnant as teenagers. *American Journal of Public Health* 60:2289–2301.

Garfinkel, B. D., Chamberlin, C., and Golombek, H. (1979). Completed suicide in Ontario youth. *Proceedings of the 10th International Congress for Suicide Prevention*, pp. 126–131.

Garfinkel, B. D., and Golombek, H. (1983). Suicide behavior in adolescence. In *The Adolescent and Mood Disturbance*. New York: International Universities Press.

Goldberg, E. (1981). Depression and suicide ideation in the young adult. *American Journal of Psychiatry* 138:35–40.

Gould, R. E. (1965). Suicide problems in children and adolescents. *American Journal of Psychotherapy* 19:228–246.

Hawton, K., O'Grady, J., Osborn, M., and Cole, D. (1982). Adolescents who take overdoses: their characteristics, problems and contacts with helping agencies. *British Journal of Psychiatry* 140:118–123.

Hendin, H. (1975). Growing up dead: student suicide. *American Journal of Psychotherapy* 29:327–338.

———— (1985). Youth suicide: a psychosocial perspective. Unpublished paper presented at symposium on adolescent suicide, Los Angeles.

Iga, M. (1981). Suicide of Japanese youth. *Suicide and Life-Threatening Behavior* 11:17–30.

Jacobs, J. (1971). *Adolescent Suicide*. New York: Wiley-Interscience.

Kaplan, H. B., and Pokorny, A. D. (1976). The self-derogation and suicide. *Social Science and Medicine* 10:113–118.

Kreitman, N. (1977). *Parasuicide*. London: Wiley.

Levenson, M., and Neuringer, C. (1971). Problem solving behavior in suicidal adolescents. *Journal of Consulting and Clinical Psychology* 37:433–436.

———— (1974). Suicide and field dependency. *Omega* 5:181–186.

Linehan, M. M. et al. (1981). Interpersonal response styles of parasuicides. *Proceedings of the 14th annual meeting of the American Association of Suicidology*, pp. 28–30.

Marek, Z., Widacki, Z., and Zwarysiewicz, W. (1976). Suicides committed by minors. *Forensic Sciences* 7:103–108.

Maris, R. (1981a). *Pathways to Suicide*. Baltimore: Johns Hopkins University Press.

———— (1981b). The adolescent suicide problem. *Suicide and Life-Threatening Behavior* 15:91–109.

Marks, P. A., and Haller, D. L. (1977). Now I lay me down for keeps: a study of adolescent suicide attempts. *Journal of Clinical Psychology* 33:390–400.

McAnarney, E. R. (1979). Adolescent and young adult suicide in the United States—a reflection of societal unrest? *Adolescence* 14:765–774.

McIntire, M. S., and Angle, C. R. (1973). Psychological "biopsy" in self-poisoning of children and adolescents. *American Journal of Diseases of Children* 126:42–46.

McKenry, P. C., Tishler, C. L., and Kelley, C. (1983). The role of drugs in adolescent suicide attempts. *Suicide and Life-Threatening Behavior* 13:166–175.

Menninger, K. A. (1938). *Man against Himself*. New York: Harcourt, Brace.

Motto, J. A. (1984). Suicide in male adolescents. In *Suicide in the Young*, ed. H. Sudak et al. Boston: John Wright/PSG.

Neuringer, C. (1961). Dichotomous evaluations in suicidal individuals. *Journal of Consulting Psychology* 25:445–449.

———— (1976). Current developments in the study of suicidal thinking. In *Suicidology: Current Developments*, ed. E. Shneidman, pp. 234–252. New York: Grune & Stratton.

Neuringer, C., and Lettieri, D. J. (1971). Cognitive attitude and affect in suicidal individuals. *Life-Threatening Behavior* 1:106–124.

Nilson, P. (1981). Psychological profiles of runaway children and adolescents. In *Self-Destructive Behavior in Children and Adolescents*, ed. C. F. Wells and I. R. Stuart. New York: Van Nostrand, Reinhold.

Otto, U. (1972). Suicidal acts by children and adolescents. *Acta Psychiatrica Scandinavica* 233:7–123.

Paulson, M. J., Stone, D., and Sposto, R. (1978). Suicide potential and behavior in children ages 4–12. *Suicide and Life-Threatening Behavior* 8:225–242.

Peck, D. L. (1980). Towards a theory of suicide: a case for modern fatalism. *Omega* 11:1–14.

Pfeffer, C. R. (1979). Clinical observations of play of hospitalized suicidal children. *Suicide and Life-Threatening Behavior* 9:235–244.

———— (1986). *The Suicidal Child*. New York: Guilford.

Pfeffer, C. R., Conte, H. R., Plutchik, R., and Jerrett, I. (1979). Suicidal behavior in latency aged children: an empirical study. *Journal of American Child Psychiatry* 18:679–692.

———— (1980). Suicidal behavior in latency aged children: an outpatient population. *Journal of American Child Psychiatry* 19:703–710.

Pfeffer, C. R., Plutchik, R., and Mizuchi, M. S. (1983). Suicidal and assaultive behavior in children: classification, measurement and interrelations. *American Journal of Psychiatry* 140:154–157.

Pfeffer, C. R., Solomon, G., Plutchik, R. et al. (1982). Suicidal behavior in latency-aged psychiatric in-patients: a replication and cross validation. *Journal of the American Academy of Child Psychiatry* 21:564–569.

Rauenhorst, J. M. (1972). Followup of young women who attempt suicide. *Diseases of the Nervous System* 33:792–797.

Rich, C. L., Young, D., and Fowler, R. C. (1984). San Diego suicide study: young vs. old cases. University of California at San Diego School of Medicine. Unpublished report.

Rohn, R. D., Saries, R. M., Kenney, T. J., et al. (1977). Adolescents who attempt suicide. *Journal of Pediatrics* 90:636–638.

Rosenberg, P. H., and Latimer, R. (1966). Suicide attempts by children. *Mental Hygiene* 50:354–359.

Schneer, H. I., Perlstein, A., and Brozovsky, M. (1975). Hospitalized suicidal adolescents: two generations. *Journal of the American Academy of Child Psychiatry* 14:268–280.

Sebastiano, S., Rieder, C., and Berk, S. E. (1982). The organization of fantasied movement in suicidal children and adolescents. In *Proceedings of the 15th annual meeting of the American Association of Suicidology*, ed. C. R. Pfeffer and J. Richman, pp. 25–26.

Seiden, R. H. (1966). Campus tragedy: a study of student suicide. *Journal of Abnormal Psychology* 71.389–399.

Shaffer, D. (1974). Suicide in childhood and early adolescence. *Journal of Child Psychology and Psychiatry* 15:275–291.

Shafii, M., Carrigan, S., Whittinghill, J. R., and Derrick, A. (1985). Psychological autopsy of completed suicide in children and adolescents. *American Journal of Psychiatry*.

Shafii, M., and Shafii, S. L. (1982). *Pathways of Human Development*. New York: Grune & Stratton.

Shneidman, E. S. (1961). Psychologic: a personality approach to patterns of thinking. In *Contemporary Issues in Thematic Apperception Methods*, ed. J. Kagan and G. Lesser. Springfield, IL: Charles C Thomas.

———— (1976). Suicide notes reconsidered. In *Suicidology: Contemporary Developments*. New York: Grune & Stratton.

———— (1980). *Voices of Death*. New York: Harper & Row.

Shneidman, E. S., and Farberow, N. L. (1957). *Clues to Suicide*. New York: McGraw-Hill.

———— (1960). Sociopsychological investigation of suicide. In *Perspectives in Personality Research*, ed. H. P. David and J. C. Brengelmann. New York: Springer.

———— (1961). Statistical comparison between attempted and completed suicides. In *The Cry for Help*, ed. N. L. Farberow and E. S. Shneidman. New York: McGraw-Hill.

Smith, K. (1983). Family and individual characteristics of suicidal adolescents and adults. In *Proceedings of the 16th annual meeting of the American Association of Suicidology*, ed. C. Vorkorper and K. Smith.

Stanley, E. J., and Barter, J. T. (1970). Adolescent suicidal behavior. *American Journal of Orthopsychiatry* 40:87–96.

Stengel, E., and Cook, N. (1958). *Attempted Suicide*. London: Oxford University Press.

Teicher, J. D. (1970). Children and adolescents who attempt suicide. *Pediatric Clinics of North America* 17:687–696.

Tishler, C., McKenry, P., and Christman-Morgan, K. (1981). Adolescent suicide attempts: some significant factors. *Suicide and Life-Threatening Behavior* 11:86–92.

Tripodes, P. (1976). Reasoning patterns in suicide notes. In *Suicidology: Contemporary Developments*, ed. E. S. Shneidman, pp. 207–228. New York: Grune & Stratton.

Wenz, F. W. (1979). Sociological correlates of alienation among adolescent suicide attempts. *Adolescence* 14:19–30.

White, H. C. (1974). Self-poisoning in adolescence. *British Journal of Psychiatry* 124:24–35.

4

SOME FACTS AND FABLES OF SUICIDE

Edwin S. Shneidman and Philip Mandelkorn

BEFORE YOU FINISH reading this page, someone in the United States will try to commit suicide. At least sixty Americans will have taken their own lives by this time tomorrow. More than twenty-five thousand persons in the United States killed themselves last year, and nine times that many attempted suicide. Many of those who attempted will try again, a number with lethal success. And here is the irony: except for a very few, most of the people who commit suicide also want desperately to live.

At one time or another almost everyone contemplates suicide. It is one of several choices open to humans. Yet any debate of suicide's sin or merit is best left to the academicians, the theologians, and the philosophers. Few suicidal persons would listen closely. Most of these deeply troubled men, women, and children are submerged in their own despair.

No single group, or color, or class of people is free from self-inflicted death. Rich or poor, male or female, Christian or Jew, black or white, young or old— to some extent every category of humankind suffers death by suicide. However, there appear to be some statistical differences. In the United States, the number of men who kill themselves is three times higher than that of women (although women attempt suicide more often than men); the number of whites twice that of blacks; college students half again as many as their noncollege counterparts (for collegians, suicide is the third leading cause of death—only accidents and cancer take more lives); single people twice that of those who are married; and among adults, it is more frequently the elderly who kill themselves.

Suicides are much less accurately reported in some places than others; nevertheless, suicide is among the ten leading causes of death in the United States. Of every 100,000 persons in this country, each year eleven choose suicide. In contrast, Hungary has 26.8 suicides per 100,000; Austria, 21.7; Czechoslovakia, 21.3; Finland, 19.2; West Germany and Sweden, 18.5; Switzerland, 16.8; Japan, 16.1; and France, 15.5. Most other countries report suicide rates lower than the United States, including Italy, 5.3, and Ireland, 2.5.

The most typical American suicide is a white Protestant male in his forties, married with two children. He is a breadwinner and a taxpayer. The sorrow his untimely preventable death brings to his family cannot be reckoned, but the financial burden on his family and community is considerable. There is a heightened probability of subsequent indigent relief. Recent studies indicate that the surviving children of suicide victims often require mental health care. Mental and physical care for a suicide's survivors usually must be provided by the city or county to whom the suicide has irrevocably bequeathed this responsibility. Counting all the taxes that he would have paid over the next quarter century, in the end, a suicide may cost his community a great deal indeed.

WHY DO PEOPLE KILL THEMSELVES?

Why do people kill themselves? This is the first question asked by anyone who knows a person who committed suicide. Certainly he was tragically upset. But this alone does not seem to explain why he took his own life. So many other people seem to carry heavier burdens in their daily lives, yet somehow persevere. What made this person different from those others? Why did he give up? People have been puzzled by suicide for centuries. Only in the last 50 or 60 years, however, have any scientifically tenable explanations taken shape.

One theory still highly regarded today was proposed initially by the French sociologist Emile Durkheim, late in the nineteenth century. Suicide, he asserted, is the result of society's strength or weakness of control over the individual. According to Durkheim, there are three basic types of suicide, each a result of the individual's relationship to the society. In one instance, the *altruistic* suicide is literally required by society. Here, the customs or rules of the group demand suicide under certain circumstances. Historically, Japanese committing hara-kiri are examples of altruistic suicides. Hindu widows who cremated themselves on the funeral pyres of their husbands were also examples of altruistic suicide. In such instances, however, the persons had little choice. Self-inflicted death was honorable; continuing to live was ignominious. Society dictated their action and, as individuals, they were not strong enough to defy custom.

Most suicides in the United States are *egoistic*—Durkheim's second category. Contrary to the circumstances of an altruistic suicide, egoistic suicide occurs when the individual has too few ties with the community. Demands, in this case to live, do not reach the person. Thus, proportionately more men who are on their own kill themselves than do church or family members.

Finally, Durkheim called *anomic* those suicides that occur when the accustomed relationship between an individual and the society is suddenly disrupted. The shocking, precipitous loss of a job, a close friend, or a fortune is thought to be capable of precipitating anomic suicides; or, conversely, poor men surprised by sudden wealth have also, it has been asserted, been shocked into anomic suicide.

As Durkheim detailed the sociology of suicide, so Sigmund Freud fathered psychological explanations. To him, suicide was essentially within the mind. Since people ambivalently identify with the objects of their own love, when they are frustrated the aggressive side of the ambivalence will be directed toward that internalized person. Psychoanalytically, suicide can thus be seen as murder in the 180th degree.

While these perceptive men, nearly a century ago, evolved their own distinctive theories to explain suicide, authorities today are melding and expanding those theories. As an outgrowth of Durkheim's original thinking, sociologists now feel they can explain suicide in the United States as partly resulting from the peculiarities of this culture, that suicide is a barometer of social tension. Meanwhile, psychologists understand suicide in terms of various levels of inner pressure on people, which sometimes parlay into suicide. Thus, a primary cause of suicide might be a traumatic experience during early childhood or youth, a physical handicap, or any of various fundamental psychological disturbances. An individual may be so affected by any of these primary problems that his outlook, manner of thought, or perspective will sustain further impetus to commit suicide.

With these underlying tensions pulsing within a person who is already somewhat vulnerable, the end of a love affair, a failed examination, a serious illness, or almost any unfortunate experience can precipitate an attempt at self-destruction.

SUICIDE NOTES

Fortunately, no one is 100 percent suicidal. Psychologists and psychiatrists today realize that even the most ardent death wish is ambivalent. People can cut their throats and yearn to be saved at the same moment. Suicide notes often illustrate the fatal illogic of the suicidal person, the mixing of cross-purposed desires: "Dear Mary, I hate you. Love, John." "I'm tired. There must be something fine for you. Love, Bill." These simple, pathetic messages are actual suicide notes. Like the iceberg's tip above the surface, they hint at the awesome mass below. When a man is suicidal, his perspective narrows and freezes. He wants to live, but can see no way to do so. His logic is confused, but he cannot clear his head. He stumbles into death, still gasping for life, even in those last moments when he tries to write down how he feels.

Although sometimes suffused with genuine emotion, a suicide note is usually written according to a specious logic that demonstrates the confusion of the author. These notes often instruct someone to do something in the future. There is an implication that the suicidal person will be there to insure that the orders are carried out. Other notes reflect a sad desire to punish persons close to the suicide, as if he would be able to observe the pity and tears he had created. Employing bizarre logic, still others identify their own death with suffering and kill themselves because they are suffering.

No one knows what it is like to be dead. At best, one can only imagine what it would be like if one were alive to watch—an invisible personality—at one's own funeral. Often, such an attractive fantasy intoxicates the suicidal mind, and tips the scale to death. But until the very moment that the bullet or barbiturate finally snuffs out life's last breath—while the ground is rushing up—the person wants to live. Until he dies, a suicidal person wishes to be saved.

Before his death, the suicidal person leaves a trail of subtle and obvious hints of his intentions. Every suicide attempt is a serious cry for help. This cry can be heard and suicide can be prevented.

PREVAILING ATTITUDES

The victims of suicide are not only those who die by their own hands; the families—spouse, siblings, parents, and especially the children—of a suicide are undoubtedly affected. There is an onus associated with suicide that has nothing to do with the loss of life. A suicide in a family irrevocably affects the relatives. Forever afterwards, the mode of death is mentioned by the family in special tones, if it is mentioned at all. They would rather their loved one died by any other mode, no matter how painful or expensive. There is a taint, a stigma, an aura of shame that envelopes the family of a suicide and marks even the closest friends and associates. The guileless remark, "Her father committed suicide," is never forgotten by anyone who hears it. Suicide is never totally forgiven. Suicide is still taboo today.

Probably the present attitude stems from the long history of suicide's condemnation. Suicide is and always has been an action that contradicts the valuation of human life, a basic democratic and social ethic. Throughout the years, various societies have responded to this insult by many crude and cruel means. The bodies of suicides have been dragged through the streets, hung naked upside down for public viewing, impaled on a stake at a public crossroads. The dead man could not be punished, of course, but his widow and children could be. Early English practice was to censure the suicide's family formally, deny the body burial in the church cemetery, and confiscate the survivor's property. As a violation of one of the Ten Commandments, suicide has been called a crime against God, a heinous offense punishable in hell, of course, but also in man's courts.

SOME ENLIGHTENMENT

With the rise of humanism in the eighteenth century, basic attitudes toward the suicidal person shifted. He came to be seen, not as a malicious criminal, but as a lunatic. As such, however, he fared little better. The mentally disturbed have been treated as society's pariahs until only recently. Even today, they are not fully accepted.

But times and attitudes have changed. Scientists have come to take a more enlightened stand on suicide, notably in the last few decades. Although the act of suicide is still socially taboo in the Western world, fortunately education and mental health advances have encouraged its study, and the effective treatment of the suicidal person has begun. Most of the early state laws outlawing suicide and punishing suicide attempts have been revoked. Those still on the books are rarely enforced. The courts have begun to interpret suicidal deaths as results of emotional disturbance. In the wake of current professional studies and news articles on their findings, the public is beginning to realize that most suicides can be prevented.

There are many misconceptions concerning this topic. Table 4–1 presents some facts and fables about suicide.

In recent years, suicide prevention activities have quickly spread across the country. In 1958, there were only three comprehensive suicide prevention centers in operation. A decade later, there were 100 of them functioning in twenty-six states. Today, in the 1990s, there is hardly a community of any size that does not have some emergency telephone hot line service devoted at least in part to suicide prevention.

Table 4-1.   Facts and Fables on Suicide*

FABLE: People who talk about suicide don't commit suicide.
FACT: Of any ten persons who kill themselves, eight have given definite warnings
         of their suicidal intentions.

FABLE: Suicide happens without warning.
FACT: Studies reveal that the suicidal person gives many clues and warnings
         regarding his suicidal intentions.

FABLE: Suicidal people are fully intent on dying.
FACT: Most suicidal people are undecided about living or dying, and they gamble
         with death, leaving it to others to save them. Almost no one commits
         suicide without letting others know how he is feeling.

FABLE: Once a person is suicidal, he is suicidal forever.
FACT: Individuals who wish to kill themselves are suicidal only for a limited
         period of time.

FABLE: Improvement following a suicidal crisis means that the suicidal risk is over.
FACT: Most suicides occur within about three months following the beginning of
         improvement, when the individual has the energy to put his morbid
         thoughts and feelings into effect.

FABLE: Suicide strikes much more often among the rich—or, conversely, it occurs
         almost exclusively among the poor.
FACT: Suicide is neither the rich man's disease nor the poor man's curse. Suicide
         is very democratic and is represented proportionately among all levels of
         society.

FABLE: Suicide is inherited or "runs in the family."
FACT: Suicide does not run in families. It is an individual pattern.

FABLE: All suicidal individuals are mentally ill, and suicide always is the act of a
         psychotic person.
FACT: Studies of hundreds of genuine suicide notes indicate that although the
         suicidal person is extremely unhappy, he is not necessarily mentally ill.

---

*From *Some Facts about Suicide* by E. S. Shneidman and N. L. Farberow, Washington, DC, PHS
Publication No. 852, U. S. Government Printing Office, 1961.

CLUES TO SUICIDE

Almost everyone who seriously intends to commit suicide leaves some clues
prefiguring that action. Sometimes there are broad hints; sometimes only subtle
changes in behavior. But the suicide decision is not impulsive. Most often, it is
premeditated. Although it might be done on impulse, and to others appear

capricious, in fact, suicide is usually a decision that is given long consideration. It is not impossible, then, to spot some potential suicides if one only knows what to look for.

About three-fourths of all those who commit suicide have seen a physician within at least four months of the day on which they take their own lives. When people are suicidal, a state of mind that comes and goes, there is no single trait by which all of them can be characterized. Always, however, they are disturbed (perturbed), and often but not always they are depressed. They feel hopeless about the direction of their lives and helpless to do anything about it. Under the weight of their own pessimism, they sink to their death.

In general, three kinds of suicidal clues can be distinguished: verbal, behavioral, and situational. The suicidal attitude may reflect itself in various verbal clues. Most obvious are the self-pitying cries of those who say, "I am going to kill myself." Not everyone who says so means it, but many people who commit suicide have said it. It may be a vague threat, testing the waters. They just haven't decided how or when. If conditions in the person's life do not change sufficiently for the better, the person may set the time and choose the method of death. All verbal indications of possible suicidal intent should be taken with some degree of seriousness. Dejected or angry asides such as "I want to die. This is the last straw . . . My family will be better off without me. . . . I won't be around much longer to put up with"—all can be real clues to suicide and, before they are discounted, need to be evaluated as possible precursors to a lethal act.

There are also behavioral hints or clues, some quite obvious. Any suicide attempt, no matter how feeble or unlikely to be fatal, can be stark testimony of a potential suicidal state. "She just wanted attention," is the exasperated comment that often follows someone's suicide attempt. Indeed, that may be exactly what she wanted. Without it, she may escalate the lethality of the subsequent suicide attempt. It is important to note that four out of five persons who kill themselves have attempted to do so previously. Of course, there are less pointed behavioral clues to suicide. Though not so readily discerned, they may predict a suicide quite accurately. Once a person has decided to kill himself, he begins to behave "differently." He may withdraw to become almost monklike and contemplative. He may drastically reduce eating or refrain from conversation and ignore normal sexual drives. He may sleep a great deal or, conversely, suffer from insomnia. He may have a will drawn up, or act as if he were going on a long and distant trip. In the final days of his life, he frequently gives away what for him have been highly valued material possessions. College students may give away their watches, cameras, even their microscopes. Wealthier people make outright grants of cash to relatives and friends; it is an even more pronounced clue if they do this with relative strangers.

Occasionally, the situation itself may be the final straw, and is the crucial indicator of imminent suicide. People already suffering from suffocating depressions may kill themselves on learning — or believing erroneously — that they have a malignant tumor. Singly, any of these rather unexpected acts may not be significant, but clustered, they often point to suicide.

The clues to suicide are not arcane or mysterious. They are not too difficult to recognize. In any event, any citizen, or worker, or friend, or relative has a moral responsibility — something akin to omnipresent fire prevention — to maintain some reasonable alertness to these possible clues.

THE SUICIDAL CRISIS

Suicidal crises almost always concern two people: the suicidal person and the significant other. It is important to determine who the significant other(s) are. If the patient is seen, it is advisable to see both, or, at the least, to make the other person aware of the situation and his or her role in the drama, and, if possible, involve him or her in life-saving efforts. In most cases, partners will show concern and even a willingness to help; in some cases, they must be disregarded, or even circumvented.

Sometimes, only a little help is needed during the period of the suicidal crisis. A person who verges on suicide also clings to life. All of his problems cannot be solved in a telephone call or a few sessions of psychotherapy — although these can have magical effects. Even a minimal response by a significant other can have an important effect.

COMMUNITY SERVICE PLANNING

There is no doubt that carefully established suicide prevention centers change the threshold of mental health response within the community; how many lives they save directly is a much more complicated question. Community mental health improves as a result. A suicide prevention service can be organized to operate autonomously or as a unit within a larger mental health facility. It can be part of a hospital or tied to the local university or mental health clinic, or a part of the community's comprehensive mental health facility. The staff of a suicide prevention center should be especially carefully selected, rigorously trained, and constantly monitored and given consultation. Without local school, university, police, mental health cooperation — integration into the community — the successful operation of a suicide prevention unit is practically impossible.

A BEGINNING

Nowadays, thousands of people are frightened and alone. They live in what Herman Melville called "a damp, drizzly November of the soul." For them, it seems that voluntary death is a viable alternative to the *unbearable psychological pain* they are suffering. The availability of active suicide prevention services may offer such a person a grasp on life. They offer the possibility of showing that life is not so fatally narrow and that death need not be the only answer.

II

EVALUATION AND TREATMENT

5

EVALUATION AND MANAGEMENT OF SUICIDAL PERSONS

Norman L. Farberow, Samuel M. Heilig, and Robert E. Litman

S UICIDE IS ONE OF the most difficult problems confronting the helping professions. This applies not only to the professional therapist but to all the occupations concerned with the health and well-being of the public. It is rare that any psychiatrist, psychologist, social worker, nurse, physician, clergyman, policeman, or educator can conduct his affairs without at some time being faced with the need to evaluate and handle a suicidal situation.

Confusion often accompanies the use of the term *suicide*. The result of this confusion is the indiscriminate application of the term *suicidal* to patients who are not in fact in commensurate lethal danger. Experience has shown that suicidal persons vary in lethal potentiality from minimal to highly serious, and that each case requires careful evaluation on his own merits.

PROMINENT ASPECTS OF THE SUICIDAL SITUATION

Crisis

The actively suicidal person is usually in the midst of a crisis. *Crisis* is defined (in Webster's) as a "turning point in the course of a situation" and "a situation whose outcome decides whether possible bad consequences will follow."

For the person in a suicidal crisis, the principal factors are the overwhelming importance of an intolerable problem and the feelings of hopelessness and helplessness. The pressure of these feelings force him toward some actions for immediate resolution. These actions may be maladaptive, as in suicide attempts.

Crisis provides an unusual opportunity for therapeutic intervention. It is in the nature of crisis that it cannot be tolerated indefinitely. Therefore, the initiation and timing of therapeutic efforts during the crisis can influence the situation toward a good outcome.

Ambivalence

One of the most prominent features characterizing the suicidal person is ambivalence, expressed through feelings of wanting to die and wanting to live, both occurring at the same time. An example of ambivalence is the person who ingests a lethal dose of barbiturates and then calls someone for rescue before he loses consciousness. The relationship and strength of the two opposing impulses to live and to die will vary for different persons, and also within the same person under different conditions. Most people have a stronger wish to live than to die. It is this fact of ambivalence that makes suicide prevention possible. In working with a suicidal person it is necessary to evaluate both motives and their relationship to each other and to ally oneself on the side of the fluctuating wish to live.

Communication

Suicidal activity is frequently a last-ditch method of expressing feelings of desperation and helplessness. Suicidal people are reduced to this method when they feel unable to cope with a problem and that others are not attending to or denying their need for help. The suicidal behavior thus becomes a desperate means to claim the attention that they feel they have lost. The communication aspect may be in terms of verbal statements such as "I no longer want to live" or "I am going to kill myself"; or it may be in terms of actions such as the procuring of pills or guns, a sudden decision to prepare a will, or the giving away of treasured possessions. The communication may also be either direct or indirect and to a specific person or to the world in general. When it is indirect it is necessary to recognize the intent of the disguised message and to understand the real content of the communication. Recognition of the communication aspects of suicidal behavior facilitates a more accurate evaluation of the various factors in the situation and allows for a more appropriate and helpful response.

THE WORKER IN SUICIDE PREVENTION

The Effect of the Suicidal Communication

The suicidal situation can further be understood in terms of the effect upon the recipients of the communication. For example, the communications may arouse feelings of sympathy, anxiety, anger, hostility, and the like, among family or friends. These feelings, arising out of reactions of helplessness under the continued barrage of desperate communications, are often projected into the situation and attributed to the patient. Similar feelings may be aroused within the worker unless he can anticipate and counteract such reactions in himself. Another feeling of which the worker must be aware is the feeling of omnipotence, the feeling of being able to solve all the problems and meet all the demands of the patient. This is, of course, impossible, but the delusion is fostered because of the intense dependency transferred to him by the patient.

On the other hand, some suicidal situations will arouse within the worker feelings of anxiety and questions of adequacy to handle the critical situations. While a moderate level of anxiety is appropriate, too much anxiety may seriously hamper the worker, especially if it is transmitted to the patient who, at this point, is depending upon the worker to help him solve his problems. If the suicidal person, who feels helpless and lost, perceives excess anxiety within the worker he may lose his confidence in the possibility of being helped. The worker may begin in the area of suicide prevention with much anxiety, but experience has shown that he soon learns to handle his own feelings of concern and develops markedly in self-confidence.

Feelings about Death

Death is a part of life and living, but in our culture it has always been surrounded by powerful taboos. These taboos and the feelings they arouse may affect the worker and even interfere in the interaction with the patient, unless the worker is sensitive to his own feelings about death. Whatever his own feelings, the worker must avoid any tendencies toward moralistic attitudes toward death and suicide. The worker's point of view, within the professional situation, must be that death is to be postponed, if possible.

BASIC PRINCIPLES OF SUICIDE PREVENTION

The following comments are offered as guidelines for effective and comfortable functioning in working with the suicidal patient. It is, of course, impossible to anticipate every situation, but the principles pertain to most situations.

In most cases, suicidal crises will go through several stages of resource activity. In the early stages, the person first comes to the attention of family, relatives, and friends. In the second stage, he will come into contact with first-line resources, such as family physician, clergyman, police, lawyers, school personnel, and public health nurses. If the suicidal tendencies persist, the third line of resources is called into play, the professional person and agency. The professions involved will include psychiatry, psychology, psychiatric social work, and psychiatric nursing. Agencies in the community most often involved will be mental hospitals, general hospitals, psychiatric clinics, social work agencies, and various service agencies such as family service, vocational rehabilitation, and employment offices. Probably, with the current development of community mental health centers and the movement toward more immediate response to both physical and emotional illnesses, the professional persons and agencies will be contacted earlier and more directly.

The handling of a telephone call from suicidal persons generally involves six steps. They may or may not occur simultaneously.

1. Establishing a relationship, maintaining contact, and obtaining information
2. Identification and clarification of the focal problems
3. Evaluation of the suicidal potential
4. Assessment of strength and resources
5. Mobilization of patients' and others' resources
6. Formulation of a therapy plan and the initiation of the appropriate actions.

Each of the steps is discussed in detail below.

Establishing a Relationship, Maintaining Contact, and Obtaining Information

In general, the worker should be patient, interested, self-assured, hopeful, and knowledgeable. He will want to communicate by his attitude that the person has done the right thing in calling and that the worker is able and willing to help. By the fact of his call, the patient has indicated a desire for help with his problems. He should be accepted without challenge or criticism and allowed to tell his story in his own way, the worker confining himself to listening carefully to the information that is volunteered. The response, both in terms of attitude and tone on the telephone, will make a significant impact.

Often, because the patient will not have a clear idea of the agencies' functions, it will be necessary to make clear the services offered. For example, the patient may request financial aid or a home visit, and, if these are not part of the service, this must be unhesitatingly stated.

A call should be initiated with a clear identification of the worker, and a request for the name and telephone number of the caller. Names and phone numbers of interested other persons such as family, physicians, close friends, or others who might be possible resources in the situation should also be obtained. The worker's immediate goal is to obtain information to be used in an evaluation of the suicidal potentiality. This is usually best accomplished by asking, including direct specific questions, about his suicidal feelings. It is the patient's reason for calling and to talk about it without undue anxiety is helpful in reducing the patient's own fear of his suicidal impulses.

Identification and Clarification of Focal Problems

The suicidal patient often displays a profound sense of confusion, chaos, and disorganization. He is unclear about his main problem and has become lost in details. One of the most important services of the worker is to help the patient recognize and order the central and the secondary problems. For example, a woman caller presented a profusion of symptoms with feelings of worthlessness, despair, and inadequacy, accompanied by incessant weeping. Questioning revealed that her main problem lay in her relationships with her husband. A statement to this effect provided her with an authoritative definition of her central conflict and she was now able to address herself to this identified problem more effectively.

In some instances the caller may be clear about his central problem, but indicate that he has exhausted all his own alternatives for solution. The worker, as an objective outsider, might be able to provide a number of additional alternatives for the patient to consider.

Evaluation of Suicide Potential

The suicide potential refers to the degree of probability that the patient may act out with self-destructive behavior in the immediate or relatively near future. The Los Angeles Suicide Prevention Center Scale (Table 5–1) has been developed to assist the office therapist and suicide prevention center or crisis center counselor in evaluating the suicidal status of a patient or caller who has identified himself as suicidal. The primary aim is to evaluate the potentiality for imminent self-destructive acting out in order to determine the need for emergency procedures such as police intervention or hospitalization, or whether personal resources, such as family, friends, neighbors, and so forth, should be mobilized.

The scale lists a varied number of items under ten categories. Each item is provided with a range of scores derived from clinical experience, with a highest score of nine and a lowest score of one possible for any one item. Most of the items have a range of scores of three points (for example, 3–5, 6–8), but a few may range over the entire scale (1–9), and a few others will have an intermediate range (for example, 5–9, 2–6). Clinical judgment determines the most appropriate score from within the suggested range, usually on the basis of the intensity or prominence of the item for the subject being evaluated.

The items are designed to provide a ready reference list of significant factors for evaluating suicide potential. Although a final numerical score is obtained, the score does not imply a specific level of suicide potential, but rather a general level, which can guide the appropriate response.

Scoring

The score for each category is the highest score on any of the variables checked within that category. The suicide potential is obtained by adding all the category scores (ranging from 90 to 10). The total is divided by 10; the degree of risk is indicated as:

High risk: 7, 8, 9
Medium risk: 4, 5, 6
Low risk: 1, 2, 3

Scoring Aids for Each Category

Age and sex

Both statistics and experience have indicated that the suicide rate for committed suicide rises with increasing age, and that men are more likely to kill themselves than women. Age and sex are useful, therefore, in evaluating the caller. A communication from an older male tends to be the most dangerous; from a young female, the least dangerous. A communication from an older woman, however, is more dangerous than from a younger boy. Nevertheless, adolescent and young adult rates have risen over recent years, increasing the level of basic suicide risk for this age group. Age and sex thus offer a general framework for evaluating the suicidal situation, but each case requires further individual appraisal, in which the criteria that follow are most useful.

Symptoms

The intensity of the symptom is the basis for scoring each item. Symptoms may appear in many different psychological states. Among the most common are depression, psychosis, and agitation. Depression may be expressed either emo-

Table 5-1. Los Angeles Suicide Prevention Center Scale.

	Ratings of items	Ratings of categories
Age and Sex (1–9)		
Male		( )
50 plus (7–9)	( )	
35–49 (4–6)	( )	
15–34 (1–3)	( )	
Female		( )
50 plus (5–7)	( )	
35–49 (3–5)	( )	
15–34 (1–3)	( )	
Symptoms (1–9)		( )
Severe depression: sleep disorder, anorexia, weight loss, withdrawal, despondency, loss of interest, apathy (7–9)	( )	
Feelings of hopelessness, helplessness, exhaustion (7–9)	( )	
Delusions, hallucinations, loss of contact, disorientation (6–8)	( )	
Compulsive gambling (6–8)	( )	
Disorganization, confusion, chaos (5–7)	( )	
Alcoholism, drug addiction, homosexuality (4–7)	( )	
Agitation, tension, anxiety (4–6)	( )	
Guilt, shame, embarrassment (4–6)	( )	
Feelings of rage, anger, hostility (4–6)	( )	
Poor impulse control, poor judgment (4–6)	( )	
Other (describe):		
Stress (1–9)		( )
Loss of loved person by death, divorce, separation (5–9)	( )	
Loss of job, money, prestige, status (4–8)	( )	
Threat of prosecution, criminal involvement, exposure (4–6)	( )	
Change(s) in life, environment, setting (4–6)	( )	
Success, promotion, increased responsibilities (2–5)	( )	
No significant stress (1–3)	( )	
Other (describe):		
Acute versus Chronic (1–9)		( )
Sharp, noticeable and sudden onset of symptoms (4–9)	( )	
Recurrent outbreak of similar symptoms (4–9)	( )	
No specific recent change (1–4)	( )	
Other (describe):		
Suicidal Plan (1–9)		( )
Lethality of proposed method—gun, jumping, hanging, drowning, knife, pills, poison, aspirin (1–9)	( )	
Specific detail and clarity in organization of plan (1–9)	( )	
Specificity in time planned (1–9)	( )	
Bizarre plan (1–9)	( )	

(continued)

Table 5-1. *(continued)*

	Ratings of items	Ratings of categories
Rating of previous suicide attempt(s) (1–9)	( )	
No plans (1–3)	( )	
Other (describe):		
Resources (1–9)		( )
No sources of support (family, friends, agencies, employment) (7–9)	( )	
Family and friends available, unwilling to help (4–7)	( )	
Financial problems (4–7)	( )	
Available professional help, agency, therapist (2–4)	( )	
Family and/or friends willing to help (1–3)	( )	
Stable life history (1–3)	( )	
Physician or clergy available (1–3)	( )	
Employed (1–3)	( )	
Finances no problem (1–3)	( )	
Other (describe):		
Prior Suicidal Behavior (1–9)		( )
One or more prior attempts of high lethality (7–9)	( )	
One or more prior attempt(s) of low lethality (4–6)	( )	
History of repeated threats and depression (3–7)	( )	
No prior suicidal or depressed history (1–2)	( )	
Other (describe):		
Medical Status (1–9)		( )
Chronic debilitating illness (5–9)	( )	
Sickness, serious illness, surgery, accident—loss of limb (3–7)	( )	
Many repeated unsuccessful experiences with physicians (4–7)	( )	
Psychosomatic illness, e.g., asthma, ulcer, hypochondria (1–3)	( )	
No medical problems (1–2)	( )	
Pattern of failure in current or previous therapy (5–8)	( )	
Other (describe):		
Communication Aspects (1–9)		( )
Communication broken with rejection of efforts to reestablish by both patient and others (5–9)	( )	
Communications declaring guilt, worthlessness, blame, shame (4–7)	( )	
Communications with interpersonal goal, cause guilt in others, force action or behavior (2–5)	( )	
Communications directed toward world and people in general (2–5)	( )	
Communications directed toward specific person(s) (1–5)	( )	
Other (describe):		

(continued)

Table 5-1. (continued)

	Ratings of items	Ratings of categories
Reaction of Significant Others (1–9)		( )
Rejecting, punishing, defensive, paranoid attitude (5–9)	( )	
Denial of own or patient's need for help (5–8)	( )	
No feelings of concern; does not understand the patient (4–7)	( )	
Indecisiveness, feelings of helplessness (3–5)	( )	
Alternation between feelings of anger and rejection and feelings of responsibility and desire to help (2–4)	( )	
Sympathy and concern plus admission of need for help (1–3)	( )	
Other (describe):		

tionally—with feelings of despair, despondency, loss of interest, apathy, loss of sexual drive, feelings of hopelessness and helplessness, social withdrawal—or physically—with sleep disorder, appetite disturbance, weight loss, lack of energy, feelings of physical and psychological exhaustion, and so forth. Psychotic states will be characterized by delusions, loss of contact with reality or disorientation, hallucinations, or highly unusual ideas and experiences. Agitated states will show tension, anxiety, guilt, shame, poor impulse control, and feelings of rage, anger, hostility, and revenge. Of most significance is the state of agitated depression in which the person may feel he is unable to tolerate the pressure of his feelings and anxieties and shows symptoms of marked tension, fearfulness, restlessness, pacing, and pressure of speech. Suicidal acting out may occur simply to obtain relief from the feelings. Alcoholics and drug addicts tend to be high suicidal risks.

Stress

Stress must always be evaluated from the suicidal person's point of view and not from the counselor's or society's point of view. What might be considered negligible stress by a counselor might be felt as severe by the caller. Stress can be considered as precipitating or long term and as inter- or intrapersonal. Most frequently the stress involves loss or the threat of loss, such as the loss of a loved one by death, separation, or divorce, or the loss of social status, such as the loss of money, prestige, or employment. The loss may also be of reputation that may occur as a result of criminal activity or sexual indiscretions; or the loss may be of physical self-image resulting from serious injury, accident, illness, and so forth. Sometimes, increased anxiety and tension appear as a result of success, such as promotion on the job and increased responsibilities.

Acute versus Chronic

Inquiry about the details and history of the current suicidal situation will determine whether it is acute or chronic. Suicidal feelings may be acute in both stable and unstable personalities; they will be chronic only in unstable diagnostic categories. The stable person will indicate a consistent work history, stable marital and family relationships, and especially no history of suicidal behavior. The current situation will be marked by sudden onset of specific symptoms. The unstable personality may include severe character disorders, borderline psychotics, and persons with repeated difficulties in social adjustment, interpersonal relationships, employment, substance abuse, and the like. Acute suicidal feelings in the unstable personality increases suicidal risk markedly because of accompanying lack of social and emotional resources and, frequently, impaired judgment and poor coping abilities. Suicide risk often stays high even when the crisis is resolved. Acute suicidal feelings in the stable personality may indicate high risk during the period of the crisis, but the severity of the risk tends to diminish quickly once the crisis is past.

Suicide Plan

Three main elements need to be considered in this highly significant criterion of suicide potentiality: (1) the lethality of the proposed method; (2) the availability of the means; and (3) the specificity of the details. A method involving a gun or jumping or hanging where results are practically immediate will be of higher lethality than one that depends on the use of pills or wrist cutting where effects are slow and intervention more feasible. If the gun is at hand, the threat of its use must be taken more seriously than when the person talks about shooting himself but has no gun immediately available. In addition, if the person indicates by many specific details that he has spent time and effort in planning his method, the seriousness of suicidal risk rises markedly. The evaluation of any suicide plan also depends on the patient's psychiatric diagnosis. A psychotic person with suicidal impulses may make a bizarre attempt as a result of his impaired judgment. Evaluation of the details of previous suicide attempts helps in assessing the seriousness of the current situation.

Resources

The suicidal person often feels isolated and alone. Suicidal risk is highest when this is factually true. It is also high when resources such as family, friends, professional agencies, neighbors, and so forth have been exhausted and refuse any longer to be further involved. Financial problems can exacerbate the situation, especially if the client's self-esteem is invested in a prosperous or effective self-image. Clergy, physician, and employer may serve to reduce the risk when available and willing to be involved. In general, it is usually advantageous for both client and counselor when the responsibility for the client is shared by as many people as possible. This helps the client feel that others are still interested and care about him.

Prior Suicidal Behavior

Research and experience have indicated that a history of prior suicidal behavior markedly increases risk. If the prior suicidal behavior is one of attempts, detailed inquiry should be made to determine the lethality. Attempts of high lethality indicate higher risk than attempts of low lethality. A history of repeated threats along with depression indicate the possible development of suicidal behavior as a means of coping with distressing problems.

Medical Status

The presence of a debilitating chronic illness that has involved much change in self-image and self-concept increases suicidal risk. Fears of a fatal illness, such as cancer or brain tumor, despite being ungrounded, may indicate a preoccupation with death and dying. For persons with chronic illness, the relationship with their physician, family, or hospital are important. It is a positive sign when they are seen as continued resources for help. However, a history of repeatedly unsuccessful experiences with doctors or a pattern of failure in previous therapy may indicate exhaustion of these resources for possible further help.

Communication Aspects

Suicidal behavior is often best understood as a communication. The suicidal person may be using it to demand attention or to effect a specific response. It usually means that the more usual methods of communicating have not succeeded. The highest risk situation is the one in which both sender and receiver are rejecting any efforts to reestablish contact. Communication may be either verbal or nonverbal, direct or indirect. Most serious are indications that the communication has become both nonverbal and indirect, raising the possibility of both missing and misinterpreting interchanges between the suicidal person and others. The content of the communications may be directed to one or more significant persons, with accusations, expressions of hostility or blame, and implied or overt demands for changes in behavior and feelings on the part of others. Other communications may express feelings of guilt, inadequacy, worthlessness, or indications of strong anxiety and tension. When the communication is directed to specific persons, the reactions of these persons are important in the evaluation of the suicidal danger.

Reactions of Significant Others

The nonhelpful significant other may reject the suicidal person or deny the suicidal behavior itself and withdraw both psychologically and physically from continuing contact. Resentment and resistance may result from the continuing demands, the insistence on gratification of dependency needs, and the frustration of insatiable requests for attention. In some instances, the significant other may react with indecision, ambivalence, or helplessness, which may give the suicidal person the feeling that help is no longer available, thus increasing his own feelings of helplessness and hopelessness.

Assessment of Patient's Strengths and Resources

It is as important to assess the patient's strength and resources as it is to evaluate the pathological aspects of the picture. Frequently the patient will present alarming serious negative feelings and behaviors. These may be mitigated, however, by positive features still present within the situation. For example, one indication of important internal resources may be the patient's reaction to the worker's first attempts to focus the interview. If the patient is able to respond to the worker, accepting suggestions and directions, this is an important hopeful sign. Improvement in mood and thinking within the course of one interview is a positive sign and indicates a patient's ability to respond to available help.

Mobilization of Resources; Treatment and Handling of the Suicidal Situation

The plan formulated for the patient will be determined by the evaluation of the patient's suicidal status and the information obtained about him and his resources. In general those cases with the higher suicidal potential will require the most activity on the part of the worker. An evaluation of acute suicidal potential in a situation that appears out of control will usually require hospitalization. In our experience, however, only 13 percent of the cases require this action. Most calls are low in suicide risk and respond to understanding, listening, and counseling. Many cases, however, will require action by the worker, usually in the process of referring the patient to another resource in the community. The type of referral will depend upon the evaluation of the problem. The referral may be to either a nonprofessional or a professional resource or to both.

    If the call comes at night, the worker should keep in mind that most problems are magnified when seen in the nighttime hours. An immediate goal would be to help the patient get through the night. The goal should be to get sufficient information to determine if it is a high-risk emergency requiring an immediate action.

In the highly unusual event that a person is calling in the midst of his suicide attempt (less than 7 percent of the calls), as much information as is necessary to identify the patient or the caller should be obtained and the informant should be instructed either to take the patient to an emergency hospital, to call his personal physican, to call an ambulance, or to call the police. The overriding aim at that time is to provide the patient with immediate medical attention.

At this point it is important to note an important aspect of the worker's responsibility. The worker might make a referral for the patient to one of the other resources within the community, but the responsibility for the patient remains his until this responsibility is assumed by the other resource. The patient is thus *transferred* rather than *referred*. The worker must not assume his responsibility has been discharged until he is assured that the patient has been accepted elsewhere.

In general, if there is any question or doubt about the evaluation of the suicidal situation of the patient, he should be referred to a professional person for a complete evaluation. A patient with a suicidal problem that is not immediately serious but who presents emotional disturbances may be referred to a psychiatric clinic, private therapist, or a family agency. Usually such resources will require a waiting period and the referral to such agencies will depend upon whether or not the patient can sustain the interim period. A resource book showing available psychiatric and social agencies in the community is especially useful.

For the worker in suicide prevention, there will always appear, despite experience and knowledge, some cases that will arouse anxiety and tension within him. The most constructive way to handle the feelings is through consultation with colleagues, which generally provides at least two measures of help. Not only is there a sharing of anxiety and responsibility, but there is benefit from discussion of the problem, which may offer further insights and alternative solutions to the problem. Consultation must not be used, however, as a device for passing the buck.

RESOURCES

The following are detailed suggestions about general and community resources for use in suicidal situations. Any one or combinations of these resources should be considered as imaginatively and constructively as possible. The worker should not allow himself to be constrained by conventional practices.

Family

The family is often neglected as a resource but is one of the most valuable at the time of crisis. The patient should be encouraged to discuss his situation and problems with his family. If it is considered important that someone be with the patient during the crisis, the family members should be called and apprised of the situation even though the patient may be reluctant. The patient is usually informed first that his family will be called. Also, the family must be involved in accepting responsibilities for the emergency and in helping the patient get the treatment that has been recommended.

Friends

Close friends often can be used in the same way families have been used. For example, the patient can be encouraged to have a friend stay with him during a difficult period. The friend may also be helpful in talking things out and in giving a feeling of support.

Family Physician

People often turn to their family doctors for help and physicians often serve as supportive authority figures. The patient usually has a good relationship with his doctor and should be encouraged to discuss his problems with him. Physicians can also be helpful in cases where medication or hospitalization is required.

Clergy

If the caller is close to his church he should be encouraged to discuss his situation with his clergyman.

Employer

When the patient's occupation is involved and there is considerable question about his feelings or self-esteem because of vocational difficulties, the patient can be encouraged to talk about these difficulties with his employer.

Police

Police should be utilized only in cases of clear and immediate emergency; for example, if the suicide attempt is about to occur or has occurred. The patient may need prompt medical attention and the police are often the ones who can procure it for him most quickly. The police are able to take the responsibility for involvement with a patient and may hospitalize when necessary. It should be remembered, however, that the police are not to be used simply as an ambulance or transportation system. As a general rule, the police should be involved as little as possible, but when the decision to use them is made it should be carried through with firmness and dispatch. The two main criteria will be the helpless-ness and injury of the patient.

Emergency Hospital

Usually the patient or his family or the caller will know of private emergency hospitals in his area. The worker should know about city and county hospitals available for emergency medical treatment hospitalization. The police will generally use city and county hospitals.

Own Agency

The worker may wish to refer the patient to his own agency in those cases in which it is felt there is a high suicide potential and in which there is a need for more intensive, careful, further evaluation. Giving the patient an appointment gives the patient a task and a purpose to his immediate future. This resource, of course, can be used only when the agency includes facilities for personal interview and evaluation.

Social Work Agencies and Community Psychiatric Clinics

In those cases in which the suicide danger has been evaluated as low or perhaps not even the primary problem, a referral to a family service agency or commu-nity psychiatric clinic can be considered. These are often the treatment medium of choice for patients in whom the underlying problem may be seen as marital discord, family conflict, or chronic personal and social maladjustment. The worker should be familiar with the social work agencies or community psychi-atric clinics within the community and referrals can be made to those near the patient. Often, a referral to an agency that works primarily with persons of the patient's own religion is more desirable. Other considerations are fees and hours that will be compatible with the patient's situation.

Private Therapists

Some calls are from people looking for psychiatric treatment. The worker should be familiar with private therapists for appropriate recommendation in such cases. If the patient indicates that he is already in treatment, he should be encouraged to return to his own therapist.

Psychiatric Hospital

If the community contains a psychiatric hospital or a general hospital with a psychiatric ward where patients can be hospitalized, a liaison with such facilities is most important. Generally, referral to such a resource is made when it is thought the patient is so disturbed that he might seriously harm himself or others, and/or he is so disorganized he can no longer exercise judgment or direction of his affairs. It might be necessary to have family or friends take the patient to the hospital if the patient himself is incapable of getting there.

SOME TYPICAL CALLS

Following are some illustrations of what may be considered typical calls:

> A woman, between 30 and 40 years old, calls at night saying that she doesn't understand why she feels so depressed. She states she is alone, complains of not being able to sleep, having troubled thoughts, and feeling that she needs to talk to someone. Sometimes she will say that she really doesn't want to kill herself but she has had suicidal thoughts over many months or years. She may be agitated, depressed, weeping, as if she is having a hysterical breakdown. She may be demanding and ask what can be done to help her right now, because she feels she is not able to get through the night. Questioning will reveal she has had many similar episodes before. Probably she is reacting to some interpersonal conflict such as argument with a family member or close friend.

It is best to listen patiently and wait for the opportunity to point out realistically that things look worse at night, but that it is not the best time when she can get help for herself. She should be advised to call her doctor or social work agency or clinic in the morning, so as to arrange a program of help for herself. It may be helpful to suggest that she call a close friend or relative to come and be with her during this difficult night.

A woman sounds as if she was between 20 and 35 years old, but will not identify herself. She asks what can the Suicide Prevention Center do for a person who doesn't want to live anymore, and generally takes a challenging position. The caller sounds controlled, makes vague allusions to a long-standing problem, and wants to know what you can do about it. Frequently, these no-name callers are either in psychotherapy or have recently interrupted psychotherapy.

The worker should point out that the caller has responsibility to clarify her request and cooperate if she is to receive help. You must know who she is and about her situation before you can assist her. If she tells you she has a therapist, and who he is, you should refer her back to the therapist. Tell her that you will call the therapist to notify him that the patient has called you.

A woman between 40 and 55 calls about herself, complaining that she is very depressed, feels lonely and tired, and feels that no one is interested in her. She talks about many physical and medical problems. She says that she feels her doctor is not helping her enough and that her husband is not paying enough attention to her. She will say that she feels like her life is over, and there is no point in continuing to live.

An effort should be made to talk with the husband and to discuss with him how his wife is feeling. Both the patient and the husband should be encouraged to talk with the family physician at the first opportunity about the patient's depression. You may offer to call the physician too, if they wish, in order to enlist her aid. If none of these resources seems available the patient may be asked to call the SPC for an appointment.

A man between 18 and 30 sounds evasive and anxious on the phone and is reluctant to give his name. He talks about having a problem that he is hesitant to identify, and states he is calling for help because the only solution he can think of is to kill himself. His suicide plan will be an impulsive one, like smashing his car up on the freeway, or cutting himself with a razor blade. This man often has a personal problem about which he feels guilty, such as homosexuality.

This patient should be encouraged to seek help for himself. You should commend him for having done the right thing in calling you as a beginning effort to get help for himself. You might suggest a resource to which he might go, such as a psychiatric clinic, private therapist, physician, or school counselor.

A man between 25 and 40 complains that his life is just a mess because of his bungling. He talks about having gotten himself into such a jam, either financially or with his family or on the job, that he feels the only way out is to kill himself. Often, he will be reacting to a specific, recent setback in his life.

He should be told that he is reacting to a specific stress, and that he needs help with that particular problem about which he feels helpless and hopeless. He should be reminded that he was able to function well before he had this setback, that he is suffering from a depression that is most often time-limited and temporary and that he needs help to get back on his feet again. He should be encouraged to call the SPC during regular office hours for an appointment.

A man about 50 or over sounds very depressed and discouraged and seems apologetic about calling and troubling you. He may complain about a physical problem that has prevented his working, and feels now that he is beyond help. His general feelings about himself are that he is old and infirm and a burden on others. When asked what his suicidal thoughts are he talks about specific plans for killing himself.

Friends, family, and resources should be mobilized and involved. The patient should be told that help is available to him. He should be told to call the SPC for an appointment and his family should be impressed with the need to follow through. If he fails to call, then a staff member of the SPC should be alerted to call him back to arrange an appointment.

A family member or friend calls about a person who is described as depressed, withdrawn, or has shown some behavioral or personality change. The patient may have told them that he is planning to kill himself and even discussed a specific plan with them; or, he may have generally talked about wanting to end his life. The caller is asking how serious the situation is and what he should do.

The caller should be advised to contact the patient and let him know he is concerned about him and trying to get help. He should be told to have the patient call you, so that the patient will have the feeling that help is being obtained for him, and, also, you will have an opportunity to evaluate the situation with the patient. You should maintain your contact with the initial caller and keep him apprised of what is happening, maintaining him as a resource to help, if need be. The recommendation to the patient will depend on the evaluation of the lethal potentiality.

The caller is a neighbor or friend and is concerned about someone he knows. He may be reluctant to identify himself or to involve himself in any responsibility but requests that you do something about the person he is concerned about. He is not able to give too much detail or information about the situation that concerns him.

You should get as much information as you can and encourage him to let the person know that he is concerned for him and to advise the patient to call you. You should point out that it would be unrealistic for you simply to call someone without being able to say who notified you. The caller should be told that it is his responsibility to be involved, if he is really concerned about a person who is suicidal. Often, such a caller will ask you to make a home visit, to which you may reply that it is impossible for you to leave the phone inasmuch as you are on duty.

A physician, minister, police officer, or similar person in a position of responsibility calls about a case. Frequently, the call is about someone who has just been rescued after a suicide attempt.

Get as much information as possible to evaluate the situation. If the patient is still threatening suicide, hospitalization should be considered. If the patient seems calmed down and under control, then he should be encouraged to seek professional help. Your informant should be encouraged to demonstrate his continued interest in the patient, if he is able to do so. The patient or family should be advised to call the SPC for an appointment, if more information is needed to make an appropriate referral.

A person calls and demands to speak to a specific staff member.

Unless there is an extreme emergency, you should talk with the patient yourself, seek to help if you can with the current problem, and ask the patient to call the staff member in the morning. If, however, the emergency is great, you can call the staff member and ask him to call the patient.

The caller tells you about a neighbor or family member who is being physically restrained from attempting suicide, and the patient cannot be left unattended. The patient is described as psychotic and determined to kill himself.

The caller should be advised to take the patient to the psychiatric unit of the general hospital. It should be emphasized that harmful drugs or objects should be removed from the patient's environment and someone should always be with him.

A call comes in from someone who is attempting suicide while telling you about it.

You should keep the person on the phone. Get his name, phone number, address, and information about his attempt. Try to learn specifically what he has ingested or what he is doing. Call the police and identify yourself as a member of the SPC staff and give them all the pertinent information and ask them to investigate.

6

LONG-TERM TREATMENT OF CHRONICALLY SUICIDAL PATIENTS

Robert E. Litman

SOME PSYCHIATRISTS find treatment of chronically suicidal patients so difficult and exhausting that they attempt to avoid these patients. In this chapter, I will offer some recommendations that will make the task less onerous. My experience in treating suicidal patients may be instructive for others faced with the challenge. In 1955, having completed training successively in neurology, psychiatry, and psychoanalysis, I became clinical director of the inpatient psychiatric service at Cedars–Sinai hospital in Los Angeles. This psychodynamically oriented treatment ward serves a financially advantaged community. I was surprised to discover that more than half the patients admitted during the next 2 years came there because they had attempted suicide or communicated thoughts of suicide. My observations on this situation (Litman 1957) came to the attention of psychologists Norman Farberow and Edwin Shneidman, who had been researching suicide through charts, notes, and other documents. They recruited me to be the psychiatrist-director of the Los Angeles Suicide Prevention Center (LASPC), a new grant-supported project of the National Institute of Mental Health. That 3-year commitment led to a lifetime career as a suicidologist. This report returns to some of the same subjects I discussed in 1957 and reviews what I have learned in 30 years about the long-term treatment of chronically suicidal patients.

THE CRISIS MODEL

My colleagues and I conceptualized suicide as a crisis, and our treatment model was crisis intervention. We thought of the presuicidal state as one of transient perturbation following trauma or serious stress, especially the loss or threat of loss of something that the patient valued highly. More generally, the presuicidal state occurs when people are overwhelmed in a given situation and feel helpless to influence the outcome. There is a painful sense of hopelessness and a constriction of perception, especially of choices or options. We emphasized the necessity for helping patients get through these time-limited stress periods so that natural healing could occur. Much of our clinical work was based on the development of a 24-hour call-for-help crisis intervention telephone service at SPC, with a limited number of follow-up interviews for clients there, if needed. The telephone service was quickly used extensively in Los Angeles, and the concept became so popular that crisis telephone services proliferated worldwide and spun off large numbers of hot lines for many purposes.

FOLLOW-UP STUDIES

We wondered what happened to clients after they were in touch with the emergency telephone service. Follow-up studies (Litman 1970) indicated a suicide mortality rate of about 1 percent after 2 years. Psychological autopsies revealed that when these (deceased) clients called the SPC, they had been chronically psychiatrically ill and chronically suicidal. More specifically, the majority had been depressed chronic alcoholic or chronic suicidal depressive individuals; their suicides had not been triggered by the crises that occur in the lives of relatively normal persons. It became clear that crisis therapy was appropriate and beneficial for persons in a true psychological crisis, that is, those persons who were fairly well adjusted until some traumatic event precipitated the presuicidal state. Given crisis therapy, such individuals almost invariably recovered and returned to their pretraumatic status. However, crisis therapy alone was ineffective in preventing suicide in chronically suicidal persons.

In a series of follow-up studies (Litman 1974), we identified differences between ex-clients who had committed suicide and those who were still alive. The statistically derived factors associated with eventual suicide in SPC callers were: older age, alcoholism, no recent rage or violence, a history of previous suicide attempts, male versus female, help rejection, longer duration of current suicidal episode, no history of inpatient psychiatric treatment, no recent loss or separation, somatic symptoms of depression, less loss of physical health, and higher occupational level. These were chronic factors, not evidence of crisis.

When asked what precipitating stress had caused them to call the center, these chronically suicidal clients often said, "Nothing special, I'm just tired of it all." They had difficulty recalling a specific time when the suicidal state began. Although they had apparently called for help, they often were unwilling to accept the help that was suggested. Typically, these persons had a long history of chronic or repetitive suicidal behavior as part of a self-destructive life-style. They were chronically depressed. Some had made repeated suicide attempts. Many had masochistic personal relationships; drug abuse and alcohol abuse were common. Their suicidal behavior did not represent crises as much as it represented repetitive behavior patterns. We learned that the treatment plan for these persons should emphasize the gradual amelioration of a self-destructive life-style, with less emphasis on active intervention to ensure their safety. The single most effective intervention was to help these people find a stable and continuing treatment resource and to encourage them to stick with it.

These chronically suicidal persons tended to be lonely, with few or mostly negative personal relationships. Hypothesizing that some relationship would be better than none for these individuals, I developed an experimental therapy called "relationship maintenance" (Litman and Wold 1976). We identified four hundred persons at high risk for suicide who had called the center, and then divided them randomly into two groups. Persons in the control group were not offered anything special or different. Many people in this group called the center when they felt they needed some crisis help. The experimental group was offered a special program of assistance. Each person was placed in contact with an experienced volunteer worker from the telephone service. The volunteer worker offered to call at least once a week and talk empathically with the client. Some of the "befriending" contacts between volunteers and clients were made considerably more often than once a week. What happened was disappointing. At the end of 2 years, six people in the experimental group had committed suicide; only two in the control group had done so. Psychological autopsies of these six people revealed that they had alienated the volunteer befrienders by making too many demands, by showing hostility, and by maintaining a chronically negative attitude; some of the clients had been rejected by the befrienders, adding one more trauma in an already maladjusted life.

We identified two main factors that contributed to the frustration and discouragement of the volunteer befrienders. When clients made unrealistic demands or expressed unreasonable hostilities, the volunteers felt that their training, clinical experience, and resources were inadequate. Even more significant were their feelings of isolation from the center's professional staff and from their supervisors. The volunteers were making their befriending contacts by telephone from their homes, and the monthly team meetings provided insufficient team support. We concluded that the task of maintaining long-term therapeutic relationships with chronically suicidal persons requires extensive training and experience and is too demanding for volunteers or paraprofessionals.

We asked ourselves how the center's professional staff was able to deal with highly suicidal patients year after year. Not only was discouragement or gloom not evident, but staff members actually grew to enjoy the challenge of meeting difficult situations and life-threatening problems. We decided that the essential element was a sense of team spirit, a feeling of mutual support. Attitudes of superiority and competitive second guessing (which can be destructive to team morale) were discouraged, and staff members who could not adapt to a team spirit were excluded. Therapists who treat chronically suicidal patients need confidence in their training and experience, and in their ability to assume responsibility and to feel that they are part of a team. The concept of teamwork is easily recognized in hospital practice or in outpatient clinics. It may take a special effort for solo practitioners in private practice.

CHRONICALLY SUICIDAL PATIENTS

Psychiatrists who have reviewed large numbers of consecutive suicides (Rich et al. 1986, Robins 1981) have described four psychiatric pathways that lead to suicide. For about half of those who commit suicide, the path is primary affective disorder (depression). Primary alcoholism or other chemical dependency is indicated in about 20 percent of all suicides, and schizophrenia in 5–10 percent; diagnoses for the rest include a sizable number of mixed personality disorders or borderline personality disorders. Often there are mixed diagnoses, for example, depression in an alcoholic person with a personality disorder. In about half the suicides, the person had never been suicidal or aroused concern in other persons over possible self-destructiveness prior to the index episode that caused death. In the other half of the suicide deaths, there had been previous episodes of suicidal concern. About 30 percent of those who committed suicide had made a previous attempt. At some time in the past, 50 percent had been in contact with the mental health system, and about 25 percent were in treatment when they killed themselves.

This chapter focuses on the treatment of those patients with a long history of suicidal episodes. Examples are many: dysthymic persons suffering from chronic apathy and anhedonia, schizophrenic persons who feel abandoned to their persecutors, alcoholic persons who face the reality of trying to be sober, borderline personalities who use the threat of suicide to control their environment. What do these patients have in common, and what are the common elements of treatment? These patients feel trapped in a hostile milieu with inadequate resources and limited hope, and so they fantasize about death, not only as an escape from pain but also often as a final vindication. Chronically suicidal patients often express appreciation for the doctor's efforts while still maintaining an inner conviction that sooner or later they will commit suicide.

I estimate that 20–25 percent of these chronically suicidal individuals eventually terminate their lives. But in any one year, the suicide rate is only 1–2 percent, even for high-risk patients. I use this statistic when I treat suicidal persons. For example, early in the treatment of those who have recently made a suicide attempt after being suicidal much of their lives, I may say something like this: "According to the statistics, you are a high-risk-for-suicide patient. That means there is a 2–5 percent chance that you will commit suicide in the next 2–5 years. However, there is a 95 percent chance that 5 years from now you will not have committed suicide—that you will still be alive—and I am gearing this treatment toward that 95 percent chance." Note that I am already thinking toward a "5-year survival." We are dealing with malignant, potentially life-threatening disease processes, and our efforts may only postpone suicide rather than prevent it.

TREATMENT

Psychiatrists focus treatment of suicidal patients on the theme of mental illness, especially depression. Mental illness plays a role, but many causal factors enter into every suicide, and only a small fraction of the mentally ill actually commit suicide. There are multiple possible interventions that might prevent a suicide, and the doctor is only one part of the configuration. Psychiatrists must admit that, for some chronic mental disorders (for example, dysthymia, recurrent depression, addiction, schizophrenia, and suicidal borderline personalities), we have no quick or guaranteed cure, either through interpretation or through medication. New developments in psychiatry and in public health have not made a dramatic change in the suicide rate.

The basic element in treatment is a continuing stable and dependable doctor–patient relationship. To achieve this relationship, the patient must develop trust in the doctor and the doctor must feel comfortable with the patient. Although it is difficult, psychiatrists must accept, understand, and live in peace with these patients' continual threats of suicide.

A national survey of randomly selected psychiatrists (Chemtob et al. 1988) revealed that 51 percent of the respondents had had a patient who committed suicide, and that this event had had a negative impact on both their personal and professional lives. Through my involvement with psychological autopsies, I have interviewed hundreds of psychiatrists and allied therapists shortly after their patients committed suicide. None of the doctors stated that the possibility of suicide as a desirable goal or "good death" had been considered in making therapeutic plans, although some acknowledged that they had thought suicide was inevitable. For many of the therapists, the death was a personal loss, like the death of a family member. Besides grief, they experienced a sense of professional failure. Some therapists felt discredited or humiliated, or they feared that they might be sued for malpractice. These are reasons why the threat of patient suicide rightly causes anxiety in psychiatrists. Nevertheless, we treat potentially suicidal patients every day. Our problem, then, is to lower the risk and to find a comfort zone where therapists can be concerned and sensitive but not anxious.

I return to the concept of a treatment team. The team includes many people, not just the psychiatrist. I usually talk with the family, especially the spouse, and sometimes others who can be of help. I hope that they will be available if needed as ancillary therapists and to communicate information that the index patient may not reveal—for example, that the patient is not taking prescribed medicine, or that family tension has increased. It is reassuring when no guns are immediately available in the home. Because suicides often occur when the therapist goes on vacation or is otherwise absent or unavailable, it is prudent to arrange for backup therapists who are acquainted with the patient to serve as substitutes or consultants. The team concept helps dilute the dependency transference, which becomes dangerous if it is too intense and too ambivalent. Intensity is generally not desirable in the treatment of these patients. Using a sports metaphor, we are involved in a marathon, not a sprint, so endurance, consistency, and steadiness are the essential parameters.

Record keeping is imperative. Early in treatment, the therapist should record the patient's history, mental status, ideas, fantasies, and plans and preparations for suicide. The chart should also include the therapist's diagnostic impression and a treatment plan. For outpatients, weekly notes are appropriate at first and should include any medications and the patient's reactions to them, as well as the major features of the patient's progress. Later notes may be less frequent and may record only significant changes or events in the patient's life or treatment and the results of periodic (quarterly or semiannual) reassessments.

After several years of treatment, these records will enable the therapist to reevaluate the original complaints, check the effectiveness of medications, and determine seasonal variations in symptoms. The records will reinforce the therapist's reminder to the patient—who thinks "now" is the worst it has ever been—that a previous time was worse, yet the patient recovered.

Failure to keep written records on a suicidal patient is dangerous. Should the patient eventually commit suicide, and the survivors allege negligence and malpractice, the therapist's best defense is an adequate written record. We live in a litigious society where lawyers and courts often decide that there should be monetary compensation for every loss. After a suicide, the family feels grief and bereavement but also guilt and anger, which often is projected onto the doctor.

Or there may be some legitimate reason to suspect that the doctor did not exercise reasonable caution and prudence in caring for the patient. I do not believe that the courts require psychiatrists to prevent every suicide (which would be quite unfair), but courts do require doctors to use reasonable judgment in making decisions about treatment. This requirement means that in organizing a treatment plan or changing it, or in giving a certain medication or stopping it, the doctor should consider the risks and benefits and briefly note these in the record.

Hospitalization

A prime example is the decision to hospitalize or not to hospitalize a suicidal patient. Hospitalization carries distinct risks as well as benefits. The benefits are obvious in cases of acute crisis due to a specific stress or loss, or to a specific toxic environment. The patient is removed from the turmoil and given a chance to reassess positions and sort out options in a protected environment. This benefit is especially true in acute psychotic states or in chemical dependency or addiction. In chronic suicidal mental illness, hospitalization sometimes is indicated for patients who change life-styles or change therapists.

On the other hand, there are definite negative aspects to hospitalization. It provides a passive remedy for problems in the world that may require an active resolution. Eventually, after discharge from the hospital, these problems will have to be faced. So discharge planning and preparation should be a central element of the hospital treatment plan. Many people think that psychiatric hospitalization is degrading, humiliating, and stigmatizing. For such people, hospitalization may mean a final loss of self-esteem or a final declaration of hopelessness. Finally, the belief that hospitalization invariably protects against suicide is false. About 1 percent of all suicides occur in hospitals (Litman and Farberow 1966). Follow-up studies indicate that the time immediately after discharge from psychiatric hospitals, when the patient returns to the community, is the period of highest suicidal risk (Hirshfeld and Davidson 1988).

It is especially difficult to decide when a long-term psychiatric patient requires involuntary hospitalization, and the influence of family and other caretakers is vital in making the decision. My criterion is whether we have available treatment resources to bring about a substantial benefit to the patient within a reasonable time (2–3 weeks). Otherwise, I hesitate to certify a patient for involuntary hospitalization because of danger to self. Of course, the patient may require involuntary hospitalization for other reasons, such as danger to others or grave disability.

I know of no evidence that supports prolonged hospitalization as a suicide prevention measure. When the county hospital in Los Angeles changed its policy and began to favor shorter psychiatric hospitalizations, my colleagues and I compared long-term postadmission experiences by tabulating suicides at a 1-year follow-up (1 year from day of admission) and found no difference in the number of posthospital suicides, although the shorter stay policy led to about one-third more admissions (Yamamoto et al. 1973). As indications have been tightened and made more difficult for involuntary hospitalization of patients who are a danger to themselves, there has not been a noticeable increase in suicides due to premature discharge from psychiatric hospitals. Nevertheless, when patients are evaluated as being at high suicide risk, community standards and expert opinion require that psychiatric hospitalization be given thoughtful consideration and that the decision should be reached after evaluating the risks versus the benefits. This mode of making and recording decisions will help keep the psychiatrist comfortable.

Chronic Depression

DSM-III-R classifies chronic depression under the heading *dysthymia*, noting that many cases of dysthymia involve superimposed major depression. Clinicians and researchers tend to focus on the more florid and episodic phases of affective illness, but in my experience dysthymia is also a significant cause of suicide, usually when there is concomitant morbidity complicating chronic depression with substance abuse, personality disorders, or multiple recurrences of major depression.

Dysthymia is common. Epidemiologic studies (Robins et al. 1984) indicate that 4 percent of all women and 2 percent of all men suffer from dysthymic disorder. Most of the suicidal patients I have treated in my private office and at the Suicide Prevention Center belong in this category. Suicidal dysthymic patients describe their joyless lives and their preoccupation with, and fear of, negative events. They are obsessed with their own deficiencies and failures. They are not psychotic, but they somehow feel strange, different, and alone. Although they may have achieved some success despite their impairment, they feel unworthy and undeserving. Their interests are constricted and their social contacts are limited. With the passage of time, their stores of hopefulness erode. Often, they are not only depressed but also shy and anxious. Because of these other traits in addition to depression, the large group of dysthymic disorders probably includes a number of subcategories (Kocsis and Frances 1987). Although there is no standard treatment, the most appropriate therapeutic approach features flexibility and a combination of antidepressant drugs with psychotherapy.

It takes time and patience to understand these patients. Keeping in mind that they commit suicide when they can no longer accept and live with their painful helplessness and hopelessness, I quickly demonstrate my empathy for those feelings, and I try to establish my office as a haven of acceptance. I am especially interested in the patients' dreams and fantasies, exploring them for gratifying aspects, although it is often hard at first to locate anything positive. A professional man reported a recurrent dream that began in childhood: "I'm outside in the cold, looking in through the window at a family gathered around the fireplace. I think to myself that I'll never belong." Depressed patients mostly report unpleasant dreams with themes of deprivation, mistreatment, rejection, ridicule, and failure. Dreams that characterize presuicidal patients feature violence and destruction, death and dead persons, and giving up and merging with death as a way to achieve peace and healing.

I employ a variety of psychotherapy tactics, depending on the patient's needs. For patients sunk in passivity and apathy, I prescribe specific activities and participation diaries, along with continuing reeducation efforts to break the habit of negative thoughts and pessimism and to substitute more realistic and optimistic appraisals of self and the world on a cognitive therapy model. I also encourage efforts to improve interpersonal relationships and melt the affective blocks that tend to freeze these persons out of the warmth they might obtain from personal relationships. These patients have often failed to respond to extensive trials of antidepressant drug therapy, but I usually continue trying other drugs, seeking a combination that will work, and offering hope that maybe a new product will be successful. Several years ago, trazodone became available and helped some chronically depressed patients. More recently, fluoxetine has been successful for others.

There is a subpopulation of dysthymic patients who respond well to dextroamphetamine (20 mg/day) over a long period of time. Unlike most people, these patients sleep *better* with dextroamphetamine. They do not lose weight. It improves their energy and mental concentration and does not precipitate mania. Most importantly, they do not develop tolerance and the need for increased amounts of medication to produce the same effect. A trial of dextroamphetamine quickly reveals its suitability for a patient.

Dysthymic patients form stable positive dependency transferences and persist in treatment. Countertransference problems arise when therapists become weary with the treatment's lack of success. A patient's persistent negativity tends to depress the therapist. A treating doctor reported to me in consultation, "The patient makes me feel like I am working in a tomb." Under these circumstances, the doctor is relieved when the patient drops out of treatment. But for the patient, the treatment failure reinforces hopelessness and doom.

Alcoholism and Drug Abuse

The first major lesson I learned as a suicidologist was the futility of attempting to treat suicidal alcoholic patients for their depression while they are still drinking alcohol. Crisis therapy helps these patients temporarily, but it is ineffective in postponing the eventual issue—that the addicted person must detoxify and abstain. The latter stages of alcoholism and the whole detoxification and abstention process carry a high risk of suicide. Effective treatment of alcoholism demands a dramatic life-style change and complete family and community support.

About 10–15 percent of all ex-alcoholic patients become dysthymic and remain permanently at high risk for suicide. In treating these patients, I emphasize the need for continuing contacts with Alcoholics Anonymous, halfway houses, and other group support and self-help programs. These patients tend to drop in and out of therapy, depending on how their personal relationships are going, and the treating doctor should be flexible in accepting these patients on their own terms, provided they do not relapse into addiction. If they do relapse, the first priority is to get them back into a detoxification program.

Schizophrenia

Paranoid schizophrenic persons commit suicide when they feel abandoned to their persecutors. This feeling of abandonment occurs especially during the posthospitalization period, or when the doctor goes on vacation, or when the patient leaves the protection of home. In our center's experience, schizophrenic patients often call in a panic several months after they have quit taking their antipsychotic medication. These individuals do best when they are in a sheltered or structured environment with friendly caretakers and with continual monitoring of their antipsychotic medication. They need to maintain contact with at least one person whom they trust, preferably, in my opinion, someone other than the treating psychiatrist. The transference problem with suicidal schizophrenic patients is that they become totally dependent on and then paranoid toward the treating psychiatrist. The countertransference problem is that the psychiatrist becomes terrified by the psychotic projections. I would recommend diluting the transference by using a team approach to the psychotherapy.

Personality Disorders

Mood lability and suicide attempts are part of the symptomatology of personality disorders, especially borderline personality. Most of these attempts are impulsive and involve self-cutting, self-mutilation, or an overdose of medication. They occur when patients experience uncontrollable tension, either because of anger or because of loneliness and frustration.

As a consultant, I spoke with a woman who had spent almost 2 years in a community hospital because every time she was discharged she attempted suicide. She told me that she did not know why. Sometimes she has stored medication deliberately and planned to take it ("I don't know how I survived taking 297 phenobarbital tablets"), and sometimes she has impulsively cut her arm or her wrist ("But I really didn't mean to die then"). In the community hospital, however, this patient had not been placed on suicide precautions, although most of the time she had been somewhat depressed. This patient's personal struggle between living and dying had been split, with the living aspect projected onto the hospital treatment team so that it had become *her* obsession to die and *their* obsession to keep her alive.

Schwartz (1979) has written incisively about such situations. He believes that the first step in the treatment program should be to make it clear to the patient and appropriate family members that the conflict is internal, not between the patient and the therapist. In this case, I told the community hospital staff members that they should now devote their total attention to devising and carrying out an aftercare program for this patient and that she should not again be hospitalized on the psychiatric service. Any future suicide attempts should be treated with appropriate medical and surgical care, and the patient should then resume her posthospital plan. The role of the consultant in such cases is to redirect the treatment plan and to share in the responsibility if the new plan does not work.

I often try medications with agitated borderline patients. Sometimes a monoamine oxidase inhibitor helps. Sometimes small amounts of antipsychotic drugs help. If there is a paroxysmal quality, sometimes antiseizure medication is helpful.

Generally, when my patients are especially anxious or preoccupied with suicide, I invite them to call me for a last discussion before they put a suicidal plan into action. Borderline patients are apt to abuse this invitation. I specify to these patients that I want to hear from them, but *only* in an emergency. "Emergencies" should occur infrequently. Repeated emergencies indicate that the treatment plan is ineffective, consultation is required, and a new treatment plan is needed. For example, brief hospitalization at this point provides an opportunity for discussions with the family, consultation with other psychiatrists, development of a new treatment plan, and, when appropriate, transfer of the patient to a different therapist.

CONCLUSION

In 30 years (1957–1987), there have been two major changes in the epidemiology of suicide in the United States. Suicide rates for older males have decreased, and suicide rates for younger persons (ages 15–30), especially males, have increased. The changes balance out so that the overall suicide rate has remained about the same, approximately eleven to twelve suicides per 100,000 persons per year. The median age for suicide has decreased from around 45 years to age 39. It is tempting, but simplistic, to attribute these changes to the helpful influence of Social Security and Medicare in the older population, and to the demoralizing influence of more easily available drugs and alcohol and decreased supervisory authority of adults for the increase among youth. However, the universal association of psychiatric disorder with suicide has stayed the same. The types of psychiatric diagnoses and the relative proportion among different psychiatric diagnoses of persons who committed suicide has also stayed the same.

Ordinarily, psychiatric treatment, especially psychotherapy, is a two-person confidential relationship between patient and doctor. But when suicide becomes an issue, the doctor must avoid feeling isolated with the patient. Psychiatrists retain responsibility for treatment, but they share responsibility for suicide prevention, mainly with their patient and somewhat with a therapy team and the social network.

I believe that chronically suicidal persons suffer from a severe chronic and life-threatening psychophysiological disease, somewhat analogous to diabetes mellitus, hypertension, or ulcerative colitis. Sometimes the treating physician has to be satisfied, not with a cure, but with an effort to improve substantially the quality of life for the patient, and to postpone death.

REFERENCES

Chemtob, C. M., Hamada, R. S., Bauer, G. et al. (1988). Patients' suicides: frequency and impact on psychiatrists. *American Journal of Psychiatry* 145:224–228.

Hirshfeld, R. M. A., and Davidson, L. (1988). Risk factors for suicide. In *Review of Psychiatry*, ed A. J. Frances and R. E. Hales, vol. 7. Washington, DC: American Psychiatric Press.

Kocsis, J. H., and Frances, A. J. (1987). A critical discussion of *DSM-III* dysthymic disorder. *American Journal of Psychiatry* 144:1534–1542.

Litman, R. E. (1957). Some aspects of the treatment of the potentially suicidal patient. In *Clues to Suicide*, ed. E. S. Shneidman and N. L. Farberow, pp. 111–118. New York: McGraw-Hill.

————— (1970). Suicide prevention center patients: a follow-up study. *Bulletin of Suicidology* 6:12–17.

————— (1974). Models for predicting suicide risk. In *Psychological Assessment of Suicidal Risk*, ed. C. Neuringer. Springfield, IL: Charles C Thomas.

Litman, R. E., and Farberow, N. L. (1966). The hospital's obligation toward suicide-prone patients. *Hospitals*, Dec. 16, 64–68.

Litman, R. E., and Wold, C. I. (1976). Beyond crisis intervention. In *Suicidology:*

Contemporary Developments, ed. E. S. Shneidman, pp. 528–546. New York: Grune & Stratton.

Rich, C. L., Young, D., and Fowler, R. C. (1986). San Diego suicide study. *Archives of General Psychiatry* 43:577–582.

Robins, E. (1981). *The Final Months: a Study of the Lives of 134 Persons Who Committed Suicide*. New York: Oxford University Press.

Robins, L. N., Helzer, J. E., Weissman, M. M., et al. (1984). Lifetime prevalence of specific psychiatric disorders in three sites. *Archives of General Psychiatry* 41:949–958.

Schwartz, D. A. (1979). The suicidal character. *Psychiatric Quarterly* 51:64–70.

Yamamoto, J., Roath, M., and Litman, R. E. (1973). Suicides in the "new" community hospital. *Archives of General Psychiatry* 28:101–102.

7

GUIDELINES TO SUICIDE PREVENTION IN THE HOSPITAL

Norman L. Farberow

Suicide, IN PRACTICALLY every culture, is a disturbing event. It is particularly distressing when it is carried out by a patient under hospital care, for the hospital is generally thought of as a place where a patient will be safely guarded from harm, including self-inflicted harm. A suicide in the hospital is therefore a special blow to the image of the hospital as life-preserving, life-enhancing, and life-prolonging. Yet the fact is that in hospitals in the United States, suicide occurs at a higher rate than among the general population.

This chapter addresses two questions about suicide in the hospital: what are the significant demographic and clinical data about suicide in the hospital, and what general principles can be used to prevent or reduce the occurence of suicide in the hospital?

Data on suicide in the hospital are available from studies undertaken in the Veterans Administration hospitals (Farberow and Williams 1978) and hospitals in Missouri (Sletten et al. 1972). The VA data are relatively similar to data on other hospital systems in the United States, even though VA hospitals have a higher proportion of males.

Over a 3-year period (fiscal years 1973, 1974, and 1975) the average suicide rate in 161 VA hospitals with an average daily population of about 81,000 patients was 150.9 per 100,000. Among the suicides, 82 percent had a primary neuropsychiatric diagnosis, and 18 percent had a primary medical or surgical diagnosis.

The average rate for the neuropsychiatric suicides was 370.7 per 100,000 population, about thirty times that found in the general population, and the modal age was 26. About 38 percent of all neuropsychiatric suicides were 34 years of age or younger, overcontributing, in comparison with their proportion in the total neuropsychiatric population, by 22 percent. The average suicide rate for these younger neuropsychiatric patients was 623.7 per 100,000. In comparison, the age group 65 and older had an average rate of 53.6 per 100,000, which made up only 4 percent of the suicides and undercontributed for their age group by 11 percent.

Diagnostically, the functional psychoses made up 72 percent of the suicides, overcontributing by 23 percent and yielding a rate of 376.6 per 100,000. About 88 percent of the functional psychoses were schizophrenics. Alcoholism made up only 7 percent of the suicides, undercontributing by 11 percent and yielding a rate of 98.2 per 100,000.

About 64 percent of the suicides occurred out of the hospital, 35 percent during authorized leave, and 30 percent during unauthorized absence. Only 35 percent of the suicides occurred in the hospital or on the grounds. In the hospital, the most frequent methods were hanging (52 percent) and jumping (21 percent). The most frequent sites of suicide in the hospital were the bathroom (23 percent) and the bed area (18 percent). Out of the hospital, the method used most often was a gun (38 percent).

The average rate for general medical and surgical suicide was 41.7 per 100,000, or about three and one-half times that of the general population. The median age was 57. The largest percentage of this population, 34 percent, fell in the age group 55 to 64, overcontributing by 8 percent and attaining a rate of 66.6 per 100,000. Although the younger age group, 34 and below, made up only 16 percent of the suicides, they also overcontributed by 8 percent and had the highest suicide rate of any of the age groups, 106.7 per 100,000.

Diagnostically, the two groups that made up the largest proportions of the suicides (18 percent in each group) were accidents, poisoning, or violence, and circulatory diseases. The accidents, poisoning, or violence category, which includes cases of attempted suicide in the community brought into the hospital for treatment, overcontributed by 10 percent. The category of circulatory diseases, which made up a much larger proportion of the hospital population (22 percent) actually undercontributed by 4 percent. Patients with respiratory illnesses made up the next largest proportion of suicides (15 percent), overcontributing by 10 percent. Patients with endocrine, nutritional, and metabolic diseases made up 10 percent of the suicides, overcontributing by 6 percent. Contrary to common expectations, patients with neoplasms made up only 8 percent of the suicides and actually undercontributed by 6 percent.

In direct reversal of what was found in neuropsychiatric suicides, 72 percent of the general medical and surgical suicides occurred inside the hospital and 25 percent occurred outside the hospital. Jumping was the method used most often in the hospital (58 percent) with hanging the next most frequent (15 percent). Outside the hospital, guns were used most often (27 percent), followed by running in front of a moving object (21 percent) and drowning (16 percent). The most frequent sites for general medical and surgical suicides in the hospital were the bed area (58 percent), an unattended room (19 percent), and the bathroom (12 percent).

Data from the mental hospital system in Missouri can be compared for rates of suicide among its neuropsychiatric patients (Sletten et al. 1972). For the period 1960 to 1969, the overall suicide rate for patients in its five state hospitals (with equal proportions of men and women) was found to be 90 per 100,000. However, this rate is based on patient-years of risk rather than average daily patient census. A previous study has shown that rates based on patient-years of risk are generally between three and four times smaller than rates based on average daily patient census (Farberow et al. 1971). Thus the rate in the Missouri state mental hospital system was about the same as that among VA neuropsychiatric patients.

Suicide risk was found to be greatest during the first month after admission and to decrease gradually as the length of hospital stay increased. Suicides were primarily by hanging, drowning, and drug overdose.

In general, suicide rates for general medical and surgical and neuropsychiatric hospital patients seemed to run about three and one-half and thirty times higher, respectively, than the rates found in the general population. The highest rates for the hospital populations were found in the younger age groups. Among the medically ill, patients with diseases of the circulatory, respiratory, and metabolic systems killed themselves most often, and among neuropsychiatric patients, schizophrenics made up most of the suicide population.

WHY DO HOSPITAL SUICIDES OCCUR?

The motivations for suicide while in the hospital, although basically the same as those of a suicidal person in any situation, are heightened by at least two factors. First, hospital patients are often at the extremes of physical or emotional distress; suicidal impulses may be energized by the debilitating inroads of a severe illness or disguised by an overlay of psychotic thinking and behavior. Second, patients (especially the long-term) are frequently without resources or relationships outside the hospital, so that the hospital and its staff assume special importance to the patient.

Most suicidal behavior contains one or more combinations of dynamic themes expressed as wishes and reflecting basic motivations. They include a wish for surcease arising out of physical and psychological depletion; a wish for expiation of guilt by self-punishment and self-destruction; a wish to destroy, kill, and take revenge; a hopeful wish to be rescued, reborn, and forgiven; and a wish for reunion with beloved dead. The feeling states accompanying these motivations are those of hopelessness, helplessness, and worthlessness, contributing to patients' feelings that they have no future and there is no reason to stay alive.

The objective of the hospital and its staff is to change these feelings. It is accomplished by instilling in the patients feelings of self-worth, showing them evidence of interested concern and care, and, most important, protecting them against uncontrollable suicidal impulses. In a previous study (Reynolds and Farberow 1976), using the experiential research method to study the treatment of suicidal patients in a mental hospital, feelings of helplessness and powerlessness were found to be the most significant characteristics of patienthood.

Powerlessness seems to present special problems. To have personal control over one's existence is essential in the development of a healthy self-concept. In the hospital, however, patients are continually impressed with a sense of powerlessness; their lives must conform to a schedule designed essentially for the convenience of the staff. Most things happen to them, not because of or for them; other people continually make the most important decisions about their lives. The hospital's dilemma is that it can treat patients most efficiently when patients are willing to accept the sick role at the same time that it tries to foster a sense of independence, self-worth, and self-control. Patients, too, are frequently confused by these mixed messages.

In the hospital, it is primarily in the relationships patients form with staff that important feelings of self-worth develop. Actions, often not considered significant in themselves, become highly meaningful because of the attitudes they imply. They include staff members thanking patients for volunteered work, taking patients' complaints about living conditions seriously, and including patients in decision making. The trauma of "staffing" for patients seems to be reduced when, rather than having the patient face an array of questioning faces in a formal staff meeting, two or three staff members talk informally with the patient in the day room, the patient's own turf.

Follow-up research on suicidal patients, after their discharge from hospitals, shows that most of the suicides occurred because the patients' feelings of self-worth and self-confidence were not yet strong enough to withstand a serious setback, and that they either did not feel the hospital could help them any more or else despaired of ever getting well again (Miller 1970; Farberow and MacKinnon 1974). These results underscore the importance of continuing relationships after discharge, either through outreach efforts by the hospital or through informed support by family and community.

A set of guidelines for suicide prevention in hospitals is detailed below and summarized in the appendix to this chapter. They have been developed from clinical experience, a review of the suicide prevention policies of a wide variety of hospitals, and discussions with colleagues. The guidelines encompass four general areas: identification, environmental and procedural safeguards, communication, and general attitudes.

IDENTIFICATION

Admissions personnel should routinely inquire about any history of previous suicide attempts and depressive or suicidal states and should include a statement about the presence or absence of such events in the report. Prior or current suicidal behavior should be described in detail, with date, method, rescue preparations, motivation, and evaluation of risk for each event. A previous history of suicidal behavior, especially two or three suicide attempts, has been noted as highly predictive of subsequent suicidal actions (Farberow et al. 1966). Obtaining this information is especially important for those patients entering a psychiatric hospital, but applies to patients admitted for physical illnesses as well.

After admission, any self-destructive impulses—whether direct or indirect, verbal or nonverbal—will appear in behavior, mood, and personality patterns. Behavior that directly expresses suicidal intentions or state of mind presents few or no problems for identification; examples are given in the appendix. Indirect behavior that requires further evidence and careful interpretation includes such actions as refusing food and medication, giving away possessions, and general uncooperativeness.

In regard to mood, probably the most significant trio of feelings indicating high suicidal risk are feelings of hopelessness, helplessness, and worthlessness. Feelings of worthlessness reflect strong feelings of unlovability and inadequacy, helplessness adds feelings of being unable to change the circumstances, and hopelessness implies the feeling that no one else can help either.

Depression is the feeling most frequently observed in suicidal persons; it is especially significant when accompanied by agitation and restlessness, but most often it is expressed through apathy and withdrawal. In such cases, changes of mood and behavior mark the danger point, perhaps indicating a decision to end life. Heightened anxiety, severe frustration, excessive guilt and self-blame, and bitter anger may also appear.

People who are severely disorganized and chaotic are unable to handle physical or psychological stresses. The disorganization may be either acute or chronic. When it is chronic, such people are frequently diagnosed as borderline or psychotic. Similar disorganization is not nearly as frequent in well-functioning individuals; however, even ordinarily capable individuals may decompensate under the stress of a serious physical illness, especially when the illness requires an extensive change in self-concept. When the decompensation is either chronic or acutely disorganized and the person becomes psychotic— perhaps schizophrenic—the suicidal risk is heightened.

Two personality patterns—dependent-satisfied and dependent-dissatisfied—have been fairly consistently observed in studies of patients with long-term illnesses who committed suicide (Farberow et al. 1963). Both groups of patients are characterized by a high level of dependency on the hospital and on the staff, but each group expresses the dependency in a different manner. Dependent-satisfied patients do well as long as they are able to remain in the hospital and feel secure in its continuing care. When discharge nears, however, they become highly anxious and restive and may act out against themselves to indicate their desire to stay in the hospital.

Dependent-dissatisfied patients need constant assurance that they are worthwhile, but obtain this approval negatively by asking incessantly for attention, medication, passes, special treatments—anything that will require attention from the staff. This behavior tends to alienate the staff and causes them to withdraw, which in turn brings about repeated and more insistent demands.

Other useful clues to heightened suicidal potentiality include recent object loss and the expression of negative feelings about the hospital, including a loss of hope for any future and the feeling that a source of help is no longer available.

ENVIRONMENTAL SAFEGUARDS

The hospital is responsible for making its environment as safe as possible. Careful inspection and evaluation of the physical plant is required to determine what safeguards can be effected without adversely affecting treatment capabilities. New construction can be based on some of the recommendations, depending on the cost.

Since jumping is a frequent suicide method, safety glass should be used in windows, or window openings should be restricted in size (6 to 8 inches) to make it practically impossible for a person to squeeze through. Stairwells should be blocked off in neuropsychiatric hospitals, and access to the roof should be impossible except for selected hospital personnel.

Similarly, opportunities for hanging can be limited through elimination of articles or materials suitable for that purpose. Shower curtain rods, clothes hooks, and railings in bathrooms should not be strong enough to support the weight of a person. Clothes locker hooks should not be able to support much weight, wooden or plastic hangers should be used instead of wire, and clothes lockers should be in full view. Exposed pipes should be covered; ventilators over grilles or porch screens should have interstices too small to admit the insertion of any cord or wire that might be used to attempt a hanging.

The hospital can also implement certain procedures to make the environment safer—for example, removing objects with which patients can injure or kill themselves and being alert in potentially dangerous situations where such objects are used, such as the dining room and occupational therapy room. Examples of dangerous items used for hanging, cutting, or stabbing are listed in the appendix. Staff should also be alert when patients are using the bathroom, where privacy often provides more opportunities for suicide by hanging, jumping, or cutting.

Staff must also be particularly alert when medication is given, at night, at shift changes, and when a suicidal patient is being taken off the ward by non-ward personnel, such as when going to X-ray, EEG lab, or dental office. The escort accompanying the patient should be apprised of the suicidal risk. When patients are being escorted outside in a group, suicidal patients should not be allowed to reach the curb first; they should be kept in the middle of the group and should also be constantly observed when being escorted since they can pick up dangerous objects.

Finally, through frequent meetings, the staff should be well aware of its individual and team responsibilities, which should be clearly defined and detailed. For some hospitals, they may include informing the patient which staff members are continually available for help at any time.

Benensohn and Resnik (1973) describe the suicide-proofing of a psychiatric unit. Patients were allowed to participate in setting their own limits and defining the ward protection, and those who helped in the suicide-proofing felt more secure. The authors believe that suicidal patients, while aware that no unit can be made completely suicide-proof, are reassured by external controls on their self-destructive impulses, especially when they are first admitted. Such controls are viewed by the patients as evidence of caring, something they often feel is lacking from significant others in their lives. The authors also found it helpful to encourage patients to care for other suicidal patients; sensitizing the patients to the needs of others provided a sense of caring about another, and thus of sharing the responsibility for each other.

COMMUNICATION

Communication is important not only therapeutically, but also legally, in relation to suicidal patients. Orders for their care must be carefully worded, especially when precautionary measures are required, and should include the locations a patient is restricted to, what objects are to be removed, who has special responsibility for observing or accompanying the patient, when or how frequently the special considerations apply, and why a procedure is ordered if the rationale is not self-evident. It is important for legal purposes that staff involved in any contact with identified suicidal patients document in the medical records that the risk of self-destructive behavior is recognized, that reasonable measures to minimize the risk have been ordered, and that those orders have been carried out.

All treatment staff should obtain consultation from outside consultants or from other staff as soon as possible about the degree of risk or about appropriate measures necessary to deal with the situation, and frequent consultation should be sought for suicidal patients.

ATTITUDES

Attitudes in the hospital toward suicide and suicidal patients are highly significant. The objective in suicide prevention in the hospital is to minimize self-destructive behavior while maintaining a therapeutic setting; it is therefore important to avoid an atmosphere of anxious preoccupation and the fear that a suicide will occur. A suicidal person should not be approached with harsh, suppressive measures for the sake of prevention; rather, the emphasis should be on positive methods that indicate genuine interest and establish mutual trust.

Hope is the basic ingredient for improvement in suicidal patients, since loss of hope and consequent despair may precipitate an unexpected self-destructive act. The staff can restore and strengthen feelings of hope by making patients feel less helpless, lending them the necessary support in the slow process of rebuilding self-esteem and self-worth. It also follows that it is necessary to accept the fact that human errors occur. There is no way that all suicides can be prevented; one can only aim to approach the minimal level.

LEGAL IMPLICATIONS

In the United States, legal attitudes toward suicide have undergone a number of changes, most of them reflecting the changing philosophy of treating the mentally ill. From the early 1890s through the present, the primary principle used by the courts in their evaluation of responsibility in cases of hospital suicides has been foreseeability—that is, whether the patient was known or identified as a suicidal risk. For many years it was assumed by the courts that if this fact was known to the hospital, it had full responsibility for keeping the patient alive; if the patient succeeded in injuring or killing himself, the hospital was liable, no matter what the circumstances. Rigid standards of care, most of which were severely repressive measures, were required (Perr 1965).

In the 1940s however, the courts began to accept that the hospitals had to have more freedom if they were to achieve their therapeutic goals. In 1943 in the *Root v. State* case, the New York Court of Claims enunciated the principle that a hospital could not "ensure" the safety of its inmates and could not be required to "maintain constant supervision of the deceased," and stated that signs of improvement indicated the need to allow the patient more freedom (Cooper 1975). In 1955, the New York appellate division adopted the principle that the degree of freedom allowed to a patient should be decided by the patient's doctor and accepted that an "honest error in judgment" might occur. The criterion for evaluation of the physician's procedures was whether they met the standards of professional practice recognized as competent in the community.

Generally, a hospital and its staff are accustomed to high-risk patients as part of daily life, and the risk is accepted with caution and care. Procedures are developed to discharge such responsibilities and to allow the hospital staff to feel they have done their best, no matter what the outcome. In the case of a suicidal patient, staff often feel the opposite, and the loss of a life is experienced as premature, tragic, and unnecessary. The guidelines are aimed at providing the staff with a feeling of confidence that they have done all that is humanly possible.

APPENDIX

Guidelines for Suicide Prevention in the Hospital

A. Identification
  At admission
    Inquire about current suicidal behavior
    Inquire about prior suicidal behavior (two or more previous events indicate
      high risk)
    Record presence or absence of above (if present, obtain details of method,
      place, motivation)
  After admission
    Watch for suspect behavior
      Refusing food, medication
      Saving medication
      Asking about suicidal methods
      Talking of death, futility

Giving away possessions
Checking locks, windows, layout of the ward
Loosening bolts, tearing sheets into strips
Watch for suspect mood
Hopelessness, helplessness, worthlessness
Depression with agitation, restlessness
Depression with apathy, withdrawal
Unrelieved anxiety
Excessive guilt and self-blame
Severe frustration
Bitter anger
Observe personality characteristics
Severe personal disorganization
Dependent-satisfied behavior
Dependent-dissatisfied behavior
Diagnosis of schizophrenia
Recent object loss
Negative feelings about hospital
Feeling of no future
B. Safeguards
Environmental
Install safety glass in windows
Restrict window openings with stops
Block off stairwells, access to roof
Use breakaway shower curtain rods, breakaway clothes hooks in bathrooms
and clothes lockers
Cover exposed pipes
Avoid grilles over ventilators, porch screens, and railings
Procedural
Remove from vicinity of suicidal patients all articles easily used in self-harm,
such as belt, suspenders, bathrobe cord, light cords, shoe laces, glass,
ashtrays, vases, razor, pocketknife, nail file, nail clippers
Be alert when suicidal patients are using sharp objects, such as scissors,
needles, pins, bottle opener, can opener, dining room utensils, occupa-
tional therapy tools
Be alert when suicidal patients are using the bathroom (to prevent hanging,
jumping, cutting)
Be alert when giving suicidal patients medication (patients may save or
discard medicine)
Observe acutely suicidal patients on a one-to-one basis
Check suicidal patients at least every 15 minutes at night
Be alert to whereabouts of suicidal patients during shift changes

Room suicidal patients with others close to nurses' station; do not room
  alone if avoidable

Warn visitors about bringing or leaving anything with lethal potential

Apprise off-ward escort of suicide concern

Keep suicidal patient in middle of escorted group; examine anything patient
  picks up

Define staff responsibility thoroughly

Ensure continuous availability of help

C. Communication

Document records completely to show that:

  Risk is recognized and evaluated

  Reasonable measures are ordered

  Orders are followed (if not, indicate why not)

Ensure that all staff record pertinent observations

Write orders specifically to show:

  Plan and rationale

  Specific restrictions

  Specific staff responsible for observation or escort

  Specific frequency of night observation

Obtain frequent consultation

D. Attitudes

Avoid preoccupation and fear

Avoid harsh, repressive measures

Use positive interest and build mutual trust

Restore and strengthen hope

Rebuilt self-esteem to overcome helplessness

Accept the reality that mistakes occur; aim for minimum

REFERENCES

Benensohn, H. S., and Resnik, H. L. P. (1973). Guidelines for "suicide-proofing" a
  psychiatric unit. *American Journal of Psychotherapy* 27:204–212.

Cooper, T. R. (1975). Medical treatment facility liability for patient suicide and other
  self-injury. *Journal of Legal Medicine* 3:20–25, 28–29.

Farberow, N. L., Ganzler, S., and Cutter, F. (1971). An eight-year survey of hospital
  suicides. *Life-Threatening Behavior*, vol. 1, 184–202.

Farberow, N. L., and MacKinnon, D. R. (1974). *Follow-Up of High-Risk Neuropsychiatric
  Patients*. Washington, D.C.: Veterans Administration.

Farberow, N. L., Shneidman, E. S., and Leonard, C. V. (1963). *Suicide among General
  Medical and Surgical Hospital Patients with Malignant Neoplasms*. Washington, DC:
  Veterans Administration.

Farberow, N. L., Shneidman, E. S., and Neuringer, C. (1966). Case history and hospitalization factors in suicides of neuropsychiatric hospital patients. *Journal of Nervous and Mental Disease* 132:32–44.

Farberow, N. L., and Williams, J. L. (1978). *Status of Suicide in Veterans Administration Hospitals: Report IV*. Washington, DC: Veterans Administration.

Miller, D. H. (1970). Suicidal careers: case analysis of suicidal mental patients. *Social Work*, 15:27–36.

Perr, I. N. (1965). Liability of hospital and psychiatrist in suicide. *American Journal of Psychiatry* 122:631–638.

Reynolds, D. K., and Farberow, N. L. (1976). *Suicide Inside and Out*. Berkeley: University of California Press.

Sletten, I. W., Brown, M. I., and Evenson, R. C. (1972). Suicide in mental hospital patients. *Diseases of the Nervous System* 33:328–334.

8

MANAGEMENT OF SUICIDAL PATIENTS IN MEDICAL PRACTICE

Robert E. Litman

AT PRESENT, AS IN the past, persons suffering from depression and anxiety consult their primary care physicians, and for the most part are treated as office patients by primary care practitioners (Eisenberg 1992). Surveys, for instance those described by Barrett and colleagues (1988) indicate that 15 percent to 25 percent of the patients in primary care practice suffer from diagnosable psychiatric disorders. This fact of life creates numerous problems, and also numerous opportunities.

One opportunity is the potential for suicide prevention. Research on suicide (Robins 1981) reveals that approximately 75 percent of persons who committed suicide had seen a physician within the 6-month period before the death. The great majority of the suicide deaths (approximately 35,000 a year in the United States, median age 40 years) occurred in young and middle age persons with great potentialities and responsibilities. Usually the families, physicians, and the community felt these suicides were unnecessary, unreasonable, and uniquely tragic. How could they be explained?

In medical practice, suicide is best understood as the final stage of a progressive breakdown of adaptational behavior occurring in an emotionally exhausted patient. Rough analogies may be drawn to states of physiological collapse; for example, in heat stroke or in untreated adrenal insufficiency. In these examples there is a progressive failure of physiological adjustment with the appearance of premonitory symptoms and signs leading to a potentially fatal crisis. Thoughts of suicide, suicide attempts, and numerous kinds of suicidal communications are part of the prodromal symptomatology of suicidal crises.

Emotional crises occur from time to time in all lives when people face problems that are temporarily beyond their ability to solve. Situations that threaten the continuity of mental, physical, and social equilibrium are powerful stressors. Confrontation with death, ill health, loss of love, or change in social status are typical examples. The person under stress feels restless, uneasy, painfully tense, and unable to adapt.

PRODROMAL SUICIDAL CLUES

There is a wide range of prodromal clues:

Verbal Communications

In more than half of the suicide deaths, there is a history of previous, spontaneous, suicidal communications. These statements are direct: "I am going to shoot myself." "I wish I were dead." Or they are indirect: "You would be better off without me." "How do you leave your body to the medical school?" Sometimes such comments are made directly to a physician, but more often the physician receives the information from concerned friends and relatives who want advice on how to respond to these messages. The most significant interpretation of suicidal communications is that they represent cries for help. As such, they tend to activate intense emotional responses in persons receiving the communications. More often than not the suicidal situation involves several people.

It should be added that many suicidal patients do not express their self-destructive thoughts spontaneously but will do so if they are asked.

Suicide Attempts

In one-third of the suicide deaths, there is a history of previous suicide attempts. These are intentional self-injuries made in an emotional context resembling suicide. Surveys indicate that physicians in California see ten to fifteen suicide attempts for every suicide. Approximately 20 percent of those who attempt suicide repeat action of this type at least once. About 5 to 10 percent of the attempters eventually kill themselves.

Considering the sizable mortality rate, physicians who treat surgical and medical self-injuries should ask about obvious sources of emotional stress as soon as possible after the self-injury. For a limited time the shock of the suicide attempt causes families and individuals to report truthfully about vital conflicts and embarrassing problems that ordinarily are hidden or distorted by half truths. The uninterested, preoccupied, or timid physician loses a golden opportunity to bring concealed problems out into the open where they can be dealt with more effectively.

Symptomatic Actions

Some suicidal persons communicate their plans by actions. One man bought two caskets, one for his wife who had just died. A student gave away his sports equipment, saying, "I won't need this any more." In struggling against suicidal feelings, some take daredevil chances, and they may have a series of accidents or near misses. Increased alcohol intake and irregular attendance at work are common. Requests for increasing amounts of strong sedatives and rapid-acting sleep producers are ominous premonitory clues to suicide.

Depression

This syndrome is of major importance to physicians because of its frequency, serious disability, danger to life—and good response to treatment. Suicide should be considered as a possibility whenever depressive symptoms are reported. The symptoms are physiological, psychological, and social. In all areas the ability to enjoy is lost or seriously disrupted.

Physiological symptoms include sleep disorder, especially sleeplessness; appetite disorder, especially loss of appetite; constipation, dry mouth, headaches, other aches and pains; and fatigue. The psychological symptoms include loss of energy, loss of initiative, absence of interest in usual pleasures, such as sex, sports, books, and television. The mood is sad and often guilty, with low self-esteem. Patients tend to feel hopeless and helpless. These emotions are experienced as painful and uncomfortable.

Social withdrawal completes the picture. The patient loses interest in social gatherings and other people, although he may attempt at times to feign interest. Often physicians or families suggest a vacation. The realization by the patient that he is unable to enjoy a vacation may be the last straw that precipitates a suicidal crisis.

The depressive syndrome tends to have a discrete onset and a limited duration. Older patients usually have had previous depressive episodes. A family history of depression is common.

Treatment Failures

In medical practice, suicidal crises tend to be associated with treatment failures. For example, Workman's Compensation has paid a number of death claims on workers who remained disabled after treatment for back injury, then killed themselves. Suicide reports often allude to vague abdominal pains or causalgias, persisting after numerous surgical operations. Diseases that impair respiration— for example, emphysema or lymphoma of the neck and mediastinum—are more often associated with suicide than other chronic illnesses.

Excessive Reactions

Some attention should be directed toward patients who have an excessive emotional preoccupation with some specific condition, such as pregnancy, obesity, or cancer. Even if the patient does not have the particular condition, the negative results of medical examinations should be carefully and repeatedly explained to such patients. It is particularly ironic when a suicide note gives "cancer" as the reason for the act but the autopsy shows no signs of the disease. In suicide histories dread of heart attacks occurs more commonly than actual coronary occlusions.

Panic Reactions

About 5 percent of suicides result from sudden blind panic. Examples: A school teacher charged with child molestation dived, in handcuffs, under the wheels of a passing truck. An older man, confused and frightened in an unfamiliar hospital room, jumped out of the window. After an automobile accident, while rescuers attended his badly hurt wife, the uninjured husband wandered off and hanged himself.

EVALUATION OF SUICIDAL POTENTIALITY

Persons who are considering suicide as a potential solution to life crises seek out physicians, hoping for answers less extreme than suicide. Although 75 percent of suicides had seen a physician within 6 months of the death, unfortunately, patients do not ordinarily reveal spontaneously that they are in suicidal crises. This information emerges readily, however, if the physician asks for it, especially if there is a preexisting patient–physician relationship of confidence and trust. When he notes prodromal clues to suicide, the physician must decide how to proceed.

Usually, the most tactful and informative technique is to approach the suicidal motivation gradually through a series of questions, working from the more general to the most specific. Such a series of questions might proceed in this manner: "How is your life going? How are you feeling in general? How are your spirits—your mental outlook—your hopes?" If the answers indicate low spirits or pessimistic attitudes or much tension or confusion, another series of questions might follow: "Do you wish you could be out of it? Would you like sometimes to give up? Ever wish you were dead?"

If the answers to the above are suggestively affirmative, then the physician might pose a third series of questions: "Have you thought of ending your life? How close are you now to suicide? How would you do it? What is your plan?"

Suicide Plan

The most important, single element in evaluating the immediate suicide emergency is the patient's suicide plan, including the proposed method, place, and time. If the patient has decided upon a specific, highly lethal method of suicide with an instrument that is readily available to him, there is a serious emergency. Usually, patients will talk to an interested physician about the details of their suicide plans, although sometimes this information is obtained from friends or relatives. We take it seriously when a patient sets a deadline for his action; for instance, his fiftieth birthday, retirement day, or an anniversary. Vague suicide plans are somewhat reassuring, as are plans to use methods of relatively low lethality, such as aspirin ingestion.

Direct denials are usually truthful and can be relied on, at least temporarily. "Yes, I thought of suicide, but I would never do it because of my children." "For me, suicide is impossible because of my religion." "I would leave town first." The exceptions to this rule—that is, patients who dissemble to friendly physicians—are nearly always obvious psychiatric cases, usually with a history of psychiatric hospitalization.

Physicians who hesitate to ask such direct questions about suicide because of possible harmful effects on patients should be reassured by the experience of the staff of the Suicide Prevention Center in Los Angeles. In interviews with ten thousand suicidal patients and reviews of three thousand suicide deaths, we found no evidence that such questions had ever harmed patients.

Severity of Symptoms

Danger signals include: severe agitation with depression; helplessness, combined with a frantic need to do something; hopelessness that gets worse in response to helping efforts from others; confusion; paranoid trends with persecution delusions or homicidal threats. Five percent of suicidal patients are also potentially homicidal.

Basic Personality

Suicidal crises vary in emergency force, according to the patient's character. Persons who have led stable, responsible lives generally respond well to treatment and return to their previous levels. Because of the favorable prognosis, such persons should be the objects of extremely zealous suicide prevention efforts. At present about half of the persons who kill themselves are of that order. Sometimes high social position, public prominence, or professional success is a barrier between patients and the help they need. Examples are physicians, military leaders, and political figures. (Many lives would be saved if persons in crises could accept help without stigma.)

By contrast, many unstable, immature, addictive, alcoholic, and deviant persons are chronically on the edge of self-destruction. These patients benefit less from emergency first aid. They need consistent firm direction and long-range rehabilitation.

Precipitating Stress

If the suicidal crisis is a reaction to an overwhelming, sudden stress, the patient needs emergency protection and support but may recover rapidly and spontaneously. This is analogous to heat stroke collapse. If the suicidal crisis represents an internal decompensation with no special external stress, the patient may need special study and special treatment, presumably by a psychiatrist. This is analogous to a physiological crisis due to adrenal cortical insufficiency.

Resources

These include physical, financial, and interpersonal assets. The willingness and ability of other persons to aid the patient often makes the difference between life and death. Some patients are emotionally bankrupt, and this must be taken into account. For example, many alcoholics, after years of self-destructive behavior that has alienated family and friends, hit bottom and are highly suicidal.

Special Indicators

These include such factors as family history of suicide, recent suicide of a close friend or relative, anniversary of a divorce or of a death in the family, complete social isolation, history of psychiatric treatment, especially recent discharge from a mental hospital, and recent suicide attempt, unrecognized or untreated.

MANAGEMENT OF SUICIDAL PATIENTS

The physician is not expected to function as a psychiatrist or skilled psychotherapist. In his practice, however, he should always maintain a *medical attitude*. This means that the physician helps whenever possible and does nothing to make matters worse. Sometimes self-destructive patients are uncooperative, provocative, and hostile. Such behavior makes the physician's task more difficult, but should be regarded as symptomatic and not taken personally. The average primary care physician will encounter half a dozen potentially suicidal patients a year and have ten to twelve suicides in his practice during a long career. Suicide prevention is not his daily preoccupation but rather an occasional opportunity. The management of suicidal crisis includes emergency medical and psychological support, plus consultation and referral in appropriate cases, and a special effort to keep in touch with patients while they are still suicidal.

Emergency Medical Care

Suicide patients require extra time, not only for examination but for management and follow-up care. Some suicidal depressions are precipitated by drugs, such as reserpine and occasionally antibiotics, or by withdrawal from sedatives or alcohol. Sometimes virus infections, nutritional deficiencies, or hormonal disturbances are important factors. Often changes in previous medical treatment plans are indicated.

It takes extra time to reassure the anxious patient or explain to the suspicious. Some physicians wisely schedule emotionally disturbed patients at the end of consultation hours, so that extra time is available if needed. If a patient requires excessive time in the office or makes repeated emergency nighttime telephone calls, it may well be a signal to transfer the patient to a psychiatrist or to put him in a hospital.

Use of Drugs

Drugs are an essential part of the medical management of suicidal patients. For sleepless patients the rapid-acting benzodiazepines and other strong hypnotics are wonder drugs. They give an exhausted patient a chance to rest and recover. But these drugs are being misused. Prescriptions should not be dispensed or refilled casually. Repeated requests for hypnotics by a patient should warn the physician to review the case and possibly get consultation.

Tranquilizers and antidepressant drugs are used freely in our clinic. I dispense tablets and psychotherapy simultaneously. I tell patients, "The drug industry spent a fortune developing these pills for you and millions of other patients like you." Side effects, such as dry mouth, are predicted, and the patient is instructed to call me daily or every other day to report. This facilitates our communication and provides for follow-up. Usually the patient gets better. If he feels worse on medication, I think seriously of getting him into a hospital.

Emergency Psychological Support

Because of his position of trust and authority, the physician is ideally suited to give emergency psychological first aid. This includes: (1) establishing communication with the patient; (2) reminding him of his identity; (3) involving family and friends; and (4) stimulating him toward constructive action.

Suicidal patients are, by the nature of their response to their difficulties, isolated and alienated from other people who could help them. They feel "different," changed for the worse, worthless. By taking the time to talk with him, the physician helps the patient to reestablish communication with the rest of the world. Psychological support is transmitted by a firm and hopeful attitude. Although the physician recognizes sympathetically that to the patient his problem is overwhelming and insoluble, at the same time he indicates that he has seen many other patients in similar crises who eventually recovered completely. Hope is a powerful medicine that should never be withheld.

The process of taking a medical history is in itself therapeutic. In reviewing his history, the patient is reminded of what he was in the past and who he is now—husband, worker, father, and the like. Thus he recreates his sense of personal continuity and identity. In answering questions about his present problems, the patient widens his view of the world, alternative possibilities can be explored, and additional solutions are suggested. If the physician can help the patient break his overwhelming, giant-size problem down into several smaller, clearly stated, and logically organized, human-size problems, it helps him overcome his panic and confusion.

The Use of Family and Friends

One of the key problems in suicide prevention is the appropriate use of families and friends. It is suggested that whenever possible the family physician talk to the relatives or friends of the patient who is in a suicidal crisis, especially if it is evaluated as an emergency. If the significant others have not appreciated the seriousness of the situation, they should be so advised. Often during an emergency there should be someone with the suicidal person at all times until the crisis is passed. An interview with the closest other person gives the physician a chance to decide whether that person can be supportive or whether he is, in fact, dangerous to the suicidal person because of carelessness, indifference, or hostility. Some of the decisions made about suicidal persons are family decisions; for example, the decision to put them in a hospital. Sometimes patients say, "My husband isn't interested" or "My wife doesn't care to bother," but a telephone call will usually reveal that relatives are concerned and cooperative. One interesting point is that where there is one suicidal patient in a family, there is often another person who is near suicide.

Constructive Action

Suicidal patients are often overwhelmed by feelings of failure, paralysis, and immobility, relieved in some by sudden impulsive spasms of action. Often the self-injury is a desperate attempt to regain the ability to initiate acts. Wherever possible, the physician should direct the patient toward planned and organized actions of a limited scope, which the patient can be expected to negotiate with a degree of success—for example, going to the physician's office for consultations and tests and making telephone reports to the physician at a certain time of the day. The patient might be asked to call a certain friend or take a simple psychological test. Persons who are recovering from suicidal states should be cautioned against prematurely resuming positions of great responsibility in which initiative is required. More routine and limited tasks have a great therapeutic value, in that they take attention away from the patient's self-preoccupation, and tend to create a feeling of confidence when they are successfully completed.

Consultation and Referral

Whenever possible, the physician should share some of the responsibility for the management of suicidal patients by discussing the situation with a colleague, associate, or consultant. The most serious suicidal crises are best treated in a hospital, preferably psychiatric. The decision for psychiatric hospitalization of a suicidal patient is a full-fledged medical emergency, since many suicides occur in persons who have had a recent recommendation of hospitalization but have not followed the recommendation. In hospitals, the same principles of suicide prevention apply. Physicians should pay attention to nurses' notes and patients' communications as possible clues to suicide.

In most patients, however, suicidal potentiality is less immediately critical, and outpatient treatment can be considered. If the patient has a long-standing, chronic personality disorder, or if his behavior has been obviously psychotic or has indicated severe emotional disturbance, or he continues to be suicidal for several weeks, a consultation with a specialist in the field of emotional problems is recommended. Most often this would be a psychiatrist, but clinical psychologists and psychiatric social workers are helpful in certain types of cases. Community agencies, such as social work and family service agencies, are very useful for assistance with reality problems such as finances, jobs, supportive care, and home visits. Mental hygiene clinics or community-supported mental health centers are available in some places. In areas in which there are no community or private agencies for care and in which there may be no psychotherapists in private practice readily available, the physician will find the public health and mental health officer of the region able to offer assistance and advice.

REFERENCES

Barrett, J. E., Barrett, J. A., Oxman, T. E., and Gerber, P. D. (1988). The prevalence of psychiatric disorders in a primary care practice. *Archives of General Psychiatry* 45:1100–1106.

Eisenberg, L. (1992). Treating depression and anxiety in primary care. *New England Journal of Medicine* 326(16):1080–1084.

Robins, E. (1981). *The Final Months: a Study of the Lives of 134 Persons Who Committed Suicide*. New York: Oxford University Press.

III

CONCOMITANTS AND AFTERMATH

9

IMMOBILIZATION RESPONSE TO SUICIDAL BEHAVIOR

Robert E. Litman

CERTAIN ASPECTS OF self-destructive behavior can be understood as an appeal for help in an intolerable situation made to one or more potential rescuers. The response of the person who receives such a communication can mean the difference between life and death. When the response is inadequate, what are the reasons?

Ordinarily suicide threats or attempts have a powerful social effect, tending automatically to induce or "release" rescuing activity from the environment. Indeed, much of the rationale of a suicide prevention center is provided by observations indicating that potentially self-destructive persons are ambivalent about death. They communicate their suicidal preoccupation, making it possible for others to give aid.

In a classic study of suicide in St. Louis, Robins (1981) found that suicidal communications were made by more than two-thirds of the deceased. The persons receiving the communications became anxious, tense, and concerned. Generally they felt helpless to act, especially since professionals offered little or no guidance. According to Robins, failure to act resulted primarily from ignorance of what to do.

The focus of this investigation are those unfortunate cases in which a suicidal communication is made to someone in a close interpersonal relationship with the suicidal individual. The tragedy is that the suicidal communication is perceived but conscious recognition of its significance is avoided, denied, or repressed. Possible solutions to the problem remain unconscious. The potential rescuer is immobilized. Such situations are common in suicide prevention center experience. These four cases were chosen for this report because in each a dream of the immobilized potential rescuer provided psychoanalytic understanding of the dilemma.

After an unhappy childhood, followed by 10 years of a disappointing and childless marriage, Mary A. met John B., a shy, introverted graduate student who was 7 years younger than she. Mary divorced her unloved first husband to marry Mr. B., who disentangled himself from his mother's apron strings to become attached to his wife. In order to make the change he had about a year of psychotherapy. Mary worked in a lab while he studied for his doctoral degree.

After several years, the balance of their quiet lives was decisively disturbed by two events. First, Mary became pregnant. Mr. B. reacted with withdrawal, confusion, anxiety, and impotence. The pregnancy terminated with a spontaneous miscarriage, but Mr. B.'s potency did not return. They never discussed this problem. Apparently each felt the other should talk about it first.

Secondly, Mr. B. received his degree and got a well-paying job, and Mary quit work. She then became aware of extreme nervous tension and the development of phobias. She was afraid to drive her car alone. She demanded more and more special attention from Mr. B. Both partners in the marriage were depressed but did not discuss it with each other. Mary consulted an internist for a series of diagnostic medical examinations, and insisted that Mr. B. accompany her to the office each time. This precipitated several quarrels. During one of these Mr. B. committed suicide by hanging. Two weeks before Mr. B.'s death, Mary had the following dream:

I walked out onto a high balcony and was horrified to see that John had fallen over the balcony railing and was dangling. He was holding onto the leash of our dog, Prince. The leash was tight around the dog's neck and was choking the dog. I stood paralyzed, not knowing what to do. If I did not act, the dog would be choked to death; if I cut the leash, John would fall and be killed on the pavement below. I woke up terrified and choking.

In the morning, Mary told this dream to her husband with the interpretation that she made herself. "I felt that I was the dog being choked by our marriage, but I couldn't end the marriage because it would kill you, John."

Mr. B. made no comment and the dream was forgotten. When she discovered Mr. B.'s suicide, Mary was at first astonished and incredulous. A full day passed by before she suddenly recalled this dream, and with the recollection came the knowledge that she had recognized her husband's suicidal state and by her subsequent actions was guilty of his death. She then made a suicide attempt with barbiturates and, following that, was brought for psychiatric treatment.

At the time of the dream, Mary knew that the marriage was collapsing and had considered the possibility of going back to work. John, she could see, vacillated between moods of humble ingratiation, with efforts to please her, and moods of withdrawal and depression. He talked about death several times. She took it to be in connection with the death of a friend. In the dream, she opens the door and walks out on the balcony of a high building. She associates to the doctor's office where she took a thyroid test. The doctor is a man she can depend on and lean on. She recalls her pregnancy and miscarriage. John liked to take the dog for a walk. Sometimes he said he lived a dog's life. He brought her slippers to her and lit her cigarette, but she could not depend on him to be a man. "I just didn't feel I could be a mother to him any more, the way I used to be. I was worn out, having a nervous breakdown myself." (The dog?) She had always wanted a dog and as soon as she could she got a big dog, a Labrador retriever. "This dog is very sensitive to my moods and very close to me." There were many associations as to how the dog can sense what she is feeling.

The dream resembles those of a traumatic neurosis. The problem is represented clearly, and the dream ends with paralysis, immobilization, and unmastered anxiety. The approaching dissolution of her marriage is felt as an overwhelming trauma and is associated with the miscarriage and previous traumatic separations from her pets and her mother. The symbolism of the leash as it appears in this dream recalls the umbilical cord. The dreamer identifies herself with the baby–mother symbiosis and she cannot cut the cord.

Mary might have saved her husband (and herself) after the dream by seeking out professional help. The dream hints at that solution in the associations to the doctor's office and her attempts to bring her husband with her to the doctor's office. Two main problems interfered with her unconscious efforts to alert the doctor and get his help for her husband. First was the absence of verbal communication between husband and wife. They were incapable of discussing feelings; their mutual sensitivity was limited to nonverbal exchange—like that between master and dog, mother and baby, and thus was extremely susceptible to repression. As we unearthed, in diaries and from friends, additional evidence of Mr. B.'s preoccupation with death, Mary was continually surprised. Secondly, an action to resolve the symbiotic relationship (symbolized by cutting the leash) was specifically traumatic to Mary, overwhelming her efforts at ego mastery. Instead of calling in a third party to cut the cord, she was compelled helplessly to maintain the symbiosis.

Mrs. C. and Mrs. D. had grown to be close friends while both were patients on a small psychiatric ward that specialized in milieu therapy. Mrs. D. committed suicide with her husband's pistol while on a trial leave of absence from the hospital. Mrs. C. had been discharged several weeks before, but continued coming to the hospital for day care activities. During this interim period, about a week before the suicide, she reported the following dream to her therapist.

> Mrs. D. tied me to a tree trunk with a rope and danced around. She piled branches around me and set them on fire. Then she was tangled in the rope, too, and we were caught. I was helpless and frightened.

Associations: Mrs. D. is much younger than Mrs. C. and reminds her of her daughter, who is a dancer. Once when they were young, this daughter tied her sister to a tree with a rope. Mrs. D. at times thinks she killed her baby. Some of the patients say she really did. Mrs. C. adds that she and Mrs. D. have been very close in the hospital. Right now Mrs. C. feels that the two of them will never get well. The fire reminds her that when she used to take barbiturates to a state of coma, she set the bed on fire. After a long silence she confesses that she and Mrs. D. have discussed ways to commit suicide, for instance, running out in front of a car or taking barbiturates or by hanging. Mrs. D. says that these are all female ways of killing oneself and like everything female it is ineffective. The men do it better. The rope reminds Mrs. C. of sex. She thinks of homosexuality. Mrs. C. feels that she is more feminine than Mrs. D. More silence, then she asks anxiously if she should warn the doctor that Mrs. D. will kill herself.

Here again we see the close connection symbolized by the rope. There is also the anxious immobility and the difficulty in communication (secrecy from the therapist). Mrs. C. knows unconsciously that Mrs. D. is in danger, but she is unable to mobilize her own ego sufficiently to recognize the danger consciously and warn the therapist directly. Instead, she places herself in the situation of danger in the dream and is helpless.

On the advice of her doctor, Mrs. E. called the Suicide Prevention Center regarding her husband. She said they were a successful television writing team. In the last year they had been having bad luck and some financial reverses, but the main trouble was a steadily increasing depressive attitude on the part of the husband. For several months he had been unable to work, was constantly on sleeping pills, and was almost bedridden. He had talked repeatedly of death and suicide. She reported the following:

> Last night I had a horrible dream. I guess that is why I decided to call you today. I dreamed that I or my husband was dead, or both of us were dead, by hanging. I was so confused—I couldn't tell which of us was which, or which of us was dead, and who had killed us, or had we killed each other.

The telephone interview revealed that she, too, had become depressed and felt helpless to contend with her problems. I suggested emergency hospitalization for the husband. She rejected it, giving many reasons. She denied the seriousness of the situation and expressed anxiety about making any decisive moves. The earliest appointment she would accept was for the next day at 1:00 P.M. The next morning she took the car to be washed and serviced and while she was gone, her husband ingested an overdose of pills and was dying when she returned.

On learning this, I went immediately to the home of Mrs. E. and found her profoundly depressed and suicidal. Her feelings were a mixture of guilt, anger, perplexity, and confusion. She was obsessed with the thought, "If I hadn't told him we were going to see a psychiatrist, maybe he would not have done this."

I was impressed by the strong identification with her husband, the intense mutual dependency, and the unwillingness to accept any type of interruption in the relationship.

The situation and dream are in some ways similar to the first three with, however, a happier outcome. The dreamer is a psychiatrist in psychoanalysis. He dreams:

> I am in my office; the lighting is dim and it seems smoggy. I am waiting for my patient Mrs. F., who is late. I try to make a phone call but I cannot. There is much anxiety. I wake up coughing.

The smoggy office reminds him that he feels tired and sick today; maybe he is catching cold. He would like to leave Los Angeles. Mrs. F. seldom comes late. Lately she has been quite uncommunicative. Her resistance takes the form of sitting silently for minutes on end and looking at him expectantly. He has interpreted the hostility with no effect. Once, years ago, she made a suicide attempt. Suicide! He had not realized he was concerned that she might attempt suicide. But only last week she talked longingly of death. He decides Mrs. F. is quite depressed. The phone call would be to Mrs. F. or maybe the doctor's analyst.

Note the traumatic quality of the dream, ending in anxious immobilization. The telephone, which links the doctor with his patient and his analyst, symbolizes the leash, the umbilical cord. The dream eloquently represents the block in verbal communication. Something in the relationship with Mrs. F. is activating in the doctor a regressed traumatic situation that he can verbalize only with difficulty. He realizes that he has been hoping that Mrs. F. would spontaneously recover and make the first move toward reconciliation. He decides to discuss the case with a third person (a consultant).

The above case reports illuminate some aspects of crises precipitated by the breakdown of neurotic symbiotic unions between adults. These are interpersonal relationships in which regressive elements predominate. There is a great deal of mutual identification; psychic representations of self and object are frequently fused. The other person is experienced as essential to survival, and a separation or divergence from the other is equated with death or disaster to both. It is as if there were an umbilical cord uniting the partners. In dreams, this may be symbolized by a leash, cord, rope, or telephone. To cut this umbilical connection is felt as dangerous and extremely traumatic. Both of the partners are immobilized under conditions of great tension and discomfort. Communication of feelings between the partners is primarily by action and gesture rather than words. "He knows what I'm thinking without my saying it."

Both partners wait for some action from the other to resolve the painful stalemate. Danger signals are exchanged but not acknowledged as such. The eventual breakthrough into action tends to be explosive and quite destructive especially when the content of the unacknowledged communications included references to suicide.

An analysis of the routes by which couples drift or are propelled into this crisis pattern is beyond the scope of this chapter. Nor is it appropriate here to discuss the treatment. In general, persons involved in a symbiotic race toward suicide respond well to emergency psychotherapy. The exhaustion of the stronger partner is the final signal for emergency intervention by a rescuing third person—friend, therapist, or consultant.

REFERENCE

Robins, E. (1981). *The Final Months: A Study of the Lives of 134 Persons Who Committed Suicide*. New York: Oxford University Press.

10

WHEN PATIENTS COMMIT SUICIDE

Robert E. Litman

MENTAL HEALTH professionals should be prepared to encounter the suicidal death of a patient sooner or later, often as early as in their training years. In a survey of suicide in San Diego, Rich and colleagues (1986) found that approximately 25 percent of the decedents were in treatment at the time of death. Chemtob and his colleagues (1988) surveyed a sample of psychiatrists and found that about half of them had encountered suicide in their practice during the previous 10 years. Moreover, the majority stated that it had been a most traumatic experience.

Considered abstractly, for instance in an educational seminar, the suicide of one's own patient strikes most psychotherapists as an unfortunate event to be averted if at all possible. On the other hand, therapists know that anxiety about the possibility of suicide could seriously impair the therapist's effectiveness in the long run. A number of philosophic notions have been advanced to make it possible for therapists to consider the idea of patients' suicides with greater equanimity. Some are legalistic: "In a free society, a person must have the right to injure or kill himself." Others are strategies that claim pragmatic success. One system of psychotherapy demands that the practitioner maintain rigid nondirectiveness and nonresponsibility. Another recommends that he communicate his indifference to the patient's possible death. As an extreme example, one therapist stated that the essence of his therapy is the quasireligious death and rebirth of the patient's soul. "If the soul insists on organic death through suicide, cannot this be considered an unavoidable necessity, a summons from God?" (Hillman 1964). In this schema, the psychotherapist has neither responsibility nor motivation toward suicide prevention.

In summary, most therapists regard suicidal potentiality as a disturbing element, complicating and sometimes restricting the therapeutic process, and requiring special care and consultation. Some theories of psychotherapy contend that the practitioner has no responsibility for the suicide of a patient and should feel no concern or anxiety about it. A small minority of psychotherapists speculate that at times suicide is a justifiable or desirable goal of therapy.

The attitudes of psychotherapists toward the deaths of patients were not in themselves the direct objectives of a systematic research program on my part. Rather, these observations about therapists are by-products of various clinical and research experiences. As the chief psychiatrist of the Suicide Prevention Center I was often sought out by therapists wishing to discuss suicide incidents. These informal discussions proved to be an important source of data for this inquiry. I also looked to previous studies that focused on the communication of suicidal intentions. These communications contain many clues to the attitudes of therapists receiving them. Finally, I returned to the investigations of several thousand suicides that my colleagues and I undertook in collaboration with the Chief Medical Examiner and Coroner of Los Angeles County. The primary objectives of these investigations were to ascertain who commits suicide and under what circumstances. The method used was to interview the survivors of the individual, not only his relatives, but also his friends, employers, physicians, and especially, when available, psychotherapists, in order to reconstruct the life situation and attitudes of the deceased as part of a "psychological autopsy." The observations reported here are derived from interviews with more than 400 psychotherapists. Each was questioned shortly after a patient committed suicide.

There are barriers to communication about such an event. The question "How do you feel about the death of your patient?" breaks taboos and intrudes into highly personal reactions. The inquiry can provoke anxiety in both the therapist informant and the investigator. Naturally, the answers given vary greatly in candor and completeness.

A majority of therapists were interested and cooperative. Some welcomed an opportunity to review the suicide. Others, guarded and uncommunicative, stated, "I can't discuss it without written permission from the family." Initially, some practitioners were casual or flippant, others superscientific: "You can't do anything about suicide, why worry?" Or, "What's the correlation between suicide and hostility?" A patient and persistent interviewer could almost always obtain cooperation and elicit many of the therapists' attitudes and reactions. Among a number of questions, the interviewer asked the following: "Is there anything you would have done differently?" "What can we learn from this?" "What effect did it have on you?"

According to my observations, therapists react to the death of a patient personally, as human beings, in much the same way as do other people. They react, secondly, in accordance with their special role in society. Their theoretical, philosophic, and scientific attitudes serve a defensive and reparative function, being used to overcome the pain they feel as human beings and as therapists.

The personal reactions depend, of course, on how the therapist viewed his patient, how long and how closely they worked together, and the degree of his professional commitment to the other. This commitment can vary from nonexistent to total. As an example of the former, a therapist refused to accept a referral when he realized that the patient was possibly suicidal. Later, when that patient committed suicide while seeing another therapist, the first therapist felt relieved and even elated over his decision. As an example of great commitment, one practitioner virtually adopted an intelligent and beautiful young woman, one of his psychology students, and when she committed suicide while in psychotherapy with him, he went through weeks of deep mourning and grief.

In recalling how they felt about the suicide of a patient, therapists have said that the first experience of this nature was the worst. One hears expressions such as "I could hardly believe it." "I was completely crushed." "It shook my confidence in what I thought I knew."

A number of younger therapists identified in themselves a strong emotional reaction after the death of an older patient who reminded them of a dead parent. Therapists who had struggled for a long period of time to help a patient overcome chronic suicidal tendencies often reacted to his death as a personal defeat, and experienced a period of hopelessness and depression. Therapists who had worked in partnership with another human being in intensive psychotherapy as a mutual relationship noted, in their own dreams or symptomatic actions, partial identifications with the deceased. For instance, a number of therapists reported having accidents in the week or two after the death of a patient by suicide.

As human beings, therapists felt a special sort of guilt that was the exact replica of a type of guilt experienced by relatives of persons who have committed suicide. This guilt took the form of self-questioning: "Did I listen to him?" "Did I try hard enough to understand him?" "Was there something in me that didn't want to hear what he was saying?" At the professional level, too, the same questions arose but with less painful guilt and more of a sense of inadequacy, taking the form of obsessive thoughts. "How did I miss it?" "If only I had done something differently."

On a personal level, painful feelings were handled in several ways. Unlike families and relatives, therapists seldom mentioned religious attitudes as a consolation, but sometimes they would say, "Maybe it's just as well that he is dead. He suffered a great deal." Personal gestures were felt to be important. "I spent several hours with the bereaved spouse trying to help her with her feelings." In some instances, the therapist attended the funeral.

Some therapists were extremely angry at someone, usually the patient's spouse, occasionally a medical colleague or psychiatric supervisor, whom they held responsible for the death. Anger at the dead patient, expressed indirectly or by inference, was common. Overtly hostile statements about the deceased were rare.

First and foremost, the psychological mechanisms that were universal in survivor relatives and in therapists were denial and repression. Therapists manifested denial in many ways. Often they questioned whether the death was a suicide. "Are you sure it wasn't a heart attack?" They forgot details of the history, or they unconsciously omitted or distorted relevant features of the case. A psychiatrist, who admitted to newspaper reporters that he had prescribed the sleeping pills with which a patient committed suicide had, in fact, not prescribed the pills. They had been obtained from other physicians.

The reactions of therapists as therapists emphasized fears concerning blame, responsibility, and inadequacy. These feelings were especially prominent if the deceased was a person of high social status or potentially great social value, such as a successful professional man, a young mother, or a college student. Therapists expressed fears of being sued, of being vilified in the press, of being investigated, and of losing professional standing. They were afraid that others among their patients would be adversely affected by the news, or ask embarrassing questions, or that there might be reproaches from the relatives. Sometimes therapists felt marked and exposed.

In these circumstances, a supportive consultation with another professional person often proved to be of great psychologic benefit. A helpful maneuver, in trying to work through a painful reaction affecting the therapist's professional role, was to review the case and present it to a group of colleagues with the attitude: What can we learn from this? It is not surprising, however, that relatively few of these cases were written up in a formal way and published.

Many therapists have stated that the suicide of a patient in an institution, for instance a psychiatric hospital or clinic, is much easier to tolerate than one that occurs in the course of private practice. A death occurring within the purview of a well-defined social institution is easier to accept and view objectively. This is especially true if there was a spirit of mutual support, shared responsibility, and cooperative teamwork among the staff of the hospital or clinic. On the other hand, the suicide of a patient being treated in private practice provokes associations of the unusual, the unexpected, the uncanny. Therapists invariably felt better if they could say that they had explored every therapeutic avenue and possibility, and had discussed the case with colleagues and with consultants before the suicide. "I felt helpless." "I did everything I could." "I guess it was inevitable."

My colleagues and I have never interviewed a therapist who advanced the notion that the suicide of his patient was philosophically acceptable to him and congruent with his theoretical expectations regarding the methods and goals of therapy. The concept of an autonomous and insightful individual initiating an act of self-validation or self-fulfillment was not mentioned in these postmortem discussions. A number of therapists said that in the future they would do everything possible to avoid working with potentially suicidal patients. Many others expressed the view that episodes of anxiety about patients were inevitable hazards of the profession. They planned to continue to try to do their best for every patient and would regard the next one with suicidal tendencies as a special challenge. No change in their general attitudes toward suicide or toward death appeared to be indicated, they said, but they would try to use the experience of the death of a patient to enlarge their own psychological horizons, to become more sensitive as persons and therapists, and to improve their professional judgments and professional actions. This is an attitude I would endorse.

Let me close this report with a vignette from Sigmund Freud (1901/1960):

> In August, 1898, Freud was vacationing in Italy with his wife when a piece of bad news reached him. "A patient over whom I had taken a great deal of trouble had put an end to his life on account of an incurable sexual disorder. I know for certain that this melancholy event and everything related to it was not recalled to my conscious memory during my [subsequent] journey to Herzegovina." Two weeks later, however, during the next stage of his journey, Freud was astounded when he could not recall the name of a well-known artist whose fresco he wished to recommend. He tried to visualize the painting and the artist in question, and the inadequacy of his associations became a source of inner torment. The missing name, which finally came to him, was Signorelli. The essential blocking thought which accounted for its loss was the repressed news of the suicide, elements of which had become associated with the name in Freud's unconscious. His analysis of this incident is the first illustrative example in "The Psychopathology of Everyday Life." [pp. 2–6]

To us it seems quite natural, even inevitable, that a patient's suicide should disturb the analyst's unconscious. Many of the therapists we interviewed reported similar reactions. News of the death was received, and part of the painful emotion was repressed. Its return from the unconscious later was expressed in various symptomatic moods and actions. Finally, the associations were made conscious and the working through of the traumatic incident was manifested in a personal change, a professional broadening, and occasionally some scientific or philosophic contribution.

SUMMARY

On the basis of information communicated by more than four hundred psycho-therapists, each of whom was interviewed shortly after one of his patients committed suicide, two types of reactions are reported. It is observed that therapists react to such deaths personally as human beings much as other people do, and also according to their special role in society. Their theoretical, philosophic, and scientific attitudes have a defensive and reparative function and help them to overcome the pain they feel as human beings and therapists.

The reactions of the therapists as human beings varied in accordance with the specific feature and intensity of the relationship with the deceased. Thera-pists felt such emotions as grief, guilt, depression, personal inadequacy, and sometimes anger. Some of them noted partial identifications with dead patients in their own dreams or symptomatic actions. For example, accident-proneness often followed the death of a patient by suicide.

Denial was the most common defensive mechanism used by therapists (and by relatives and friends of the patient as well). A psychological maneuver that was helpful in working through pain affecting the therapist's professional role was to review the case and present it to a group of colleagues with the object of learning from it. Occasionally, the incident was worked through in the form of a scientific or philosophic contribution.

REFERENCES

Chemtob, C. M., Hamada, R. S., Bauer, G., et al. (1988). Patients' suicides: frequency and impact on psychiatrists. *American Journal of Psychiatry* 145:224–228.

Freud, S. (1901/1960). The psychopathology of everyday life. *Standard Edition* 6:1–310. London: Hogarth.

Hillman, J. (1964). *Suicide and the Soul*. London: Hodder and Stoughton.

Rich, C. L., Young, D., and Fowler, R. C. (1986). San Diego suicide study. *Archives of General Psychiatry* 43:577–582.

11

THE LOS ANGELES

SURVIVORS'

AFTER-SUICIDE PROGRAM

Norman L. Farberow

INTRODUCTION

Suicide is a self-destructive act, most often carried out by a person when alone, feeling isolated and alienated from family, community, and society. Unhappily, the impact of the act does not end with the death. After most suicides, there is a long-lasting residue of distressed feelings in family and friends, feelings that may continue for years. Within the last decade concerted efforts have been made to provide relief for these distressed feelings, especially by means of survivor group programs.

A review of the literature on suicide survivors before 1980 reveals a number of articles reporting studies of the effect of suicide on survivors, but relatively few describing group programs directed toward helping the survivors. Osterweis and colleagues (1984) summarize nine studies carried out between 1975 and 1984 that report the results of interventive psychotherapy with bereaved. The interventions, however, are all individual therapy or family counseling, and the populations have experienced losses from various types of death.

In suicide, the pioneering work of Cain and Fast (1966) found guilt and distorted communication between children and the surviving adults after a parent suicide. There was also identification with the deceased parent, and sometimes a feeling among the children that they were themselves doomed to suicide. Herzog and Resnick (1967) identified three common reactions within five families who had experienced the suicide of an adolescent: denial, hostility toward authorities who certified the death as suicide, and long-term guilt about the death. Cantor (1975) also found parental denial, long-term guilt, and depression in reaction to a child suicide. Augenbraun and Neuringer (1972) found that the relationship to the deceased affected the grief process. Where the relationship had been positive and the suicide could be attributed to factors outside the survivors' control, adaptation occurred more readily and there was less need for help with bereavement. Conversely, when the relationship had been ambivalent or conflicted, mourning was difficult.

Addressing the process in bereavement, Schuyler (1975) discussed the elements involved in working through a suicide: (1) a search for meaning, (2) denial, (3) guilt, and (4) anger. He recommended therapy in which the nonjudgmental setting allowed the survivor to examine these feelings and the associated distortions in thinking. Foglia's (1984) review of the literature on suicide survivors voiced concern about several areas in programs to help survivors: (1) professional background of the leader(s); (2) sponsoring organization; (3) timing of intervention; (4) education for natural community care givers, such as clergy, doctors, teachers, social workers, and so forth; and (5) research of existing survivor programs.

In the 1980s, Hatten and Valente (1981) conducted a 10-week bereavement group for parents of children who died by suicide. The group met weekly and dealt with the need to find meaning in the act. The feelings discussed were guilt, depression, denial, and anger; the social prohibitions on mourning; inadequacy of usual coping mechanisms; isolation; and a sense of crisis in parental identity and control.

A few studies attempted to evaluate the process. Osterweis and colleagues (1984) described four studies involving group interventions. Barrett (1984) studies widows using three different treatment approaches in one meeting per week for 7 weeks and a "waiting list" control group. He found at posttest that both groups had higher self-esteem, more intense grief, and more negative attitudes toward remarriage. Of the three formats, most positive changes occurred in the consciousness-raising group, moderate changes appeared in the confidant groups, and least positive changes occurred in the self-help group. Vachon and colleagues (1980) worked with newly bereaved widows by using trained "widow helpers" for 1:1 support followed by group mutual support. They found no differences between the intervention and nonintervention groups at 1 month, better intrapersonal adaptation for intervention groups at 6 months, and better interpersonal adaptation at 12 months.

Lieberman and Berman (1981) twice surveyed by mail, a year apart, widows and widowers in THEOS, a postbereavement mutual support group, and those who had declined joining the group. They found that improvement in both depression and self-esteem was positively associated with more intense involvement with the group. Videka-Sherman (1982) also surveyed by mail, a year apart, both members and nonmembers of Compassionate Friends, and found that personal growth seemed to vary directly with the intensity of the involvement in the group. However, there were no differences in depression scores by level of involvement.

Rogers and colleagues (1982) established a Survivors Support Program (SSP), using both survivor and nonsurvivor volunteers who were trained to be leaders of the groups, and a structural program with a specific focus for discussion in each session. Participants attended eight 2-hour weekly sessions and then were invited to attend four biweekly groups after the program was completed. Subjects were tested before and after intervention and improvement was found in reduced levels of somatization, obsessive-compulsive and phobic-anxiety behavior (Derogatis 1973). The program was rated as helpful but, unfortunately, no controls were used in the study.

Battle (1984) used pre– and post–group-experience questionnaires on his group participants (who attended one to fifteen sessions), and on both bereaved who did not attend group and nonbereaved controls, some of whom were in individual therapy. Attendance in groups was open-ended, but most participants left after twelve sessions. Battle found the predominant problem to be guilt and self-blame about the loved one's death, so much so that 50 percent had considered suicide for themselves compared with none among the controls. The postgroup questionnaire indicated that 71 percent felt helped, 27 percent said the group could not help them further even though they were still suffering, and 12 percent reported no help.

In 1984 an AAS-appointed committee studied the growing phenomenon of survivor groups by sending out seventy questionnaires to identified group programs; forty-one were returned (Heilig 1985). About half, twenty-one, had been started by survivors who had themselves recently experienced a suicide loss; the other twenty were started by people with a professional interest. In twenty-nine of the groups, leaders had professional training; thirty-two groups had co-leaders, seven of them survivors. Formats were mixed, with some open-ended, some closed; some with a set number of meetings and others indefinite. Most (twenty-four) reported a positive attitude toward professional participation, nine were clearly negative, and five were ambivalent. The most commonly mentioned problems listed by the groups included lack of community support, leader burnout, inappropriate members, a need for more help than the group could provide, and suicide of a member.

LOS ANGELES SPC SURVIVOR SUPPORT GROUPS

The concept on which the Los Angeles Suicide Prevention Center Survivors' After-Suicide Program has been based is that the survivors are not psychiatric patients, but rather are essentially normal people who have been subjected to severe emotional stress, and who have needed help in the working through of their grief. The process differs from the traditional group therapy in which psychiatrically ill persons seek understanding of their dynamics and resolution of longstanding intrapsychic conflicts. The format used in the SAS is limited to eight sessions, once a week, conducted by two leaders, one a mental health professional and the other a survivor who has gone through the program and has then received additional training. Kinship losses are mixed, as are sex and ages of adults. Following the eight weekly meetings, members are invited to attend monthly meetings as long as they wish. At each of the group sessions, reading material is distributed along with suggested topics for group discussion. Most of the time, the suggestions serve merely as possible topics for discussion.

Population

The subjects in the study are sixty participants (E) in the SAS program who completed the 8-week course and who also completed the research questionnaires before and after. The controls (C) are survivors who applied for admission to the program and who filled out the preprogram questionnaire, but either did not attend or else dropped out after one session. They were contacted by letter, phone, or both after 2 months had passed and asked to complete the postprogram questionnaire. The first twenty-two subjects to return their questionnaire constituted the controls, with 82 percent received within 3 months and the rest within 6 months. Reasons given for not joining or not continuing with the group were most often: location too far away, found help elsewhere, and, in a few cases, fee, although no one was excluded because of inability to pay.

Comparison of the study controls (C) with those potential controls (Cp) (N = 20) who did not complete the postprogram questionnaire indicated similar age distribution, 73 percent youth and midyears among the controls (C) and 60 percent among the Cp's controls; 77 percent women among the C's and 60 percent among the Cp's; and 77 percent time lapse of 6 to 8 months since the death for the C's and 70 percent among the Cp's. Kinship losses varied, with the Cp's experiencing loss of a child, 30 percent, and 15 percent each of the loss of a parent, spouse, and sibling. Among the study C's, these losses were 18 percent child, 27 percent parent, 27 percent spouse, and 18 percent sibling.

Results

Comparison of Participants and Controls

Demographics indicate that more women than men sought help through the group process for their bereavement, 70 percent among the E's and 77 percent among the C's. The age distribution was relatively similar, with most of both groups in the young adult and mid-years, 81 percent E's and 73 percent C's. Sex and age distributions of the E's and C's were not significantly different (Table 11–1).

There were significant differences between the two groups, p less than .05, in the kinship to the decedents (Table 11–1). In the E's, the most frequent loss was of a sibling, 35 percent compared to 18 percent among the C's. Other significant differences in losses were of a child, 23 percent and 18 percent, and of a parent, 20 percent and 27 percent for E's and C's respectively. Twice as many of the C's had lost a spouse, 27 percent, than did the E's, 13 percent. A few subjects in both groups reported multiple losses by suicide, three among the E's and two among the C's.

Table 11–1. Percentage Distributions for Participants and Controls of Ages, Kinship Losses, Time Lapse since Death, and How Learn about the Program.

Ages			Kinship Losses		
	Percent			Percent	
Ages	E	C	Losses Of	E	C
10–19	0	5	Child	23	18
20–29	23	32	Parent	20	27
30–39	33	27	Spouse	13	27
40–49	25	14	Sibling	35	18
50–59	10	14	Sweetheart	5	14
60+	8	9	Other	10	5

Time Lapse since Death			How Learn about the Program		
	Percent			Percent	
Months	E	C	Source	E	C
–3	32	9	Friend	28	18
3–5	33	50	Media	13	23
6–8	14	18	SPC or Hot Line	20	18
9–11	0	5	Therapist/Physician	12	14
12–23	2	5	Family Member	13	5
24 +	19	15	Book	5	9
			Self-Referred	5	5
			Other	3	0

Most subjects sought help within the first 6 to 8 months after the suicide, about 77 percent for both E's and C's (Table 11-1). Some, however, had experienced the death 2 or more years previously, 19 percent of the E's and 15 percent of the C's. The death occurred 4 or more years ago for seven persons among the E's and for one person among the C's.

Among the E's, 28 percent had heard about the SAS program from a friend, 20 percent through calling the suicide crisis lines, 13 percent through the media, and 13 percent through a family member (Table 11-1). Among the C's, 23 percent had learned about the SAS through the media, 18 percent through a friend, and 18 percent through calling the SPC.

Health

About 55 percent of each group stated that their health has been about the same, while 33 percent of the E's and 41 percent of the C's stated that their health has been worse. A few, 8 percent and 5 percent of E and C respectively, said their health has been better. Differences between the E's and the C's were significant (Table 11-2).

Table 11-2. Percentage of Participants and Controls Reporting Health Changes, Life Changes and Helpful Coping Activities since Loss.

Health since Loss			Major Changes since Loss		
	Percent			Percent	
Condition	E	C	Types of Change	E	C
Same	55	55	Job	15	18
Worse	33	41	Residence	18	32
Better	8	5	Divorce	3	0
No Answer	3	0	(Re)Marriage	7	0
			Other Deaths	12	18

Helpful Coping Activities		
	Percent	
	E	C
Talking with Family/Friends	85	91
Reviewing Pictures	55	50
Work	40	55
Visiting Grave	42	36
Rearranging/Storing Belongings	33	41
Changing Residence	10	18
Psychotherapy, Individual	50	45
Psychotherapy, Group	22	23

Among both groups, those who indicated their health was worse since the death described symptoms such as stomach problems, sleeping, headaches, anxiety, tension, mood changes, fatigue, anxiety, and others. The most frequent illnesses were colds and the flu; a number of symptoms were indicative of various psychosomatic illnesses.

Major Changes

Both groups have experienced additional deaths, 12 percent of E, 18 percent of C; and job changes, 15 percent of E, 18 percent of C (Table 11-2). Change of residence has been the most common change, more among the C's, 32 percent, than among the E's, 18 percent. Among the E's, four persons have married and two have divorced during this period (Table 11-2).

Impact of Loss

The subjects revealed the severity of the impact of the suicide and the ensuing disruption of their lives with statements such as:

"There's no future now."
"Things don't matter."
"I feel empty and lost."
"I feel on hold."
"Thoughts of the act repeatedly intrude."
"I've been trying hard but nothing is the same, or ever will be the same."
"Sometimes things go along wonderfully and suddenly I can't go for a second without thinking of him putting that damn rifle up to his head."
"I was in a severe depression and didn't know why."
"I felt myself disintegrating every way."

Coping Activities

The activity most often used and also found to be the most helpful by both E's and C's in coping with the loss was talking with family and friends, 85 percent E, 91 percent C (Table 11-2). The other activities used frequently and found helpful were: reviewing pictures and mementoes, 55 percent E, 50 percent C; work, 47 percent E, 55 percent C; visiting the grave, 42 percent E, 36 percent C; and rearranging and storing the belongings of the deceased, 33 percent E, 41 percent C. About one half of each group, 50 percent E's and 45 percent C's, have found individual psychotherapy helpful, and about 22 percent in each group have found group therapy helpful. A few subjects in both groups listed a number of other individual activities they found helpful, such as AA and Alanon, reading, writing to the deceased loved one, exercise, spiritual searching of self, gardening, and looking for ways to be good to oneself.

Feelings

Each of the subjects was asked in his preprogram questionnaire to estimate at two different times the level of intensity for nine feelings: depression, grief, anxiety, shame, guilt, anger at self or others, anger at deceased, puzzlement, and own suicidal feelings. The first time (T1) is retrospective, asking for a rating of the level of feelings within the first 4 weeks after death; the second time (T2) is a rating of the current level of feelings as the program was about to start. A third (T3) measurement was requested postprogram, a rating of the level of the feelings immediately after the 8-week program was concluded. The controls were asked to provide the same ratings for the same times, with the third rating (T3) sought about 2 months after the second rating.

Group Comparisons at T1

Table 11–3 indicates the high, medium, and low self-ratings of the nine feelings for the three time periods. Comparison of the feelings of the E's and C's at T1, within the first 4 weeks after the death of their loved ones, indicated no significant differences in the rated levels of any of the feelings. Feelings rated highest (high and moderate combined) by both groups included depression, 99 percent E's and 96 percent C's; grief, 94 percent E's and 91 percent C's; anxiety, 88 percent E's and 100 percent C's; puzzlement, 82 percent E's and 86 percent C's; and guilt, 83 percent E's and 81 percent C's.

Ratings of other feelings were more varied. Self-rating of shame or stigma, for example, showed that approximately half of each group rated their feelings as high and moderate, while the other half rated feelings of shame as low. Anger at self or others within the first months was intense for a surprising number of the survivors, 67 percent E's and 81 percent C's. Anger at the person who committed suicide was also surprisingly high with more than half in each group, 55 percent E's and 54 percent C's, rating their anger as either moderate or high.

Most people had no or few suicidal feelings themselves at this point, with 77 percent E's and 91 percent C's rating themselves as low. Although 22 percent of the E's rated themselves as moderate or high compared to only 9 percent among the C's, the difference was not significant.

Generally, comparison of the ratings of levels of feelings for the two groups within the first 4 weeks after death indicated no significant differences between the groups.

Table 11-3. Percentages of Participants and Controls Rating Selected Feelings High, Moderate, and Low within One Month of Death (T1), at the Time of Start of the Program (T2), and After Completing the Program (T3)

	T1						T2						T3					
	E			C			E			C			E			C		
Feelings	H	M	L	H	M	L	H	M	L	H	M	L	H	M	L	H	M	L
Depression	72	27	2	64	32	5	33	53	13	27	50	23	10	70	20	18	41	41
Grief*	77	17	3	77	14	9	33	53	8	18	55	27	15	55	28	9	68	23
Anxiety	53	35	7	59	41	0	20	55	22	18	41	36	10	48	38	5	45	45
Shame	25	30	40	23	27	50	10	32	52	5	18	77	2	28	68	0	18	82
Guilt	43	40	12	36	45	18	18	63	13	9	32	59	5	35	53	14	32	55
Anger/Self	32	35	15	45	36	18	23	45	28	9	50	41	8	45	45	14	41	41
Anger/Suicide	27	28	43	27	27	45	18	35	45	23	18	59	10	23	67	18	23	59
Puzzlement	60	22	13	59	27	9	38	35	23	27	36	32	17	53	27	27	14	50
Suicidal	10	12	77	9	0	91	2	16	82	9	5	86	0	10	90	5	14	82

Significant	T1, E v. C	T2, E v. C	T3, E v. C
Differences	None	Guilt, E > C	Puzzlement, E > C

T1 v. T2   T2 v. T3

E = Depression, Grief   E = Grief, Depression, Guilt
   Anxiety, Suicidal
C = Grief, Anxiety,   C = None
   Anger/Self

*Ratings totaling less than 100 percent indicate absent ratings

Changes between T1 and T2

Differences in self-ratings of the feelings at Time 1 and Time 2 were tested for statistically significant changes. It should be remembered that for about 77 percent of each group, the changes noted took place within 6 to 8 months after the death. The remainder described changes that took place generally 2 and more years later.

Among the E's a significant decrease in intensity of the feelings was found for four of the nine feelings, $p < .05$. Depression (99 percent T1 to 86 percent T2), grief (94 percent T1 to 86 percent T2), anxiety (88 percent T1 to 75 percent T2), and suicidal (22 percent T1 to 18 percent T2) showed significant differences over the intervening 6 to 8 months. However, the level of feelings for depression, grief, and anxiety were still high at the time the group started. In addition, guilt (81 percent), puzzlement (73 percent), anger at self and others (68 percent), and anger at the suicide (53 percent) were also still relatively moderate or high. Suicidal feelings decreased for those marking it high, from 10 percent T1 to 2 percent T2.

For the C's, decreases between T1 and T2 were significant for grief, anxiety, and anger at self and others. A smaller number among the C's rated selves as high than among the E's, but depression (77 percent) continued to be high and moderate, while puzzlement (63 percent), anxiety (59 percent), and anger at self (59 percent) were still at least moderate. Shame and feeling suicidal continued to be rated low by a majority of the group, 77 percent and 86 percent, respectively.

Group Comparisons at T2

The comparison of the two groups at T2 (just before initiating the group) showed significant differences for one feeling only, guilt, with the rating by the E's significantly higher than by the C's (81 percent as against 41 percent high and moderate, $p < .01$). Many more C's rated themselves low in guilt compared to E's, 59 percent as against 13 percent, respectively. With no further significant differences between the E's and the C's, one could conclude the two groups were experiencing essentially the same pattern of feelings (except for guilt) at the time the group sessions were about to start.

Changes between T2 and T3

Significant changes in the rating of levels of feelings between T2 and T3 were indicated by the participants in the SAS program in three of the nine feelings: depression, grief, and guilt. For each feeling, the change was again a decrease in the intensity of the feelings, often from high to moderate or moderate to low. Thus, while depression (80 percent) and grief (70 percent), high and moderate, were still much present, the high ratings were considerably lower, for instance, depression, 33 percent T2 to 10 percent T3; grief, 33 percent T2 to 15 percent T3; and guilt, 18 percent T2 to 5 percent T3. The shift in ratings of guilt were to predominately low, 13 percent T2 to 59 percent T3. Other feelings, though not changing enough to be significantly different, showed similar changes — puzzlement, 38 percent T2 to 17 percent T3; anxiety, 20 percent T2 to 10 percent T3; and anger at self, 23 percent T2 to 8 percent T3.

Suicidal feelings showed little or no change because most of the participants, over 80 percent, had already rated themselves low in this feeling.

In contrast to the E's, the C's showed no significant changes between T2 and T3 for any of the feelings. Ratings were still high and moderate for grief, 77 percent; depression, 59 percent; anger at self and others, 55 percent; and anxiety, 50 percent. The percentage rating high for guilt and anger at self and others actually increased from T2 to T3 — guilt, 9 percent to 14 percent, and anger at self and others, 9 percent to 14 percent, respectively.

Group Comparisons at T3

When the E's and the C's were compared with each other at Time 3, only one of the nine feelings was found to be rated significantly differently, puzzlement, with the E's rating themselves higher, 80 percent as against 59 percent. Puzzlement ratings at T2 had not shown a significant difference between the two groups. The shift for the E's was a marked decrease in their rating of this feeling as high (38 percent T2 to 17 percent T3); and an increase in the rating of moderate (35 percent T2 to 53 percent T3). The rating of low showed practically no change (23 percent T2 to 27 percent T3). For the C's, however, the shift was primarily from moderate to low (moderate, 36 percent T2 to 14 percent T3; low 32 percent T2 to 50 percent T3). The percentage of high ratings remained the same at both time intervals, 27 percent.

Guilt, which had significantly differentiated the two groups at Time 2, no longer distinguished them at Time 3. The E's, who had shown a significantly higher level of guilt at Time 2 than the C's (twice as many E's, 81 percent, as C's, 41 percent, rating moderate and high), lowered their level of guilt by Time 3 to the point at which there was little difference in the percentage rating it high and moderate, 40 percent by the E's and 46 percent by the C's.

Ratings of the SAS Experience

Approximately nine out of ten, 92 percent, of those who attended the SAS groups rated their experience favorably, stating the group helped them (Table 11-4). Four persons, three females and one male, did not feel the group had helped; one person did not answer. On a scale of 1 to 7 (with 7 high), 56 percent rated it 7, 24 percent rated it 6, and 10 percent each rated it a 5 and 4. There were no ratings below 4.

Only one person felt that the eight sessions were too many; most, 51 percent, thought eight sessions were not enough, and 41 percent thought the number of sessions was just right. When asked how the process had been helpful, some of the responses were:

> "It lessened the shock."
> "It made me more aware of my feelings."
> "I was helped to face the reality of my loss."
> "It was helpful to talk and share with others."
> "I feel more normal, it put things in perspective."
> "I feel more in control."

In answer to a request for suggestions on how to improve the group, some wanted more structure, such as more informational material, more practical

Table 11-4. Percentages of Participants Feeling Helped, Ratings of Degree of Helpfulness, and Opinion about the Number of Sessions in the SAS Program

Has Your Experience in the Program Been Helpful		How Helpful was the Program*	
	Percent	Rating Levels	Percent
Yes	92	4	10
No	7	5	10
No answer	2	6	24
		7	56

The Number of Sessions Was	
	Percent
Too few	51
Just right	41
Too many	2
No answer	5

* 7 = High, 1 = Low

advice, more professional input about suicide and mental illness, how to handle friends who mean well but don't know what to say, how to handle holidays, and so forth. Most indicated a preference for having a variety of losses represented in the group rather than putting only people with similar losses together. Some wanted more reading resources and the establishment of a library. One comment was simply appreciative: "Perfect, the process just happens, and goes where it needs to."

DISCUSSION

If the impact of the SAS group experience were to be judged solely on the basis of comparison of the two groups at each of the time measurements, it might well be concluded that there was relatively little impact inasmuch as there were practically no differences in the general pattern of feelings and their intensities reported by each group at each time. Thus, at Time 1, immediately after the death, no significant differences were reported. At Time 2, approximately 6 to 8 months after death, only one difference appeared, with the participants indicating a higher intensity of guilt than the controls. (One might speculate that this explains, at least in part, the fact that the controls did not continue in the program.) At Time 3, 2 to 3 months later, again only one difference was reported, a higher level of puzzlement among the participants than was found among the nonparticipant controls.

The impact of the SAS group experience becomes much more apparent when the changes within each group are noted over the three time measurements. Both groups show relatively similar changes between Time 1 and Time 2, with each group reporting a lessening in the intensity of their feelings, significantly so for grief and anxiety. In addition, the participants reported significant drops in the levels of depression and suicidal feelings, while the controls showed a significant drop in anger at self and others. However, on measurement at Time 3, after the SAS group experience for the participants, additional significant decreases in ratings for depression and grief appeared. Ratings of anxiety and suicidal feelings also changed in a positive direction, but not enough to achieve significance. In addition, a crucial lessening of the feeling of guilt appeared, a change commented on below. The controls at Time 3, on the other hand, had not decreased significantly on any of the feelings, indicating that the pattern of their feelings remained substantially the same over the 2-month period. One can conclude that in 2 short months the SAS group experience had made a significant impact on the levels of some of the most difficult, unhappy feelings experienced by survivors following the suicidal death of a loved one.

The levels of the ratings at Time 2 indicated that the participants were still experiencing most of the feelings intensely, with six of the nine feelings still rated high or moderate by at least two-thirds of the group. Only three of the nine feelings were rated high or moderate by two-thirds of the controls at this time, indicating that the controls had improved during the interim more than the participants. Approximately 2 to 3 months later, however, with the benefit of the SAS program behind them, the participants no longer rated themselves significantly higher than the controls on the feeling of guilt. The sharing and learning about the ubiquity of such feelings had apparently lessened its intensity. However, differences had now appeared in the ratings of another feeling, puzzlement, with the participants rating themselves higher than the controls. A possible reason is that the SAS experience had, through its intensive discussions and repeated reviewing of the loss, restimulated questions of "why." The controls, on the other hand, had continued to suppress their feelings during the interim, causing the question of "why" to subside further.

The obvious question is: Do these trends hold up in the long term; if not, what changes do occur? An effort was made to obtain follow-up data 2 years later by sending the subjects questionnaires which asked them for information on their current emotional status and to rate the same feelings on the same 7-point scale. Sparse returns (twenty of the sixty E's, and eleven of the twenty-two C's) permit only an estimate of their bereavement and emotional status approximately 2 years later. Briefly, they may be summarized as follows:

1. All the feelings were rated low by almost half of the members of both groups. Grief among the participants was the exception, with a low rating by only 20 percent of the group.

2. The mean score of each feeling varied by less than one interval on the 7-point scale between Time 3 and Time 4.
3. Some feelings, like feeling suicidal, shame, and guilt (especially among the controls), have almost completely subsided by follow-up. A few feelings, like depression, grief (especially among the participants), and anger, seem to be relatively persistent even after 2 or more years.

The time limitations of the SAS program ($1\frac{1}{2}$ hours once a week for eight weeks, with monthly meetings afterward if desired), seem to have been acceptable to the participants, with nine out of ten rating the experience favorably. For some who wished to continue longer, the monthly meetings served well, allowing the separation to occur more gradually. Those who did continue to come reported on the problems of picking up again the continuity of their lives, reestablishing their identities, and filling the gaps resulting from their loss. As in Rogers and colleagues' program (1982) comments by the participants indicated that they found help in facing the reality of the loss, were reassured that their feelings were normal, and felt that they had regained control of their lives after its severe disruption. Almost all stated that they would recommend the program to others, with 89 percent indicating yes, 9 percent no, and one person not answering.

Whether the participants are best served by forming each group with those with similar kinship losses only is a question that remains unanswered. At times, comments indicated concern whether sharing and understanding could occur when someone who had lost a parent contrasted his feelings with someone who had lost a sibling. However, the distinct clinical impression was that the feelings discussed were universal regardless of the kind of loss, and that most participants were able to identify readily with the others. In some instances it was even felt to be highly advantageous, as when two participants with sibling losses remarked at the end of their program that they were glad they had been in the same group with some parents who had lost a child. They stated that they had been angry at their own parents, who they felt had never really understood nor even tried to help their siblings. Listening to the parents in their group had helped them to see how much effort had been made to help, as well as how much pain had been experienced by everyone involved.

Despite Rogers and colleagues' (1982) experience of success with leadership of the groups by volunteer survivors only, it is our strong impression that most benefit is derived from the combination of professional and survivor as co-leaders. The two serve overlapping but very different and necessary functions. While it was generally the professional to whom the members turned for information and security, it was to the survivor-facilitator that they most often turned to share their feelings: the intensity of their pain, the ravages of their guilt, the depth of their depression, and the pressures of their anger. The survivor-facilitator also served as an important role model, of someone who has been there and has successfully gone through the experience. It was almost a promise for many that it would be possible to function again even though they felt at the time that they would never recover.

The professional is important also in providing a sense of security both to the members and to the survivor co-leader in the not-too-infrequent occasions of emotional disturbance, suicidal feelings, or severe depression in one of the participants. In such instances the professional provided the authority and skill that was necessary to handle the situation. In some instances, expressions of guilt, self-blame, and suicidal feelings indicated the need for the more traditional therapeutic interaction. A primary prevention purpose was served in treating a potential suicide before the impulses fully developed.

The feelings and their course as measured in the SAS program were similar to those described by other researchers (Hatton and Valente [1981], Rogers et al. [1982], Battle [1984], McIntosh and Wrobleski [1988]). Hatton and Valente (1981) identify particularly the search for meaning in the act, a need that was expressed in this study by the continuous high rating for puzzlement by both groups. Perhaps, one of the more significant benefits of the SAS experience was reaching the point of tolerating the fact that there was no answer. Our findings on suicidal feelings among the participants is different from Battle's (1984), who reported 50 percent had considered suicide for themselves. Among our participants the most that reported suicidal feelings was 22 percent, and that was in the first 4 weeks after the death.

Contrary to Rogers and colleagues' (1982) experience of finding by testing the subjects before and after intervention that there had been reduced levels of somatization, the participants in the SAS program reported no changes. In general, when asked about their health since the death, most felt their health had been either the same, 55 percent, or worse, 37 percent. About 7 percent said their health was better. For those reporting that their health was worse, most of the illnesses were psychosomatic in nature, with such illnesses as ulcerative colitis, ulcer flare-ups, dermatological problems identified. Headaches and respiratory illnesses were also reported along with depression symptoms including loss of motivation, loss of zest for life, problems sleeping and eating, and social withdrawal.

A major contribution of the SAS program, similar to the programs of Hatton and Valente (1981), Rogers and colleagues (1982), Battle (1984), and the programs described by Osterweis and colleagues (1984), has been to provide support through the sharing of mutual experiences, problems, and losses. Many of the participants reported difficulties because their usual sources of support were lost as a result of the fact that the death was a suicide. Friends turned away or were unable to overcome their own awkwardness in discussing the suicide. Often this was reported as occurring within families as well.

Finally, from the experiences of many of the controls, it is possible also to agree with the conclusion of Osterweis and colleagues (1984) that not all bereaved persons need formal intervention. The results of this study support the conclusion that some intervention programs help people move faster through the grieving process, but ultimately most people get through it whether or not they have formal support.

REFERENCES

Augenbraun, B., and Neuringer, C. (1972). Helping survivors with the impact of a suicide. In *Survivors of Suicide*, ed. A. Cain, pp. 178–185. Springfield: Bannerstone House.

Barrett, C. J. (1984). Effectiveness of widows-groups in facilitating change. *Journal of Consulting and Clinical Psychology* 46:20–31.

Battle, A. O. (1984). Group therapy for survivors of suicide. *Crisis* 5(1):48–58.

Cain, A., and Fast, I. (1966). Legacy of suicide. *Psychiatry* 29:406–411.

Cantor, P. (1975). The effects of youthful suicide on the family. *Psychiatric Opinion* 12(6):6–11.

Derogatis, L. R., Lipman, R. S., and Covi, L. (1973). The SCL-90; An outpatient psychiatric rating scale. *Psychopharmacology Bulletin* 9:13–28.

Foglia, B. (1984). Survivor victims of suicide: a review of the literature. In *Suicide: Assessment and Intervention*, ed. C. L. Hatton and S. M. Valente, 2nd ed. New York: Appleton-Century Crofts.

Hatton, C. L., and Valente, S. M. (1981). Bereavement group for parents who suffered a suicidal loss of a child. *Suicide and Life-Threatening Behaviors* 11(3):141–150.

Heilig, S. M. (1985). Survey of 41 survivor groups. In *Proceedings of the 18th Annual Meeting of the American Association of Suicidology*, ed. R. Cohen-Sandler. Toronto, Canada: American Association of Suicidology.

Herzog, A., and Resnik, H. (1967). A clinical study of parental response to adolescent death by suicide. In *Proceedings of the 4th International Conference on Suicide Prevention*, ed. N. L. Farberow. Los Angeles: Delmar.

Lieberman, M. A., and Berman, L. D. (1981). Researcher study THEOS: report group's effect big help to members. *THEOS* 20:3–6.

McIntosh, J. L., and Wrobleski, A. (1988). Grief reactions among suicide survivors: an exploratory comparison of relationships. *Death Studies* 12:21–39.

Osterweis, M., Solomon, F., and Green, M. (1984). *Bereavement: Reactions, Consequences and Care*. Washington, DC: National Academy Press.

Rogers, J., Sheldon, A., Barwick, C., et al. (1982). Help for families of suicide: survivors support program. *Canadian Journal of Psychiatry* 27:444–449.

Schuyler, D. (1975). Counseling suicide survivors: issues and answers. *Omega* 4(4):313–321.

Vachon, M. L. S., Sheldon, A. R., Lancee, W. J., et al. (1980). A controlled study of self-help for widows. *American Journal of Psychiatry* 137:1280–1284.

Videka-Sherman, L. (1982). Effects of participation in a self-help group for bereaved parents. *Compassionate Friends Prevention Services* 1:69–72.

12

RESPONSIBILITY AND LIABILITY FOR SUICIDE

Robert E. Litman

I${}$T IS NOT POSSIBLE to predict every suicide or to prevent every suicide. When a suicide is not prevented, then who is responsible and who is liable? With respect to these two questions, we are in a time of confusion and controversy, when moral and legal attitudes are undergoing reevaluation.

RESPONSIBILITY FOR A DEATH

In Britain, it was the practice for hundreds of years to assign responsibility for a death according to four categories: natural, accident, suicide, or homicide. In natural and accidental deaths, God was held to be responsible and the case was closed. In homicide or suicide, however, human beings were held to be responsible and in that case it was appropriate for society to impose punishment. For suicide, these punishments included mutilation of the corpse, degrading burial ceremonies, and financial penalties laid on the family. However, as social attitudes changed, it became more difficult to inflict these punishments after a suicide. Juries would find that the dead person had been distracted, was out of his senses, didn't know what he was doing, in a word, that he was "insane," and therefore not a suicide. Mercy was smuggled into the law via the concept of insanity. But if the insane person himself was not responsible, who was? Presumably God, who had inflicted the madness. Gradually, the laws were changed to reflect new social attitudes. The last of the British laws against suicide was repealed in 1961. Those American states that had adopted the British common law have also decriminalized suicide. In California, suicide was never illegal.

LIABILITY FOR A SUICIDE

The legal system turned away from punishment toward an attitude of trying to protect people from committing suicide whenever possible. Gradually, the idea of compensating the victims (survivors) assumed importance as part of a general movement in the courts toward the concept that wherever there are victims, there should be monetary compensation. In tort law this concept has led to a considerable stretching of cause and effect. For example, if someone is injured in an automobile accident and after the injury becomes depressed and some years later commits suicide, in many lawsuits it has been alleged that the persons who caused the original injury in the automobile accident are responsible and liable for the eventual death by suicide.

The issue of a monetary award to the survivors of suicide involves life and accident insurance in certain cases. For example, there has been a long tradition in life insurance policies that they contain an exclusionary clause that says that if the person commits suicide within a year, or sometimes 2 years, then the face value of the policy is not paid. Instead, the premiums are returned. Now courts are being asked to void this type of exclusion on grounds that the deceased was insane when he killed himself and therefore not responsible.

If persons who commit suicide are held not to be responsible for their self-destructive acts, then who is responsible? More and more, the courts are being asked to hold mental health professionals responsible! Society has come to expect hospitals and mental health practitioners to be able to prevent suicide if they can "reasonably" be expected to do so. Much of that expectation is a legacy of the mercy smuggled into the law and into religion and morality that is based on the assumption that persons who commit suicide cannot be held accountable since they must have been mentally ill.

But, in fact, the relationship between mental illness and suicide is most complex and a worthy subject for clinical research. As they approach suicide, the great majority of suicidal persons are not psychotic, nor are they legally "incompetent." They are painfully upset and perturbed, usually psychiatrically diagnosable as depressed, alcoholic, schizophrenic, or personality disordered. But mental illness is only one in the multifactorial causation of suicide. Other factors include stress; loss; physical illness; disrupted social supports; personality traits of pride, independence, and help rejection; and demographic features such as age, sex, and occupation.

SUICIDE AND MEDICAL MALPRACTICE

The basic theme of this chapter is that the law's view of suicide faithfully mirrors society's view, which is confused, ambivalent, and contradictory. While some people think of suicide as requiring courage, independence, and self-sacrifice, the majority view continues to be that suicide represents cowardice, defeatism, selfish hostility, and social irresponsibility. The law sees suicide as a social evil, but it is quite unclear as to what extent the justice system should be involved in suicide prevention. Medical personnel and medical institutions are caught up in this conflict.

For every individual in our society who commits suicide, there are as many as 100 who seriously consider committing suicide. These suicidal people often consult physicians because of complaints such as sleeplessness, fatigue, inability to concentrate, anxiety, weight loss, muscle tension and muscle pain, indigestion, or because of recognized abuse of drugs and alcohol. If the physicians allow the patients to talk about how they feel, or if family members act as informants, physicians may discover that a patient has been thinking and talking about committing suicide. Furthermore, suicidal actions may occur in any medical practice, including general, medical-surgical, primary care, psychiatric clinic, or hospital.

If a patient commits suicide, under what circumstances may physicians and hospitals be liable in lawsuits alleging negligence or malpractice? Ordinarily, the general practitioner or specialist in medicine or surgery is not expected to detect a high suicide risk in office practice, or necessarily to take preventive antisuicide action, although ideally the physician would do both. If the patient dramatically calls suicidal tendencies to the attention of a general physician, a reasonable evaluation is called for, and a consultation with a psychiatrist should be considered. One area of practice in which office physicians may be accused of negligently contributing to a suicide is when they prescribe large amounts of hypnotic drugs to a person who is known to have been a drug abuser or alcoholic, especially if such a person has made suicide attempts in the past. The same rule would apply to psychiatrists practicing with outpatients.

There is a growing tendency for society and its courts to expect hospitals and hospital-like institutions to prevent suicide if it can be done reasonably. In general and psychiatric hospitals, suicide is a rare event, accounting for only 1 percent of the total annual number of suicides. According to experience in Los

Angeles County, the average 400-bed community hospital might expect no more than one suicide every five years. If the occurrence of suicide is appreciably greater than this, it should arouse self-criticism and self-scrutiny in the administration. After any suicide in a hospital, there should be a complete investigation and a report setting forth the contributing causes and making recommendations for future prevention of a similar event. One essential for suicide and accident prevention in medical and surgical wards is to protect patients who are temporarily depressed, agitated, or confused from falling from a dangerous height. Safety devices that limit the opening of windows and safety screens on doors and windows might prevent a majority of hospital suicides. Attention should be paid by physicians to clinical notes by nurses that a patient has been confused, demanding to go home, threatening suicide, or testing the strength of the windows. If a psychiatric consultation is requested, there should be a reasonably rapid response, and the recommendation from the consultant should include clear, direct-action recommendations.

The changing nature of psychiatric hospital practice has been confronted head-on by the problem of malpractice liability. In recent years, there has been a strong emphasis on the civil liberties of psychiatric patients with promotion of ambulatory crisis therapy, short-term hospitalization, open wards, and the earliest possible discharge from the hospital. There is a widespread trend in psychiatry to strip away the prisonlike features from the mental hospital, to abolish restraints, and to encourage a maximum of patient self-responsibility. Psychiatrists find themselves responsible for suicidal patients in psychiatric settings which have been deliberately designed to give the patients maximum freedom of action as part of the therapeutic milieu. Most psychiatrists regard suicide potentiality as a disturbing element complicating and sometimes restricting the therapeutic process and requiring special care and consultation. In psychiatric hospital practice, the possibility of suicide should be explicitly considered and entered into the record as part of the therapeutic program plan. The best defense against the accusation of malpractice is proof that the possibility of suicide was explicitly considered and a treatment decision reached.

LAWSUITS AND STANDARDS

When there is a lawsuit against the health care providers after a suicide, the attorneys for both sides will usually ask experienced and qualified practitioners to consult with them on the case, and if necessary give testimony in court.

How does an expert evaluate the performance of the staff of a hospital concerning the patient who committed suicide? The data consist of the hospital chart (which includes the observations and reports of physicians, nurses, aides, and other hospital personnel) and files from the police and medical examiner's office. In addition, the attorneys obtain sworn statements and depositions from a variety of witnesses, such as doctors, nurses, friends, relatives, and associates of the person who committed suicide. These witnesses are asked, under oath, to provide information about the deceased persons and the circumstances connected with their deaths. In many ways, the information thus obtained resembles a psychological autopsy. What are the standards against which these data must be evaluated?

The law demands that patients receive reasonable care in foreseeable situations. At present, however, the standards for reasonable psychiatric care with regard to suicide prevention are unclearly stated and inconsistently applied. These matters have been reviewed in depth by Litman (1980) and by Perr (1974). Generally, courts tend to hold a given institution to standards of care which are equivalent to those standards prevailing in the community. I have suggested that all hospitals, and in particular, psychiatric hospitals, formulate written administrative and professional policies bearing on the care of psychiatric patients and especially suicidal psychiatric patients. Such policies should be in accord with the recommendations of the American Psychiatric Association and the Joint Commission on Accreditation of Hospitals and should be compared with the established customs and practices of other hospitals in the general geographic vicinity. Then, for a case of litigation, the appropriate standard of care would be the guidelines established by the institution for itself.

The first issue in a medical liability case is to determine if the patient had presented evidence to warrant the conclusion that the patient was at high risk for suicide. It is important that the staff take sufficient time and effort to evaluate the patient accurately. The next issue deals with the manner in which the patients were protected against themselves. Here again, facts will reveal whether there was carelessness or insufficient attention which created the opportunity for suicide.

This is a report on four lawsuits against hospitals in which I participated as a suicidologist expert witness.

Mr. A. was a 22-year-old from California, attending a prestigious east-coast law school. Shortly before the end of his first semester, he became discouraged and depressed. He appeared at the student health clinic complaining of inability to study, feelings of failure, and a classic cluster of depressive symptoms, including suicidal ideas. For the next two nights he slept in the infirmary, and an off-duty police officer from the university was assigned to sit with him. His parents flew in from California, intending to take him home with them, but they were told by a psychiatric social worker and by the psychiatrist in charge that they were being overly protective and that better treatment could be provided in the

University City, so they returned home. On Saturday morning, Mr. A. was transferred to University City Hospital.

Because the admission was on a weekend, the young man was seen briefly by an on-duty admitting doctor, and briefly by the attending staff psychiatrist making rounds. There was no thorough evaluation of his suicidal potential, nor was there a definite plan or disposition. On Sunday afternoon, apparently, he called an ex-girlfriend in New York. He then ingested a lethal amount of caustic poison which he found in an unlocked utility room where it was used for urine testing, and then jumped from a window to a lawn three floors below. He survived the fall, but died subsequently of the poison. The danger posed by caustic soda in an unlocked utility room had been of great concern to the nurse in charge of the psychiatric unit, and she had called this to the attention of the chief psychiatrist several times, asking for an order that this door be kept locked. But a decision had been postponed because this particular utility room was also used by a rehabilitation unit, and the charge nurse there wanted her diabetic patients to have the testing equipment available.

No effort was made by the hospital staff to talk with the bereaved parents. It was very difficult for the parents to obtain any information at all about what had happened to their son. Finally, they consulted an attorney in order to find a way to obtain information about what had happened, and, eventually, this led to a malpractice and negligence lawsuit. I was asked by mutual friends to become involved in the case. It was the first time I had agreed to be a witness against psychiatrists. At the point I became involved, two years after the death, the hospital could still have settled this case by giving the parents a full explanation, publicly admitting guilt, and paying the legal expenses already accumulated, and this is what I tried unsuccessfully to arrange. In the end, after many delays, the case went to trial five years after the death. One week into the trial, when it became obvious there was no defense, the hospital and staff settled for $185,000 in damages and a public admission of negligence.

Even a hospital staffed by renowned doctors from the world's best medical schools, such as this one, must establish strict protocols for the treatment of potentially suicidal patients. In this case there were numerous gross violations of minimal standards of care and prudent judgment both before and after death. The major problems stemmed from indecision by the leadership concerning the degree to which security would be emphasized on this ward.

A 25-year-old male, driving aimlessly through the California valleys after abandoning his job and apartment in Los Angeles, attempted suicide by deeply slashing both his wrists with a razor on the morning of July 21.

He was treated in the emergency room of the local community medical center, where he first refused surgical treatment. The chief of the neuropsychiatric unit interviewed the patient, and applied for a 72-hour involuntary commitment because the patient was gravely disabled, actively suicidal, and a danger to himself. After this, the patient agreed to have the cut tendons in his wrists repaired. At 3:00 P.M., July 22, he was transferred to the psychiatric unit with the diagnosis of depressive reaction, severe, and the doctor ordered "active suicidal precautions" for 24 hours and placed him in a room close to the nursing office, where he could be closely observed. He was given the routine hospital bathrobe with an attached cloth belt. At approximately 6:00 P.M. on July 22, he closed his door. Personnel were not aware of this for about 10 minutes. When they entered the room, they found the patient had hanged himself with the belt.

In this case, as in the preceding case, the parents were notified belatedly and there was no attempt at bereavement counseling or open discussion. Rather, the parents had the impression that the hospital was trying to cover up something, which was probably true. In suing the hospital and staff for negligence, the parents were more interested in vindicating their sense of outrage than obtaining the money, for they were financially well-off. Attorneys for the parents alleged that the hospital staff failed to exercise the care, skill, and diligence ordinarily used by persons generally in the same or similar locality, and under similar circumstances, primarily in allowing the patient to be out of their observation for 10 or more minutes, and secondarily, for allowing him the robe with a belt. At the time he was transferred to the psychiatric unit, and continuously until his death, the patient expressed suicidal ideas. In a closing note on July 25, the doctor stated, "In spite of the close one-to-one observation, the patient closed door to room unobserved at about 6:00 P.M. and he hanged himself from the clothes locker using the bathrobe cord around his neck."

I directed special attention to the hospital's own training and procedures manual, which was dated September of the year before. This manual stated with regard to "suicidal precautions: Patient is to be on a one-on-one regime . . . with continuous observation. . . . Do not allow belt." An important aspect of my testimony was to indicate to the jury that the Accreditations Board was requiring hospitals to have a training and procedures manual which included, among other things, a section on suicide precautions. The award to the parents made by the judge and jury was $125,000.

In this case, the high risk was diagnosed but there was a failure to follow correctly the order for active suicidal precautions. It seemed reasonable to the court that the legal concept of standard of care in the community should be replaced by the standard of the hospital's own procedures and policy manual.

Mr. C. was a 29-year-old veteran who was admitted to a veterans hospital on September 24 because he was confused, had violent dreams, and had attacked his wife, who then left him. At admission time, he was depressed, sleepless, with amnesia for many of the things he had done. Two days later, he told the doctors that he had been drinking too much alcohol and taking too many other drugs. The diagnosis was reactive depression or depressive neurosis and he was discharged after being in the hospital 4 days. His wife returned to the home.

One month later, on October 29, he was seen in the VA out-patient clinic and given a refill on his medications, which were Tofranil and Valium. Later that day, he overdosed on the Tofranil and Valium in a suicide attempt, and he was treated for coma at an emergency hospital and transferred back to the Veterans Administration psychiatric ward. The doctor's notes on this hospitalization reflect a contemptuous attitude toward the patient. The doctor minimized the seriousness of the suicide attempt, which he characterized as an effort to get more attention from the wife. In fact, there was no detailed psychiatric evaluation or history or mental status examination on the chart, only the doctor's three-or four-line progress notes. I could find no consultation report. The patient was discharged November 5, sent home with 100 Tofranil tablets and 100 Valium, enough to last a month if he took them three times a day as directed. Within 48 hours, however, he took them all, and this time he died.

The case was tried in Los Angeles Federal Court. The attorney for the government seemed flustered and poorly prepared and did not have an expert witness. I stated that in my opinion, the seriousness of the patient's condition was misunderstood by the doctors the first time he was admitted, and negligently underrated the second time he was admitted to the hospital after a serious suicide attempt. There was no diagnostic or evaluation effort, no treatment plan, no rational approach, and the notes in the chart were scanty and reflected a disrespectful attitude toward the patient and his wife.

Judgment was against the government to the amount of $90,000. The plaintiff's attorneys appealed the award, stating that it was insufficient. I was called back to the court many months later at the judge's request to help her evaluate what the earning potential of this man would have been had he not been given the Tofranil that he used to kill himself. Based upon my testimony, the judge awarded $150,000 to the widow.

Suicide attempts should be taken seriously. Each patient deserves a complete workup. There should be a diagnostic evaluation with an appropriate therapeutic plan. There was negligence in this case because the physician did not take sufficient time to evaluate the patient adequately. If a patient has made a suicide attempt with Tofranil, one does not ordinarily send him out with more Tofranil without at least a staff conference or a consultation. Finally, note that the court used an expert suicidologist to try to evaluate what would have been the earning power of a person who committed suicide had he lived.

Mr. G. was a 28-year-old man who had a long history of psychiatric treatment with several hospitalizations. He had been able to work regularly as a post office employee, but had continuous marital problems and would become depressed and suicidal when his wife threatened to leave him. He was hospitalized in January and talked about committing suicide. However, the physician thought he could be managed on an open unit. There was a staff conference with other psychiatrists. They all noted the patient was depressed with suicidal ideation, but decided to treat him with minimal hospitalization. He was discharged on an outpatient status. He was being treated with Lithium Carbonate and Elavil. Then, his wife actually did leave him, taking the children and moving to her parents' home. He was readmitted February 19. Once again, after a consultation, he was managed on an open ward. He asked his doctor for a pass to take care of cleaning things up in his new apartment and when the doctor seemed reluctant, the patient pointed out that the doctor gave him weekend passes before and the patient was on an open ward. The patient went to his apartment, paid the rent for the next month, and then jumped to his death from a nearby bridge.

In the hospital chart, there were daily lengthy progress notes. The specific treatment plan was to get him out of the hospital as quickly as possible and help him cope as an outside patient. The day before the patient died, he reported a dream to his psychiatrist, who entered it into the hospital record. "I'm in a car by the harbor. There is a military jet plane flying, barely above, and then a fiery plane crash. I'm driving with someone else. We turn off the rocky road to see where the accident was. No one knew who was the mechanic who had been working on this plane." Because the doctor had been seeing the patient daily, and was aware of all the information that was available on this case, and had made a decision to give the patient a pass based on a consistent treatment plan, I felt there was no negligence, and the case should be defended.

In this case, there was a treatment plan based on psychiatric consultation, which was recorded and followed. It is not negligent to have taken a calculated risk, even if, in fact, the patient did commit suicide.

Institutions benefit from self-knowledge. Hospitals should ask themselves, "Do we treat persons at special risk for suicide?" If yes, then there must be a security area and policies for special management of suicidal persons. These policies are best determined by a suicide-prevention committee representing staff and administration. The committee establishes written guidelines after surveying the security areas and talking with staff and patients. *Suicide management policies are then incorporated into the training and supervision of staff.*

A reasonable performance requires that the patient be evaluated for suicide risk, that a treatment plan be formulated, and that staff follow the treatment plan according to the hospital's own policies.

LIABILITY IN OUTPATIENT PRACTICE

As discussed above, outpatient practitioners are held to a much lower standard of accountability and responsibility than hospitals. This is because outpatients are much less subject to the control and authority of their treatment resources. An important issue is to what extent a doctor is responsible for effecting the hospitalization of an acutely suicidal patient. Court decisions on this issue have been inconsistent, even contradictory. In an excellent review, Perr (1974) has described the results of court actions. He stresses that the law demands reasonable care in foreseeable situations. The key words in the cases are "reasonable," "anticipated," "foreseeable," "preventable," and "controllable."

After an introductory phone call to Dr. Helen Grey, a senior psychiatrist, Mrs. F. brought in her husband because he had appeared depressed for 24 hours, and this morning she found him in the kitchen holding a knife to his throat. The doctor suggested immediate hospitalization, but the patient said no. He had been through a depressive illness 10 years before and had been hospitalized twice back in Illinois by a psychiatrist recommended then by the patient's brother, a physician. Since then, Mr. F. had taken imipramine periodically as prescribed long distance by his brother. The patient was an attorney working at a fairly low level for the government and he greatly resented being moved periodically from one office location to another. Apparently, this type of move precipitated the present depression. Dr. Grey took an hour and a half to complete the history and mental status and then strongly recommended hospitalization and called the hospital to arrange for a bed. The patient said he hated hospitalization. He would refuse to go and he would fight it every inch of the way. The doctor made the clinical judgment that the patient would be very difficult to hold on an involuntary basis and that to hospitalize him against his will threatened to produce an even more precipitous loss of self-esteem than he had already experienced, which would increase his depression and the risk that he would harm himself. "I decided as an alternative to immediate hospitalization to see Mr. F. on a daily basis as an out-patient for further evaluation and psychotherapy." The patient said he would see the doctor on a daily basis, and he was sure he would not kill himself. The doctor recommended an increase in the daily dosage of imipramine. Then the doctor talked with Mrs. F. and learned that there were no guns in the house. The doctor recommended that somebody be with Mr. F. Later that day, however, Mr. F. slipped away from his monitor unnoticed and the next day his body washed up on the beach at Santa Monica. Later, Mrs. F. sued Dr. Grey, claiming that the evaluative interview had made her husband even more suicidal and that the doctor should have put Mr. F. in the hospital immediately on an involuntary hold. As an expert consultant, I advised the attorney that the doctor was not liable for damages and recommended a strong defense. However, the insurance company settled the case.

For Dr. Grey, this was the most painful experience of her life, lasting about 2 years until a settlement was reached and before that, threatening to last for 5 years until the case would come to trial, I had considerable sympathy for Dr. Grey, for the decision not to enforce involuntary hospitalization was one I might well have made myself under the circumstances. It's not easy to commit a lawyer. If the papers were made out, and he ran away toward the beach, would the police shoot him? Hospitalization does not insure safety. Many suicides occur in psychiatric hospitals, and the few weeks immediately postdischarge from a psychiatric hospital are recognized as a time of very high suicide risk.

When I reviewed the case, I noted that Dr. Grey did the following things right:

1. She took enough time to acquaint herself with the history and do a complete mental examination, and she talked with the wife. The doctor even made a phone call to the physician brother in Detroit to verify that the previous medicine was imipramine.

2. The doctor made written notes of the history and the mental status together with a provisional diagnosis and a plan of treatment. (There should be no controversy about the value of notes in the practice of mental health treatment. My opinion is that after the therapist is familiar with the patient, notes are needed only for turning points, or dramatic events, but there should be extensive evaluatory notes at the very beginning of the treatment, and I recommend that a question about present suicidal ideas and previous suicidal experiences be included in every mental status examination.)

3. The doctor investigated the patient's suicidal ideas and elicited a strong denial. The doctor asked about possible weapons at home and was assured that none were available. In fact, the patient committed suicide by drowning, a method which is unusual in California and therefore unexpected.
4. The doctor discussed the suicide potential with the family (the wife) but possibly did not emphasize dramatically or strongly enough the need for constant surveillance. This was because the doctor herself had formed the opinion that the patient would not commit suicide that day.
5. Dr. Grey discussed this case with a colleague while they were arranging to have a hospital bed available. A more formal consultation would have been even better as a way of insuring against liability.

I recommended defending this case and bringing it to trial, but Dr. Grey was glad to agree to a settlement for the full amount of her insurance ($250,000). She told me that the experience of being sued precipitated her retirement from practice.

CONCLUSION

With regard to responsibility for suicide, we are passing through a time of rapid change, both in legal attitudes and in psychiatric practice. What can reasonably be anticipated, foreseen, controlled, or prevented is limited by what is desirable and what is beneficial. We can look forward to a fairly long period of confusion, discontinuity, and contradiction as our ideas of justice and of medical and psychological practice struggle to keep pace with each other.

REFERENCES

Litman, R. E. (1980). Psycholegal aspects of suicide. In Modern Legal Medicine, Psychiatry and Forensic Science, ed. J. Corran et al. Philadelphia: F. A. Davis.
Perr, I. N. (1974). Suicide and civil litigation. Journal of Forensic Science 19:261–266.

ADDITIONAL READINGS

Aitken, R. C. B., and Proudfoot, A. T. (1969). Barbiturate autonatism—myth or malady? Postgraduate Medical Journal 45:612–616.
Curvey, C. E. (1974). Effect of the manner of death in medicolegal cases in insurance settlements. Journal of Forensic Science 19:390–398.

Dorpat, T. L. (1974). Drug automatism, barbiturate poisoning and suicidal behavior. *Archives of General Psychiatry* 31:216–220.

Litman, R. E. et al. (1963). Investigations of equivocal suicides. *Journal of the American Medical Association* 184:924–929.

Litman, R. E. (1966). Police aspects of suicide. *Police* 10:14–18.

Litman, R. E., Farberow, N. L., Wold, C. I., and Brown, T. R. (1974). Prediction models of suicidal behaviors. In *The Prediction of Suicide*, ed. A. T. Beck et al., pp. 141–159. Bowie, MD: Charles Press.

Litman, R. E. (1975). The assessment of suicidality. In *Consultation-Liaison Psychiatry*, ed. R. O. Pasnau, pp. 227–236. New York: Grune and Stratton.

Motto, J. D. L. (1969). Toward suicide prevention in medical practice. *Journal of the American Medical Association* 210:1229–1232.

Murphy, G., et al. (1974). On the improvement of suicide determination. *Journal of Forensic Science* 19:276–283.

Perr, I. N. (1965). Liability of hospitals and psychiatrists in suicide. *American Journal of Psychiatry* 122:631–638.

ACKNOWLEDGMENTS

APPRECIATION IS expressed to the following for permission to reproduce materials that appear in this volume:

American Medical Association for permission to reproduce "Immobilization Response to
   Suicidal Behavior," by Robert E. Litman, published in *Archives of General Psychiatry*, 1964, volume 11, pp. 282–285. Copyright © 1964, American Medical Association.
American Psychiatric Press for permission to reproduce "Guidelines to Suicide Prevention in the Hospital," by Norman L. Farberow, published in *Hospital and Commu-
   nity Psychiatry*, 1981, volume 32, pp. 99–104. Copyright © 1981, American Psychi-
   atric Press.
American Psychotherapy Association for permission to reproduce "When Patients
   Commit Suicide," by Robert E. Litman, published in *American Journal of Psycho-
   therapy*, 1965, volume 19, pp. 570–576. Copyright © 1965, *American Journal of
   Psychotherapy*.
Family Services of America for permission to reproduce "The Suicide Prevention
   Center: Concepts and Clinical Functions," by Norman L. Farberow, Samuel L.
   Heilig, and Howard J. Parad, published in *Crisis Inventory, Book 2*, edited by H. J.
   Parad and L. G. Parad, 1990, pp. 251–274. Copyright © 1990 Family Services of
   America.
F. A. Davis Company for permission to reproduce "Psycholegal Aspects of Suicide," by

Robert E. Litman, here entitled "Responsibility and Liability for Suicide," published in *Modern Legal Medicine: Psychiatry and Forensic Science*, edited by J. Curran, 1980. Copyright © 1980 by F. A. Davis Company.

Guilford Publications for permission to reproduce "Hospital Suicides: Lawsuits and Standards," by Robert E. Litman, here entitled "Responsibility and Liability for Suicide," published in *Suicide and Life-Threatening Behavior*, 1982, volume 12, pp. 212–220. Copyright © 1982 by Guilford Publications.

Hogrefe & Huber Publishers, for permission to reproduce "The Los Angeles Survivors' After-Suicide Program," by Norman L. Farberow, published in *Crisis*, 1992, volume 13, pp. 23–34. Copyright © 1992 by Hogrefe & Huber Publishers.

The Menninger Clinic for permission to reproduce "Long-Term Treatment of Chronically Suicidal Patients," by Robert E. Litman, published in *Bulletin of the Menninger Clinic*, March 1989, pp. 215–228. Copyright © 1989 by The Menninger Clinic.

Prentice-Hall/Atherton Press for permission to reproduce "Orientations toward Death," by Edwin S. Shneidman, published in *The Study of Lives: Essays in Honor of Henry A. Murray*, edited by R. W. White, 1963, pp. 201–219. Copyright © 1963 by Prentice-Hall.

Superintendent of Documents, U. S. Government Printing Office for permission to reproduce "Preparatory and Prior Suicidal Behavior Factors," by Norman L. Farberow, published in *Report of Secretary's Task Force on Youth Suicide*, volume 2, pp. 2–53, 1989.

Western Journal of Medicine for permission to reproduce "Management of Suicidal Patients in Medical Practice," by Robert E. Litman, published in *California Medicine*, 1966, volume 104, pp. 168–174. Copyright © 1966 by *Western Journal of Medicine*.

NAME INDEX

SUBJECT INDEX

207